Ideally Speaking

Interviews with South African and
ex-South African Jews

Stephen Hellmann & Lindsay Talmud

Lexicon Books

Requests for permission to make copies of any part of this work should be addressed to Lexicon Books. Email address: lexiconht@gmail.com

Book design and production by Joel Friedlander
http://www.TheBookDesigner.com

Cover design: Daniel Goldfarb

ISBN: 978-0-9831820-1-6

British Library Cataloguing in Publication Data. A catalogue record for this book is available from the British Library.

Printed in the United Kingdom by Lexicon Books

how long does it take
for a voice
to reach another
in this country
held bleeding between us

ANTJIE KROG

Ideally Speaking

Interviews with South African and
ex-South African Jews

Contents

Introduction

The sight of Afrikaner rugby players singing *N'kosi Sikelele* arm in arm with their black teammates brings many a tear to South African eyes. For those of us who grew up in apartheid South Africa and adhered to the prevalent view that there would be no reconciliation between the races in our lifetime, this scenario is mind-boggling. Now living in Israel, we are inevitably struck by the irony of a democratic South Africa having made significant progress in the area of peace and reconciliation, while the expectation of peaceful coexistence between Israelis and Palestinians appears to be the "not in our lifetime" problem. The attempt to come to terms with this contradictory reality was one of the original spurs for this book.

The book is also a product of a desire to better understand our own lives. We are graduates of *Habonim* South Africa who, confronted with the realities of apartheid and the choices available in the sixties, chose the Zionist option which appeared to promise personal and national redemption. Within the broader Zionist context, we both chose the path of kibbutz to implement our socialistic ideals and beliefs. We honestly believed we had the obligation and the ability to create a just society and to make the world a better place.

Reflections on our current stage of life and different trajectories since that time led us to ask ourselves questions about the nature of our beliefs and the choices we made: How did we acquire those fervent beliefs? What prompted us to make the radical choices we made? To what extent do our present lives reflect our youthful ideals? In search of answers to such questions, we embarked on an exploration of the part ideology played in the lives of people from a similar background to ours, before and after our time, and with different experiences of childhood and youth.

A further stimulus to investigating the role of ideology was the lingering qualm about whether we have 'done enough'. Particularly for people living in Israel, doubts exist regarding the extent to which fundamental aspects of the ideology we brought with us have been realized. South Africans who came on *aliyah* holding strong beliefs in social justice, equality, and freedom from oppression have perhaps tended to forsake those beliefs, abandon activism, and lapse into lethargy. We wanted to find out what a broad range of people think about this contentious issue.

We proceeded to interview almost fifty South African and ex-South African Jews and identified three geographical groups of people: 1) people who believed they had a role to play in the South African liberation struggle; 2) people who chose the Zionist option; and 3) those who chose to pursue a cause in other places – the UK, Canada and Australia.

As youth movement graduates, terms such as 'ideology', 'belief', and 'commitment', came very naturally to us. It soon became clear, however, that that many of the people we decided to speak to did not define themselves according to youth movement terminology. Consequently, our guideline was modified to encompass a broader spectrum: people of conscience or people who wanted to make a difference.

Deciding who to interview was a difficult task owing to the large number of eligible people. We had to rely on what we knew, had heard or read about people, as well as suggestions from friends who were interested in our project.

People we did not interview include: 1.Well-known Jewish activists who were involved in the liberation struggle in South Africa. A fascinating book called *Cutting Through The Mountain* edited by Immanuel Suttner gives voice to a large number of these deservedly celebrated personalities. 2. Bnei-Akiva graduates. We did not feel we could do justice to what is a very specific and complex ideological outlook.

The transcripts of the interviews we conducted have been edited and collated to produce this book. For reasons of space we have reduced the length of each interview, though the text that appears remains essentially as it was recorded. In some cases we have altered the order in which things were said as interviewees sometimes wanted to include a point they had forgotten to mention earlier in the interview.

We were often surprised at the frankness displayed by many of the interviewees as they grappled with the complex issues raised. They shared memories of influences on their early thinking and beliefs, their certainties and their doubts and how their lives had panned out. Some time has elapsed since we began the interviews and in that interval the world around us has changed. The result is that in certain cases, answers relating to current political situations or to predictions and expectations might not be the same today as they were back in 2007.

In deciding on the format of the book we have adhered to the basic geographical division of the three groups. We did not opt for a thematic approach because we feel that the interviewees' individual stories convey the essence of our quest. Nevertheless, appreciating the significance of drawing out the principal themes from the interviews, we have added a concluding chapter.

We hope that besides being a source of interest and nostalgia, the book will also prompt introspection, questioning, and enjoyable discussion.

Stephen Hellmann and Lindsay Talmud
Tzora and Ramat Raziel
May 2010

South Africa

Lael Bethlehem
Johnny Broomberg
Jules Browde
Selma Browde
Geoff Budlender
Johnny Copelyn
Dennis Davis
Mickey Korzennik
Michael Kuper
Leon & Lorna Levy
Alan Lipman
Ronnie Miller
Illona Tip

Lael Bethlehem

Johannesburg
28/05/08

Lael Bethlehem is the CEO of the Johannesburg Development Agency. The JDA is an arm of the City of Johannesburg, responsible for inner city and township regeneration. Lael has been with the City since 2002. Prior to that, she worked in national government and in economic policy research.

Lael has an MA from Witwatersrand University University, where she was active in the anti-apartheid movement. She serves on several company boards including the Industrial Development Corporation. She has previously served as a Trustee of several international organizations in the natural resources sector, including the Centre for International Forestry Research, based in Indonesia, and the International Institute for Environment and Development, based in London.

Lael is married to Emilia Potenza and they have two daughters.

Who or what do you identify as playing key roles in the way you thought as a young person?
Lael - Temple Emanuel, the Reform *shul*, certain rabbis and the movement (*Netzer/Maginim*) were totally formative and shaped my life choices to a very large degree. What is interesting is that my sister Louise and I both had these experiences but made different choices though based, I think, on similar motivations. For me it was a conscious decision: Was I going to go to Israel or was I going to stay?

In *Maginim* there were various ideas about what we were trying to achieve. Basically it was about changing the world, a light unto the nations. The way it was explained was as *tikkun olam*. The questions were about the right method. Was it through *aliyah* and trying to make a difference there so that Israel could become an example of how you can overcome conflicts? A lot of us believed then that it was possible but it has turned out not to be. Others said, "Now hang on a second, I was born here and here we are in the mid 1980's. I want to play a role, to change things and for *tikkun olam*, you don't have to look very far." In the end this was the path I chose. But I remember our debating this, on and on.

Who were the active participants in this debate?
Lael - Well there was Rabbi Dickie Lampert. He was the first person in authority who I remember saying that apartheid was not okay and that one should say so publicly. My parents both had quite strong political views. My dad had been involved in some activist work around the bus boycotts. But he got a bit of a shock when his passport was revoked. The message we got from many people was that apartheid was not okay, but very few were active against it.

Rabbi Isaacson was also a big influence on all of us, a very inspiring figure, charismatic, and a real example of passionate belief. "If you believe in something you go out and do it." I got a very strong sense of the need for a mission in life. You know you don't just wander along. You should have a clear ideology and pursue it.

These issues were a constant part of my life in my high school years. My sister was my *madricha* and I remember her raising them with my mother: leave the country or stay and contribute? What do we mean by Reform Zionism? What are our ethics, etc.?" My decision to stay was actually made after school.

Can you elaborate a little on the role of the Jewish aspect of your life?
Lael - It has been enormous. I feel it has been the bedrock of all my ideas. In fact at one point I decided that what I should do is become a rabbi. I took my Reform Judaism helluva seriously. I was religious. Rabbi Assabi and others spoke about Reform not being a watered down version of Orthodox Judaism. It was making a conscious decision about what was most meaningful and important in the Jewish tradition and pursuing it. We used to think that engaging with these matters and deciding for yourself made them more profound. You were not just

carrying out *mitzvot* because somebody told you to do so. I can remember going through the *siddur,* going through each *tefila* and deciding what was problematic about it. We'd sit around in our study groups and amend them. We were a pretty serious bunch. I used to lay *tefillin* and the whole thing every morning.

In standard nine I joined Jews for Justice which was the first political move I made.

Standard nine? Wasn't that very young for …
Lael - I suppose so Ja. Eventually when I went to university I started Jewish studies and Hebrew One. The mine workers' strike was in 1987. I became involved in a peripheral way and then I knew I had to decide: "Stay or go?" If you are interested in *tikkun olam* and making a contribution that comes out of the Jewish tradition then surely the place to do it is here. This was 1988 and a very tough time in the country. All sorts of organizations were banned. Lots of people were arrested, there were hunger strikes; things looked really bleak.

I started thinking less and less about being a rabbi, though I still taught for *barmitzvah.* I retained an involvement in the Jewish community for quite some time. But it became clear to me my path was not about Zionism, not about kibbutz in Israel or about being a rabbi – it is here. And then I dived into NUSAS. I went into this very concerned with my life as a Jew. I was doing all this as a Jew. I guess over the years, the more universal principles and the politics of it overtook that. Now my involvement in organized Jewish life is very little. But I still feel that it is a wellspring of my being and my ideas.

Did this affect your choice of what to study?
Lael - Ja it did. I majored in sociology and politics and did an MA in sociology. Sociology was the recommendation of my high school history teacher at King David - Michelle Friedman. She was a wonderful teacher who made a very big effort to "conscientize" us. Before I went to the States on AFS (a student exchange program) she said, "Don't go there and pretend that South Africa is just a nice country with animals. Please don't allow yourself to become an ambassador for South Africa."

I took her very seriously. When we were still at school, she invited us to her flat regularly and showed us a video of the Steve Biko inquest. She had a big influence but not a Jewish one. Apart from Ms. Friedman I would say in fact that of all the ideology in my life, the percentage that came from King David school was little more than zero. King David was uninspiring, uninspired, and ideologically backward. I believe it is very different now. At that time, it was all *Maginim*.

How did the AFS experience turn out?
Lael - I was in Buffalo, where I started giving short talks on apartheid. I went to schools, read poetry, and just talked about South Africa as I knew it. I knew very little but people started asking for me to talk. I was even asked to give a talk to a Jewish group in Canada. Here I was, just a nice Jewish girl from Johannesburg who had got from her parents and from people like Michelle Friedman this idea that I must now try and do something. These experiences made me feel that I could be an activist.

Did fear not deter you from becoming an activist when you returned to South Africa?
Lael - Not really. I joined NUSAS, which had the idea that you had to start with people where they were. Nice Jewish boys and girls from King David or non-Jews from Parktown were not going to jump into NUSAS from the first day and call to join in the armed struggle. They took us through a process. Slowly I began to understand things and see myself differently. NUSAS was reasonably safe. It was not what the ANC was doing. Having said that, quite a few NUSAS activists were harassed and some were arrested. Our cars and flats were vandalized a number of times.

How would you compare the NUSAS experience to what you had known in Maginim?
Lael - In *Maginim* we were on a collective mission to change the world. We used to sing that song. *Ani ve'ata neshane et ha'olam* (You and I are going to change the world). We were kids of privilege who had to give

something back if we were going to stay in South Africa.

It felt very similar in NUSAS. We were a collective and in the end that collective became quite serious. There was no such thing as: "I am off to play tennis" or to study for an exam. That would be letting down the team. As in *Maginim*, it was a collective with a serious sense of accountability not only to the ideology and to the principles but also to each other. We always shared flats with other activists. It was a strongly-lived, intense experience.

I used to drive tourists around Soweto and it was there that I met Albertina Sisulu. On one occasion she took me into her house and there were Walter Sisulu and many of the treason trial people sitting in the lounge. You have an experience like that and it completely changes you.

How do you feel about the future of the rainbow nation?
Lael - Clearly the honeymoon is over and we are at a turning point. But what happens now is partly going to be a result of our own actions. A lot of course depends on what the new leadership of the ANC decides and does. A lot of whites feel disempowered and there is a lot of alienation in the country. For the first time now people who were activists with me in NUSAS are emigrating. It is quite a shock. People with a long history in the struggle are going to Australia in numbers.

I am very clear for myself - I don't want to emigrate. These are tough times. People feel that whatever they do it won't make any difference.

But you don't feel that way?
Lael - Well you know that is my history – *Maginim*, NUSAS, you must throw in your lot and you must try and do good things. In the end the world is partly about what the Jacob Zumas do or don't do, but it is also about which philanthropic project is happening in Diepsloot and how that is changing lives and which teacher is doing a good job. The world is built through small actions, not only through big ones.

We understand that collectivism still plays a role in your life...
Lael - A group of seven of us got together and decided to build a

collective housing project. People are doing this for different reasons but for my friend Nina Cohen and me, there is a certain language that is reminiscent of our youth movement days. We think of it as a *kupah meshutefet*. The whole idea of the project is to have a more collective less individualistic emphasis. We think of it as a *moshav*. Geographically this project is in Dundalk Avenue, two hundred meters from the old *Habonim bayit*. (laughter and agreement on the appropriateness of the venue).

Jonathan Broomberg

Johannesburg
8/11/07

Dr. Jonathan Broomberg is Deputy CEO of Discovery Health, South Africa's leading health insurance company, with operations in South Africa, the UK, the USA, and China. He qualified in Medicine at Witwatersrand University in South Africa, and subsequently obtained an MA in Economics and Politics at the University of Oxford while on a Rhodes Scholarship, followed by MSc. and PhD. degrees in Health Economics from the University of London.

From 1994, Jonathan worked for several years advising the first post-apartheid government on reform of the health care system. In addition to his work at Discovery Health, Jonathan plays an active role in international public health affairs. He served as a member of the Technical Review Panel of the Global Fund to fight AIDS, TB, and malaria for five years, including two years as Chair, and is on the Board the Alliance for Health Systems Policy and Research, based at the WHO in Geneva.

As the *mazkir klali* of Habonim, your life seemed to be headed in a Zionist, perhaps socialist direction. At some point, however, you obviously took decisions to follow a different path. Can you tell us about those decisions?
Johnny - I think a lot of those decisions simply evolved, in a way, rather than my sitting down in an organized fashion and saying, "I used to be a Zionist, but I am not any more, or I used to be a socialist but now I am something else." How did I end up making the decision not to ever go and live in Israel? I think it was probably a combination of two different aspects of my life. One was probably the fact that I spent quite a lot of time here after (involvement in) the movement, having finished medical school but out of *Habonim*. I spent more than three years immersed

in the reality of South Africa, student politics and so on without the movement around me. Undoubtedly, during those years, the reality of South Africa just became more significant for me.

On top of that, I then went to Oxford on a Rhodes scholarship. I just drifted further and further away from the influences that were originally drawing me in that direction. I didn't even know whether I would come back here. I ended up coming back and really getting immersed in politics. By the time I got back, there was a real sense that transition was starting to happen. I got quite involved in the development of the ANC's health policy though it was still two years before Mandela's release.

So to summarize, there was never an active decision not to live in Israel. It was more of a drift, getting sucked into what was happening here rather than any pull of the movement or my friends or Israel as an ideological idea – it kind of just happened.

Was it a problem for you to make the shift from being so involved in Habonim to such a different path?
Johnny - That's a good question. At the time, those evolutions seemed very slow and gradual. When I first got out of *Habonim*, I felt happy to just be a student again. Medical school was demanding enough anyway.

I do remember on a post-movement visit to Kibbutz Tuval, being struck by some people's hostility, and anger I suppose. In my mind I had moved on in quite an organic way. They had an image of me from then. I was very comfortable with who I was and my own transition. They seemed to be saying, "You were with us and were part of our decisions. We did it and what happened to you?" No one actually said it. I was surprised that some people would perceive or see a dissonance that I did not feel.

This seems to say something about ideology doesn't it?
Johnny - I think that's true. I think though, that it says something else which may be related, which is that ideology and beliefs are quite conditional on participation in a group. I think the Jewish religion has

always understood the importance of keeping people close. And I think it is about that. When I started drifting off and there weren't those inputs… and maybe it does raise questions about how deeply ingrained those beliefs were for me personally, or how conditional they were on my environment at the time.

Are you saying ideology might just have been skin deep while it was the social context that was more the powerful element?
Johnny - Who knows? My sense is that each person who was in the movement in each generation has a different and quite unique relation to that ideology. At one end of the spectrum were people whose involvement was entirely a function of the group while at the other end you had people for whom it ran very deep personally. So where do I fit in on that spectrum? I don't think my position was entirely conditional on my environment.

At the time you were most active in Habonim how did the Zionism v. anti-apartheid struggle express itself?
Johnny - There was quite a heady blend of Zionism on the one hand and a social cover – being switched on to the reality of apartheid. But for me, what was more appealing were liberal left-wing and general humanitarian values, and therefore revulsion of apartheid and prejudice was actually more resonant with me than Zionism.

When I look back, those things have been more consistent in my life since then. It has been actions and reactions around that stuff and I have drifted quite far from Zionism in any sort of active or day-to-day sense. I am identified very strongly as a Jew, not particularly religious as you'd expect, but it is a central part of my identity. In a way I think that that is also what I took from *Habonim* and it still lives with me quite strongly.

How did your period of study in England affect your thinking?
Johnny - I deviated quite far from my dry academic path. I did a degree in economics, politics, and philosophy over two years. This was a huge awakening for me intellectually and politically, reading all sorts

of political theories of liberal and left-wing writers as well as South African history.

When I came back, my work was combining social policy that I had been studying with my health care background. It was not particular individuals who influenced me so much as the times and the natural opportunities and challenges that were there for a person like me with my particular interests and skills.

Tell us about your professional activity after your return…
Johnny - I spent two or three years doing a bit of clinical work at Baragwanath hospital but then getting quite involved in health policy work. I was part of a small group at Wits University doing research and writing about what the health care system should look like in a post – apartheid South Africa. By then it was clear apartheid was going to end.

After a couple of years I went back to England. I went much more deeply into the economics of health care systems. I did an MA and eventually a doctorate in London. I came back in 1992 and transition was imminent.

From that base I got pulled in as adviser to the woman who had just been appointed Minister of Health, Dr Nkosazana Dlamini Zuma, Jacob Zuma's ex- wife. I worked with her for close on two years, pretty much full-time.

Give us a sense of that time. What kind of period was that for you personally?
Johnny - The time around 2000 was a period of intense engagement, incredible optimism, and excitement for me - seeing the system change, knowing that I could pick up the phone and talk to the minister, whereas now we are miles away from that. I'm certainly not alone, but it is a completely different discourse. It's not as if my ideas or my relationships with a lot of those people or my ability to contribute have changed. It is just that the work of rebuilding of this country, with regard to the senior positions and advisers to government, is much more of a project around empowering black people. It has been an important but difficult transition in some ways.

Did you end your work with Dr. Zuma because of a sense of what was coming down the line?
Johnny - I felt I had done a lot and I could still do some stuff with them if I continued but I didn't really want to build a career in government. To be honest, it wasn't because I was looking ahead and seeing that I didn't have a chance of lasting. There are particular ministries where the leadership was far-sighted. Look at the treasury.

To sum up that time then. It was an incredibly heady time. There was a lot of hope and one had a lot of personal influence and I had a sense of contributing. It is much harder now.

How did you get from there to here?
Johnny - The consistent theme has been that I stayed within the health care system, with different degrees of involvement with business or industry aspects. In different ways all along I have maintained a strong public policy type of involvement as well. I left government at the end of 1992 and I went into the consulting business for a few years.

I started here at Discovery about three years ago. It is a very big private health and life insurance company. My first role here was to manage the whole interface between the company and government. Fifteen percent of the population has private health insurance.

I still have quite a role around government and issues about health policy. My main focus over the last ten years has been business, but I have managed to keep my hand in social stuff as well. There have been constant themes.

We understand Discovery has interests and goals beyond the pure business aspirations...
Johnny - It is a big issue for me personally and for this company, not only for commercial reasons. We have quite a values-driven business here.

For me the values of the business and of the leadership, as well as my ability to influence them are quite important. Shortly after I got here, the government launched an investigation into what it would take to dramatically increase health insurance coverage. For us the questions were: What could we do to reduce the cost of health care to make it more affordable, what laws needed revision, how could doctors and hospitals be persuaded to lower their fees, etc? I had just joined the business here but they said, "Go do it, we'll pay your salary." That is still very much part of what drives me.

Where do you find yourself when meeting with those people whose main interest is the business?
Johnny - There are environments where it is clear that people are there to make profits and that is all that matters. This in my experience is not the ethic here. Outside the company there may be those with a different view, who see Discovery as a major capitalist beast looking after its own interest.

So does the Johnny Broomberg of today sit quite comfortably with the Johnny Broomberg ex-mazkir klali of Habonim?
Johnny - Maybe there were periods when I was more extreme or more focused in one direction, but if anything, maybe those were all the aberrations rather than now. I think I have always been someone with a strong social conscience but unlikely to end up a socialist in the narrow sense. If then I argued such a position strongly, that was probably because I was out of touch with who I really was or would become. At that time, it was quite natural. I don't feel any dissonance.

What were your feelings about your friends who gave up on South Africa in favor of an active Zionist path? Did you feel perhaps that they were abandoning what had become important to you?
Johnny - No, not at all. I have a view of the people and a view of the politics with a bit of overlap. My sense of the people is one of unequivocal admiration for people who made choices, stuck to them, and remained committed.

What about Israel? Is that tougher?
Johnny - I have many moments when I feel upset and anxious about the current manifestation of Israeli politics and how its leaders choose to behave in defense of the state.

It is an incredibly difficult and complicated situation. We often have serious arguments about it all, especially when visiting my sister in Israel. I would definitely count myself among the critics of the way Israel currently manifests itself. At the same time, I have strict limits about where I take that. And this is not about just not wanting to be a traitor in public. They are kind of internal limits, so that when people talk of a one people state with an eventual Arab majority, this is beyond discussion for me. I can't go there. I think there needs to be a Jewish State. I don't feel in any way that living in Israel is a betrayal of some ideology.

Jules Browde

Johannesburg
6/12/07

Born in Johannesburg in 1919, Jules Browde was educated at King Edwards and Witwatersrand University. A classmate and lifelong friend of Nelson Mandela's, Jules is well-known as a human rights lawyer of unashamed passion and commitment. For 25 years he combined his legal work with his role as the legendary Manhig of Habonim.

As a young advocate Jules argued and won the case preventing the eviction of the law firm of Mandela and Tembo from its premises. He appeared in many significant cases of a political nature such as the State v Adams which played a significant part in the repeal of the Group Areas Act. Jules was chairman of the Johannesburg Bar Council in 1983 and 1985 and has been an acting judge and Judge of Appeal on various occasions. A founder member of Lawyers for Human Rights in 1980, he became national chairman in 1984 and held this position for ten years.

In 2000 Jules was awarded an Honorary Doctorate by Witwatersrand University. His commitment to securing human rights through the legal system was described by the awards committee as playing a vital part "in the ultimately crucial decision by the ANC to endorse the path of constitutionalism and human rights in South Africa."

A long and distinguished career was recognized as recently as 2010 when Jules was appointed an Integrity Commissioner to the Johannesburg Metropolitan Council.

Jules in married to Selma Browde. They have three children and seven grandchildren.

What sort of home did you grow up in?
Jules - My father came here from Lithuania and he spoke with a

pronounced Lithuanian accent but he became a very devout freemason. He was a *yeshiva bocher* with a fine knowledge of the Talmud but he was a liberal thinker.

The one side of the street where we lived in Yeoville was mainly Jewish. My dad befriended an old Scotsman from the non–Jewish side and asked him to teach me chess.

We employed an African chap by the name of Solomon who I befriended. He drove a cart which delivered sugar and flour in sacks. My father often used to sit with Solomon in his room in the yard of our house and learned a bit of his language from him. I think he had a feeling for other human beings which he imparted to me. I say that with humility because I don't profess to be a great humanitarian. That was the sort of home in which I was brought up.

Who were the other people who influenced you?
Jules - I was lucky enough to have Louis Pincus, who later became the head of the Jewish Agency, and Colin Gluckman (Gillon), later the Attorney General in Jerusalem, as my *madrichim* in *Habonim*. They were both young advocates in those days. I would have done anything that Colin wanted me to do. I neglected my school work for example for five years. He had a profound influence on my life.

To this day, I remember the words of a play called The Eternal Jew that Colin wrote. In 1934, at the age of fourteen I played the leading role. (Jules recites with great pathos): "G-d I'm tired, I'm very tired... O lord why didst thou not let me rest, my punishment be abated, my sentence remitted?"

He taught me a lot, not only about our Jewish heritage, but about compassion for people within the legal profession. As the State Attorney in Israel, he denounced the killings carried out at Kafr Kasim.

Was there an emphasis on Jewish issues and Zionism in the early days of Habonim?
Jules - Oh yes definitely. *Habonim* was started in England because of the anti-Semitism which existed there at the time. The scout movement didn't welcome young Jews. Norman Lourie came back to South

Africa and brought it with him. And we needed it in South Africa; there was a great deal of anti-Semitism here too.

When did you start studying law?
Jules - I started in 1940 before I went to the army. I was only at university for three months before France fell. By that time it became imperative that we fight against Hitler's Germany, and I joined the army.

When I was in Egypt during the war, at the first opportunity I had, I went over to Palestine. I've always felt very strongly that there should be a Jewish homeland but that South Africa was my home.

How did you get back into Habonim after the war?
Jules - It had to do with the difference of philosophy in the movement after the Second World War. The leaders of the movement came to see me and told me of a very big problem they had with Sam Piper Stern who was about to expel members from the movement on ideological grounds. I agreed to come back for six months to see what I could do. This became twenty-five years in a role that became known as *Manhig* of *Habonim*.

How did your legal work fit in with your role in Habonim and interest in Jewish issues?
Jules - When I went to the Bar, I did a large amount of *pro deo* work. I started taking cases that were unpopular at that period of time. And my wife Selma of course is a strong humanist and always has been. I'm skipping twenty years but in 1970 she went into politics, by which time I was pretty heavily involved in matters pertaining to a legal bill of rights.

Were there people in the legal profession who were looking for radical change?
Jules - Definitely. I came into contact with Bram Fischer for example who was a wonderful role model for me. He found time for everything - amazing man. And then there were other people who influenced me in that way too. Harold Hansen was a great humanitarian who went to Israel for a short time.

In 1979 I went to the first International Human Rights conference in Cape Town. Sydney Kentridge was there as well as George Bizos and Johann Kriegler. We got together and decided to start an organization to be known as "The Lawyers for Human Rights." I became chairman after Johann Kriegler and was chairman for about ten years.

Did this kind of prominence not attract invitations from the left to play a more active role in the struggle?
Jules - Not really. I was very friendly with Joe Slovo, a devout card-carrying communist. We were friendly but he never tried to influence me. They didn't try to do that. I don't think they were great proselytizers. They didn't try it on me at any rate.

I'll tell you where I was perhaps different from many of my contemporaries and privileged, in a way. When I came out of the army in 1945 and started second year law, I was in the same class as Nelson Mandela. He and I became quite friendly. I also spent a lot of time with Oliver Tambo. Now that was unusual; not everybody befriended those chaps at that time, but I did.

Ultimately I was briefed by them and did a lot of work which my colleagues who had started with me at the Bar didn't get. I had the rare opportunity to meet these people and to maintain friendships with them.

I became involved in attempts to get everybody together around a table and to talk about what was called The National Convention Movement. Van Zyl Slabbert started this together with Buthelezi. I was elected National Chairman and devoted a year of my life to this.

I went to Lusaka to try and persuade Oliver Tambo to come in. Round the table were Joe Slovo, Mbeki, all these guys were there. I really was quite involved.

Were you involved in Jewish community affairs?
Jules - I became a member of Jewish Board of Deputies and I went to a couple of meetings. I could see that they would not speak out against the atrocities being committed against the black people and I resigned. I couldn't stand it.

Did Habonim consult you on their relations with the government?
Jules - Oh absolutely. There were very strong feelings on that issue. In 1961 when South Africa became a Republic, they held a huge camp in Bloemfontein. The Scouts, the Girl Guides, the Voortrekkers, and *Habonim* were invited. The question arose as to whether *Habonim* should attend or not. We sat up until all hours of the night discussing this. Ultimately the *hanhaga* felt that for the sake of the Jewish community we should go and I should be the head of the delegation. We had a scout craft competition and *Habonim* won it hands down. But the fact is that we were on thin ice.

At what point did it become clear to you that despite your deep involvement in Habonim, you were not going to leave South Africa and go on aliyah?
Jules - At this juncture in my life looking back I can't say I decided to stay here and do what I could for South Africa. It wasn't a conscious decision of that nature. It was just that I was here, I became one of the leaders of the Bar but I retained my love for, and great interest in Israel. I often felt embarrassed that I was saying goodbye to one *garin* after another without myself doing anything about it. But I just never brought myself to decide. Look, it would have required more than me, and Selma was very involved in this country.

Do you recall ever being inclined to advise Habonim to rethink its position on South Africa?
Jules - Well at the time of that camp in Bloemfontein we thought very hard about this issue. We felt that *Habonim* was an intrinsic part of this country; not everybody was going on *aliyah*. I wanted *Habonim* to be a liberal movement in the South African context, which it was. It was always leftist-orientated and I believed in that.

I actually think that *Habonim* played quite a big role in the Jewish community in this country, I really do. I meet people even at this old age of mine who say "I remember you when you spoke here, when you spoke there..." I remember speaking to members of the movement about political things that weren't always orientated towards Zionism.

The *Habonim* promise spoke of being a loyal member of the country in which I live. We used to talk about what that meant.

I invited a lot of attorneys including many chaps that I knew from *Habonim* to form a body that did a lot of work trying to put an end to the problem of evictions. We fought in three courts and it took over two years of my life. In effect this helped break down the Group Areas Act in South Africa.

I don't want to exaggerate my role, but I believe I influenced the Bar Council. It all goes back to my dad and the early days of *Habonim* that had a profound impact on me.

Were there times when you felt that Habonim graduates in South Africa behaved in ways that were disappointing to you?
Jules - Yes. I felt very badly about that. I'll tell you an anecdote to illustrate why I say that. I had been very close to someone who was with me in *Habonim* from the day Colin recruited us. He served in *Machal* in the War of Independence. He came back to South Africa and became an attorney. He was one of the people I called to my office to help with the eviction case. He worked for one of the biggest firms of Jewish lawyers in South Africa and decided not to get involved because the head of the firm would not have approved of doing anti-government work. This kind of thinking was tremendously disappointing for me.

I once defended a young woman who set off a bomb in the Hillbrow police station. I had good reason to think she was mentally unstable and asked an ex-*Habonim* psychiatrist to help me with the case. He said he was sorry but preferred not to get involved. I lost respect for him. However, I must tell you that the answer to your question is not easy; it is a multi-faceted thing.

Do you feel that you have seen the fulfillment of much of what has been important to you?
Jules - I wouldn't have missed the last twenty-five years in South Africa for anything. This has got nothing to do with whether I should have gone to Israel or not. I am not ashamed to tell anybody that I was a Zionist then and I am a Zionist today. I believe in the Jewish homeland

very fervently. I believe that if it were to fail it would be the end of the world, for me, and for anybody who says he's Jewish.

But having lived through this period in South Africa after the difficulties we experienced during the time of apartheid, I look back and say, "Thank God I was here to see this."

As to the comparatively small contribution I have made, I've seen it come to light. I've seen the Promised Land in a way. It is absolutely extraordinary. We never believed we would see this day in our lifetime and that made it worth fighting for.

Selma Browde

Johannesburg
15/10/2007

Selma Browde's life has been dedicated to the promotion of health, both as a cancer therapist and as a politician.

Selma studied and graduated from Witwatersrand University in 1967 as a specialist in radiotherapy. She served as Professor and Head of Radiation Therapy and Oncology in the Johannesburg hospital, until taking early retirement for health reasons in 1986. However, she maintained a research program and also became deeply involved in organizations that would influence the profession and the quality of patients' lives.

In 1972 Selma embarked on a parallel career in politics as a member of the Transvaal Provincial Council and an active leader of the Progressive Party. She was passionately committed to improving conditions for the disenfranchised majority. Notable and successful projects in which Selma played a leading role were: high-mast lighting in Soweto and the removal of the quota system for access to Soweto high schools. Her influence was felt in a plethora of organizations ranging from the South African Institute of Race Relations to the Soweto Basketball Association.

In recent years her work has become increasingly Aids-related, with an emphasis on education activities. She has also influenced policy with contributions on issues such as euthanasia.

Acknowledgement of her success in changing policies and attitudes was expressed in the conferring of an honorary Doctorate of Medicine by Witwatersrand University University in 2003.

Selma is married to Jules Browde. They have three sons and seven grandchildren.

We would like to hear a little about early experiences that foreshadowed later events in your life.

Selma – I remember an incident when we were driving to Hermanus. It was raining and I noticed people coming out of some huts in a field. I started to cry. My aunt asked, "Why are you crying?" I said, "Those poor people. How can they live in the rain in those places?"

It seems I have an obsession about suffering in the world. It's inherent. It is not normal and I have suffered as a result. My kids used to say to me, "Don't take the whole world onto your shoulders." Where it comes from, I don't know but it is a kind of phobia. I am a phobic person – about the dark and about public speaking.

I realized in later life that my parents were non-racist, though not political. In the mid-thirties, when I was about ten, my father had a medical practice in Maitland, a lower income suburb of Cape Town at that time. There were both white and colored people living there. We lived in a nice double-story house and nearby along a gravel road there was a row of tenement houses. I had no idea that these housed only colored people. It made no difference to me. I went to the local convent and my best friend was a girl called Renee Shaw, who was colored. My mother never told me she was colored. In her house the five sisters slept in one bed and I was very envious because I had a big room to myself and it was lonely. I thought: how lucky she is to live five in a room.

My father used to do house-calls in the colored areas, something very few doctors did. And he took me with him. I suppose that had an effect on me - people are people and I never saw them as different.

I got my political induction through my friend Ruth Rome, whose father Boris was the cantor of the Gardens Synagogue. He was a communist and an agnostic! In their house I heard real politics. When I was about eleven, I remember saying, "What does d-e-m-o-c-r-a-c-y mean?" I had another friend who had an older brother who was a medical student. He was a member of the Young Communist League and we really looked up to him. He told me that I was also a member of the YCL. I believed him because I believed in communism. My bible at that time was The Socialist Sixth of the World, written by the Dean of Canterbury, known as the Red Dean. He went to Russia in the thirties and was totally taken in. He described how everybody got the opportunity to do what they wanted professionally and got enough to eat and a place to live, according to their needs. To him it was utopia and I believed every word.

There was one chapter on prisons and the prison system. He described a jail that I can still see in my mind's eye: large grounds with rolling grasslands and trees, a large building, the prison, where everybody was rehabilitated. To me this was ideal. Because I believed everything in this book I used to argue with my friends about communism. I did not have any religious belief after leaving the Catholic convent at the age of twelve.

I have always remained with socialistic tendencies although I realized that the Russian model of communism was a rip-off. It might have sounded good on paper but the world is not like that. I am for social democracy and that is what paved the way for what I became later. I was never interested in being in politics. It never occurred to me.

Were there other books and people that influenced you?
Selma – I remember the Spanish Civil War. I was violently anti-Franco at the age of about twelve. We were living in Muizenberg at the time and there was a group of people who decided they were going to stage an anti-Franco march with banners. We marched in the parking ground of the pavilion. Can you imagine the effect it had on the world? Then I wrote a play about two children living under Franco, how they hid in a cave. I was absolutely passionate about that. When Russia invaded Finland in 1939 I was selling the Guardian, a left-wing newspaper, on the streets until my father stopped me. I was very upset. Anyway the older people at the YCL convinced us that Russia was justified in invading because it needed Finland as a buffer against attack. At the cinema, when the newsreel showed Russian tanks advancing most people booed but a few of us sat there clapping. It was crazy.

When did you turn towards South African politics?
Selma – There was no apartheid then, so it was concern for the suffering of black people, poverty, and discrimination that drove me.

When I came up to Johannesburg in 1946, I was in touch with my cousin Monty Berman, who was a communist. We were told by his mother that we had to attend a cocktail party for a relative's engagement. They were rich people who dressed very smartly and we were anti-rich. Monty and I said we are not going. My aunt said, "You can't do this to me." So Monty put on a sheepskin waistcoat and I dressed in a horrible green outfit with heavy shoes. This was our rebellion against going. The other women were beautifully dressed, with little hats. I was totally out of place but I actually think I felt a bit superior.

At the party, I met Jules Browde. This was a period in my life when I was anti-Jewish. I was a Universalist, no nationalism. Zionism to me was ridiculous and I was put off Judaism at the synagogue in Maitland. I preferred non-Jewish boys, too. It all had to do with my fear of Hitler. I did not want to be Jewish. As a Jew you don't belong anywhere and I wanted desperately to belong. I wanted to be South African, not Jewish.

That night Jules took me to a party of his friends from the army, none of whom were Jewish. I thought, "Wonderful, here is a Jewish man but look who his friends are." To my amazement I learnt that he was a big noise in *Habonim*, which despite my mother's pleas, I was determined never to join. Later that year I went to meet him at a camp in East London. I was amazed to see the people there. They were socialists. They didn't wear make-up and they didn't shave under their arms. But I could not really identify with them because I knew no Jewish history. I was alienated and now I think it is important to know your history, where you come from, even if you reject it later.

How did you get into politics?
Selma – I had a stroke in 1968 and it affected my ability to recognize faces. After recovering I went back to work as a radiation oncologist, doing research as well as treatment at all hours of the day and night. I was deeply hurt and angry when I learnt that the doctors I had been

working with had produced a paper and barely acknowledged me. To add insult to injury the head of the team said all I had done was "switch on a light" (given radiation). I was furious.

The following week I got a phone call from Helen Suzman who told me that there was an election (local, city council) the following month. I felt guilty because I should have been addressing envelopes in her office. But that was not what she wanted from me. She wanted me to be the fourteenth candidate on her list and gave me forty-eight hours to think about it.

I consulted with Jules, who thought I would never get in. So he suggested I take six weeks leave from the hospital, fight the campaign and when the election was over and I had cooled down I would go back to the hospital. I told Helen I would be a candidate on two conditions: 1) no publicity, as I was a doctor and 2) no public speaking. She agreed.

I had never been a Progressive Party member and I knew nothing about political procedure. I was standing against Alec Jaffe, who had been a provincial councilor and mayor, so I had little chance of beating him. I knew I was not going to get in.

When the count was done, it turned out that I had won. Alec Jaffe demanded a recount. News got out and people all converged on the park where we were. What I did not know was that all the other Progressive candidates had lost. When Alec realized he had lost, he started to cry. I said, "Alec, you can have it. I don't want it." I thought, "I can't be on the council. I have to go back to work." When I went outside the tent, I could not believe my eyes. The people, the excitement. I was carried with my umbrella shoulder high in the rain. I looked like Mary Poppins in the paper the next day. When we had a party to celebrate the victory, I could not believe it was for me. They put me on a table and started shouting, "Speech, Speech." I wanted to say something simple and honest so I said, "Thank you" to all the people who had helped me. Then I added, "There is just one thing I want to say. It is so wonderful to be out of the rat-race of medicine into the sincerity of politics." I meant it, but they thought I was being witty. So I got a roaring cheer.

Initially I combined the council work, which was only one meeting a month, with work at the hospital but it nearly killed me. The one big issue that I latched onto was the state of the electricity in Soweto. Most people had coal stoves so the place was full of smog, which was very unhealthy and dangerous. I pushed for high-mast lighting in the whole of Soweto. I had a fight with the council but I had the support of the press. "Let there be light," they said. In the end I won through and the whole of Soweto was done. It transformed people's lives.

Another issue I took up was Indian football, where they were not being allowed to play on their own ground. Here, too, I took up their fight and I won. There were lots of other cases.

What do you think was your greatest political achievement?
Selma – There were two. One was the electricity in Soweto. The other was related to education. One day a delegation came to me to complain that there was something amiss with the way their children were being graded for standard six, which was the key to further study or learning a trade. The children were being failed when by all accounts they should have passed, even after extra lessons. After doing some research I realized that a quota had been imposed on the number of children 'allowed' to pass. I spoke to the inspector of schools in Soweto. As it happens this man was dying of cancer and I eventually went to his house to get his answer. He got out of his death bed to say, "Dr. Browde, you were right. There is a quota system and I did not know about it. I have changed it already." Then he went back to his death bed. The next day parents called me to say they were so excited because they had read in The World (a local newspaper) that the quota system had been abolished.

With hindsight, how do you feel about your decision to go into politics?
Selma – I do not regret my decision to go into politics. It was what needed to be done. However, I am very disappointed with the way the Progressive Party including Colin Eglin, its leader, ignored me and failed to give me the recognition I deserve. At one point, I wrote a letter

to Helen Suzman saying that I wanted to resign because I could not play the game of politics. I did not send it because I could not let the people down. Eventually I resigned in 1982 after ten years of work.

Do you see any incompatibility between the black culture of the ANC leadership and western style democracy?

Selma - We do not understand black culture. Their understanding of democracy may be different from ours. People we have met recently accept the idea of an authoritarian figure, modeled on the tribal chief. There is growing westernization but we don't know how far that has penetrated. Some blacks have taken the bad things from the west – aspects of the economic culture, like greed, but it is uncertain how democracy will continue. We are not like Zimbabwe, but which direction we take will depend on who our future leaders are. There are wonderful people and maybe they will emerge.

How do you explain that the fire in your belly at this stage of your life is still so strong?

Selma – I think it is because I have got a passionate nature. In many ways it is a handicap. I feel very deeply about things and I express those feeling too forcefully. I have made a lot of enemies by not taking a gentle, persuasive approach. Maybe I lack the sheath that most people have to protect them from other people's suffering. I can't distance myself from suffering. I feel I have to do something about it. In the old days if Jules and I were coming back from a movie in town I would ask him to stop at the hospital so I could check to see if anybody was suffering and see if I could do something to help. One night at about midnight I phoned the ward to find out how a boy of twelve who had a tumor in his mouth was doing. The nurse who answered said he was fine but I asked her to go to his bed to check. She came back and said he was in pain. I immediately told her to give him an injection and I would write it up in the morning. I have difficulty driving past a beggar.

I have a model for treating AIDS that I hope will be used throughout the country but I don't believe it will. Now, at the age of eighty-one, I realize you cannot tilt at windmills all your life. You have to accept.

Geoff Budlender

Cape Town
29/09/07

Geoff Budlender SC was active in the anti-apartheid movement as a student activist in the 1970s. In 1973 he was National Chairperson of the National Union of SA Students.

Geoff qualified as an attorney and was engaged in political trials and human rights litigation under apartheid. He was one of the founders and later National Director of the Legal Resources Centre. His work there focused on the pass laws, forced removals, citizenship, and detention without trial.

From 1996 to 2000 he served as Director-General of the Department of Land Affairs in the Mandela administration.

He is now an advocate practising in Cape Town. He works mainly in the areas of constitutional law, human rights, administrative law, and other aspects of public law.

Geoff has acted as a judge of the High Court in Johannesburg and Cape Town. He is a trustee of the Sigrid Rausing Trust, a London-based international philanthropy working in human rights.

What do you see as the background to your outlook and activism on human rights issues in South Africa?
Geoff - I grew up in a moderately liberal home with a consciousness of what apartheid was about. And so it was a natural direction in which to go I suppose.

I was very heavily influenced in my student days by the Black Consciousness Movement, by Steve Biko in particular. NUSAS was white-dominated even if open to all. Blacks in the late sixties under the leadership of Biko promoted a philosophy of black consciousness. They said they were being submerged in these multi-racial organizations, subject to the wishes of whites and dominated by them. They needed to break away, form their own organizations, and regroup in order to confront white power. Here were black people who were our allies who were saying they didn't want to be engaged with us politically. They wanted to conduct their own struggle.

All this disturbed the equilibrium of liberal white movements who were seeking to make common cause. Biko always used to say, "It's as if we are separated by a mountain. We have to go round the mountain by different paths and we will meet again at the end of the day, but we have to separate in order to do what we have to do."

Was any pressure put on you to become involved in militant or illegal activities?
Geoff - Well, we were on the margins of the law. It was always on the edge of what was permitted and you broke the law in various ways. I was arrested for organizing a riotous assembly on the steps of the Cathedral. I thought it was a legal protest but the police said it was unlawful. I wasn't involved in any underground activities of any sort at any time. There was pressure – a friend who was in the ANC in Botswana tried to recruit me to join an ANC cell in Johannesburg. I felt that the most useful contribution I could make was the work I was doing at the Legal Resources Center. We were working with people who were obviously part of the ANC and we represented them, but I made the choice to stay on the other side of the line.

During that time did you have a sense of what was to happen in 1994?
Geoff - Well I never knew that it would lead to something as positive as that in my own time. I had no great sense of confidence about that. What I did think was that the work had its own value because we were assisting people who were resisting apartheid and through the legal system we were trying to crack some of its structures, e.g. the Forced Removal and the Pass Law Policies.

There was a question about being a lawyer in South Africa. I mean, what does a lawyer do in a fundamentally unjust system? That was always a subject of debate. I took the view that as long as people in positions of political leadership said they wanted decent lawyers representing people, then one should do it. The ANC in its various guises clearly supported the work that was being done inside the system and so it seemed to me to be the right thing to do.

There was a time in the mid-eighties when we had a succession of states of emergency and the courts were completely supportive of the government. At that time, I began to wonder if there was a point in being a lawyer in South Africa because law is in part about restraints on power. And then the politics started turning so quickly that I never really came face to face with that question.

It is actually an odd thing looking back now. I had struggles with myself about whether it was a useful thing being a lawyer, but no one ever said "You should get out of this, this is lending legitimacy to the system." I actually feel better about it now than I did then. Looking back, one can see it was a contribution. Nobody was fooled into thinking that our work legitimized apartheid.

Can you give us a sense of how your colleagues viewed these issues?
Geoff - There was a community of liberal and progressive lawyers who knew each other well, worked together, and cooperated quite closely. That was very important so that people didn't feel isolated. There was a sense of community of people doing similar work, like-minded people. There were very few of them when I came into the legal profession as an articled clerk in 1976, the time of the Soweto uprisings. We could meet around one small table. But that started to turn and by the 1980's there were quite a lot of people involved.

Something that characterized the attorney-client relationship was that none of them could pay for the legal help. So either you had to give it for free or raise the funds. The Legal Resources Center where I worked, raised money from American foundations and other institutions.

Was there any common denominator that marked the lawyers doing this sort of work other than the belief that this was the right thing to do?
Geoff - Predominantly white in the early days but that was for a variety of reasons, not least that there were very few black lawyers. They were disproportionately Jewish.

Do you have any explanation for that?
Geoff - Well you have to ask yourself why, in a very conservative community in which the leaders of that community abandoned ship on the issue of apartheid, or perhaps more accurately stayed on board, you didn't find the same phenomenon amongst the lawyers. I can't explain it. I don't think it had anything to do with Jewish teachings because Jewish teachers were silent on the subject. If you wanted to hear a religious critique of apartheid you had to go to the Anglican Cathedral. I certainly wouldn't go to *shul* for that. It's an interesting question. I really don't know the answer.

Were you in any way critical of the official Jewish stand of non–involvement?
Geoff - I gave up on it after my experience in student politics. The sixties and seventies were very rough years. I don't know how many churches I spoke at during my time in student politics. I did a lot of public speaking. I spoke once at the Reform *shul* in Cape Town. The organized Jewish community was silent when we were in trouble and one had the sense that we were an embarrassment to them. So I gave up on them. There were better battles to fight. I thought they were hopeless. I had an enormous amount to do with the Christian community and I enjoyed that.

Did this color your connection with things Jewish today?
Geoff - I have drifted away really because I felt the community had nothing to say or declined to say anything about the society in which I was living. I lost interest. I mean, I never made a conscious decision not to go to go to *shul* or do this or that. It just ceased to be part of my life because it seemed to be irrelevant.

Did you ever think about leaving South Africa?

Geoff - No. I always wanted to stay except in the mid to late eighties, when I did wonder if it was a sensible thing to be doing. But if you were engaged with something it gave your life some meaning and some value. The reason to leave was that argument being offered by the Black Consciousness Movement, "You can't be white in apartheid South Africa and not benefit from it." Just as you can't be white in South Africa today and not have benefited from it. That was an issue.

Tell us something about how you see things today.

Geoff - Well, in legal terms the changes are astonishing. Almost uniformly positive. More generally speaking, I think we all had very inflated expectations because things changed so dramatically, overwhelmingly, and favorably in 1994. So it depends on your time horizon. If in 1987 you had said to me, "This is what it will be like in 2007, how do you feel about that?" I would have grabbed it with both hands. If you'd said that to me in 1997, I would have said, "That is a bit disappointing." Our expectations changed and I suppose the question is, "What will we be saying in 2017?" We haven't done nearly well enough in areas where we should have – in poverty and inequality, which is a huge fault line running right through the society and it still has a racial component. We haven't done nearly well enough on unemployment, on violent crime, which is partly but not only a consequence of these things.

I am fundamentally optimistic but there is more than enough to worry about.

Who are going to be the Geoff Budlenders of the future? Are there young people out there with the resolve to take on the obvious challenges facing this young democracy?

Geoff - I think social mobilization is a difficult issue when the government is doing the right thing and failing. It is another thing to be energized and mobilized when you are against the government. It gives it a strong moral force. But what is going to energize the students today? You don't see protests on the campus. What are they going to protest about - the failure to deliver housing more quickly?

I think, however, there are the beginnings of social mobilization among black and white people who are saying, "We have to do something, we have got to get our hands dirty." But what has to be done is not so obvious. There are deep moral issues in the nation. Paradoxically it was easier under apartheid. The enemy was clear; it was obvious.

Do you still have the energy to get your hands dirty?
Geoff - I do. I do quite a lot of work in the 'rights' area. I do a lot of work for the Treatment Action Campaign, HIV issues, on housing, and on social welfare issues.

In what way has your legal work changed most significantly?
Geoff - The name of the game has changed. You go into court as a lawyer for a poor person and your back is not immediately against the wall as it used to be. Now very often your opponent's back is against the wall. For a lawyer that's an amazing sea change. You stand up in court and say, "My clients are poor people." And that is strike one. That was usually strike one against you. Our generation is the lucky one. There are very few generations who have a clear moral cause in their lives on which you can have no equivocation, the opportunity to fight against something, to see the victory and to have an opportunity to participate in building something new. That is a privilege. The crossover generations are the lucky ones.

It must be disappointing for you to see those who do not see a future here and are leaving or planning to do so ...
Geoff - I have friends and family who have said that it is time to leave – that is really awful. I do think it is a mobile world. People have the right to go where they like, but white people who have taken the benefits of apartheid of a post- apartheid education, and then say, "It's time to leave" are, I think, on very shaky moral ground. I think it's intolerable. They've kept black people out of those positions by taking the education, and then they say, "I'm going." I think if you are going to go then you should go. You shouldn't take all the fruits you can and then go.

Not when you have an unjustifiably racially advantageous position. I think it is one thing to go live in America, study at Harvard and then go live somewhere else. That's fine. Not here.

Johnny Copelyn

Cape Town
23/09/2007

*John Copelyn grew up in Johannesburg and attended Parktown Boys'
School. While studying African Government at Witwatersrand University, he
became involved in the textile industry in Natal.*

*In a twenty year career as a trade union leader John, a licensed attorney,
was part of the central leadership caucus that negotiated the first agreement
recognizing an unregistered non-racial union and the merger of several union
groups into South Africa's giant broad-based federation COSATU. He drafted
the constitution for COSATU, served on COSATU's central and national executive committees and was one of three central ANC/ COSATU/ SACP representatives that negotiated the National Peace Accord. From 1976 – 81 he was
a banned person in South Africa.*

*John worked in several different roles in the trade union movement, among
which were: National Organizer of the Textile Workers Industrial Union; General Secretary of the Amalgamated Clothing and Textile Workers Union South
Africa; CEO of the SACTWU Investment Group (Pty) Ltd, the commercial
operation of a welfare trust of SACTWU established for its members and their
families.*

*From 1994-1997 John Copelyn served as a Member of Parliament for the
ANC. He is currently the Chief Executive Officer of Hosken Consolidated In-
vestments Limited (Pty) Ltd. and also a board member of various other subsid-
iaries and associates of the group and a Trustee of HCI Foundation.*

*John lives in Cape Town with his spouse Corinne Abel. They have six chil-
dren between them and they foster a seventh.*

Did you have a typical Jewish South African childhood?
Johnny - My interest in Jewish matters was exceptionally low. There

was very little Jewish content in my life. Generally I was focused on sport and mates.

Likewise I had an incredibly apolitical background. My dad was a dentist; my mom a speech teacher. We weren't especially wealthy but we were never short of anything. I was certainly pretty cushioned from problems poor people experienced.

In 1967, my matric year, there was such a lot of buzz at the school about the Six Day War. It woke things that were far removed from me and got me excited about them. I was friendly with a number of guys who dragged me along to *Habonim*. I was very excited by the intellectual framework, debates, etc. that had never been part of my life before. I got very interested in the utopian, socialist ideas that *Habonim* stood for.

We started an urban collective *garin* aiming to bring the kibbutz into the cities. It was a fantastic set of ideas though probably the town we picked was too remote to fulfill them. The first wave of our *garin* settled in Carmiel but the group became disillusioned with the idea and decided to give up about three or four months before I was due to go on *aliyah*. When they closed it down, I suddenly realized I did not want to go to kibbutz and had not really thought about what I would do in Israel. The whole idea of going on *aliyah* and skipping the collective side of things wasn't that compelling to make me rush away from South Africa.

At the time, I was doing an Honors degree in African government. There were quite a lot of strikes in that year and I started focusing on worker organizations in South Africa.

What was the atmosphere at the time? Were people politically conscious?

Johnny - There were a few interesting lecturers on campus. Sheldon Leader and Michael Nupin were two people whose academically oriented left-wing ideas influenced me. They had different ideas, but both within the framework of scientific socialist thinking. At the time, anything leftish was banned, so you could not read Marx or Lenin. People went out of their way to find left-wing books.

Are scientific socialism and utopianism still part of your political outlook?
Johnny - From that point I began to think of myself as a communist. I never joined the Communist Party but I certainly always thought of myself as a Marxist through the seventies and eighties. Since then I have come to the view that things are much less predictable than anyone might think. In that sense I have become a lot less ideological than I was at different points. I think that is very common for left-wing people. The whole breakup of the Communist world and the exposé of all the dictatorial tendencies within it and all the stupidity have been incredibly disillusioning for anybody that was in that space.

How did you become involved with Rowley Arenstein?
Johnny – As part of my Honors degree I did a dissertation on the 1960 Pondo revolt. Rowley was actively involved in representing a large number of the Pondo leaders who were charged with arson, etc. I went to see him a number of times for information. He was under house arrest in Durban so it was quite a big secret thing. He was the most laid-back, relaxed character you could ever come across. He was very well-informed, a great intellect.

Did Rowley encourage you to take the path he had taken?
Johnny - Anybody who came into contact with him was unquestionably fascinated by his ideas. He was absolutely non-prescriptive - "You do what you think is right." But if you got into trouble then he was there for you.

On the other hand, he gave great practical advice. For example, when I got banned Rowley was quick to strongly advise against leaving the country: "You are a trade union man and you can't do any useful trade union work from outside." Likewise he was pretty helpful about how to manage the banning order, encouraging me to develop as many interests and hobbies as I could, each of which could justify a personalized variation of my banning and afford opportunities to meet other people despite the general prohibition on being with more than one other person at a time.

Tell us about your move from student to political activist.
Johnny – All the debates going on at NUSAS at the time were very remote from me. I just stuck to reading left-wing ideas and coupled it with all the *Habonim* ideas, which were very comparable – an antagonism to a world in which rich and poor are sharply divided. By the time I was finishing university, I was pretty keen to find a politically active role to play.

As soon as I finished varsity I managed to get an invitation to come down to Durban and work with some activists who were organizing black workers into unions. About a week before I was due to go, the state suddenly gave out all these bannings and house arrests to the group I had been chatting to. I arrived a week after they had all received their bannings and instead of being trained by them as I had planned, I found myself being just about the only guy there. The worker committee appointed me as the general secretary of the textile workers' union in the first couple of weeks I was there.

I started working with workers and there was nothing that could have been more interesting than that for me. I had had no contact with black people, with workers, their issues, and their generosity. I had never mixed with people like that and it was a whirlwind of new experiences for me. Intellectually I felt I had rocketed into the real world from outer space. I did not know anything about workmen's compensation, unemployment benefits, and the law governing dismissal. I had no idea what rights people had in their factories.

Were you not moving into dangerous territory?
Johnny - I never saw it that way. Trade union work was lawful. It is true that every time there was a strike it was regarded as a matter of national security. If workers stopped work to protest against a worker having been fired, the security branch would be on to it. But our role in that was taking people off the streets so they would not get beaten up. None of it seemed precipitously dangerous to me. The banning was

not a very heavy *shtick*. I never had the sense that I would be beaten up. I came along at a time when it was good to be a trade unionist. A lot of people did what I did before and got their heads bashed for it, but I didn't.

I began in the trade unions in 1973 and in 1976 there were the Soweto struggles. People were getting shot and brutalized. That was a different brand of politics. We were reform-orientated: organize meetings, tell people their rights, try and persuade employers to deal with the trade union.

Were there 'politicos' who tried to use you for the purposes of the armed struggle?
Johnny - A lot of political people who had been given ten-year jail sentences in 1964 came off Robben Island in 1974 and they made a bee-line for the trade union movement. Jacob Zuma was one of those. Billy Nair and Harry Gwala appeared pretty much the same time. They saw South Africa as a police state that could only be stopped in its tracks by armed struggle. They thought of the trade union movement as a weak structure whose main significance was being a nursery school for a cadre before they were guided into more serious underground work where they could be trained in needs of the armed struggle.

I thought of this line of thought as being a complete abuse of the trade union movement and I resisted it strongly.

Were you the only white union leader at that time?
Johnny - No, there were quite a lot. There was Taffy Adler, Rod Crompton, Bernie Fanaroff, Chris Albertyn, Mike and Jeanette Murphy, and several others. Unions often appointed a white general secretary. It made a lot of sense at the time. He could do things that black could not do, especially in relation to white employers. You were English-speaking, had been to university, you had an idea how management think and work. You had access to so many tools that an ordinary worker did not have.

Was it difficult for you to integrate into the black working environment?
Johnny – Worker meetings were all conducted in Zulu. Since I could not speak Zulu, I mainly had to rely on translators to participate in worker meetings. Nevertheless I never felt resented; quite the contrary, I felt incredibly warmly welcomed. Workers always wanted to hear my suggestions before they made a decision. People opened their homes to me and invited me in. A typical day for me would end with a shop steward meeting, after which I would drive everybody home as there was no public transport into the townships at night. People would invariably say, "Come and have something to eat with us." You would meet their family, etc. You were a child in the world of adults.

Subsequently I qualified as a lawyer and I spent a lot of time negotiating contracts with employers. Nevertheless I always felt okay about representing workers because I felt able to walk easily in the world of workers and to report in a language that workers talk. A lot of the skill of trade union work is being able to walk and talk easily across two totally different worlds.

Were you content with trying to improve conditions for workers in the factories?
Johnny - In Lenin's book *An Infantile Disorder*, the question he asks is: What should a good revolutionary do in a non-revolutionary time? People who try to make revolution in a non-revolutionary time are bound to fail. They should be branded as adventurists.

The work that we were doing was building up class solidarity, organizational capacity, all of which was very good for the working class and very important for revolutionary-orientated people to engage in without trying to manipulate it. This is the real political significance of union work.

Nevertheless, when you work for a trade union, everything revolves around getting a decent increase. If you get an extra rand, that is a victory. Does it change the world? It doesn't. But helping workers realize their collective power if they organize effectively unquestionably helps.

Did you see this as Stage One of an eventual revolution?
Johnny - The thing about South Africa was that the state was so over-whelmingly strong. The idea that you could overthrow it seemed impossible to me. I was never clear where this was all going to lead to. It just seemed very unjust. We could help people up to a point but there was a sharp-edged cliff that you had to avoid going over. The whole technique was putting the brakes on at a time when you were about to go over the edge of the cliff.

The change came in a series of steps. While I was banned, the trade union movement was recognized by the state. When they lifted my banning and I went back to the union in 1980, it was a whole different world. Trade union work in the eighties became much more sophisticated; negotiating with employers around grievances, rights, wages, shift patterns, etc. This wide range of issues became the daily bread of a trade unionist. Likewise the power of the organization grew in leaps and bounds. Suddenly we not only had the power to raise issues in individual factories but we could bring the whole country to a halt by calling a stay-away if there was a compelling issue.

When did you start to sense that things were going to change in the country?
Johnny - In 1985 they declared a State of Emergency. The trade unions were not the centre of what was being targeted by the state. However, as often happens with these things, you get drawn in at the periphery and you start to feel the heat anyway. So suddenly we got caught up in more militant behavior because the whole world was more militant around us.

In Natal, Inkatha was a mass organization that was used by the state to smash up the ANC. The result was that there was an unbearable amount of violence in townships. The question was: What should the ANC's view be? Should we try to shoot our way past Inkatha or not? The idea that we were going to bash our way to power did not appeal to me.

In the event I think we were influential in persuading the ANC to promote peace and develop a peace movement, where there was a propensity for violence. In that process I got drawn more and more into political work.

In 1994 twenty leaders of the union movement were chosen for inclusion in the ANC's parliamentary list and I was among them. I really felt it as a great honor for the union movement to include me in their delegation. I was an MP for three years. In truth, however, it only took a few months before I realized it was a mistake for me.

What was so unsatisfactory about being a member of parliament?
Johnny - It was a disappointment for me. I had always been part of a group of strategic thinkers in the union. There I was in a group of four hundred people, where I was just a pro-government backbencher. Everything was pretty much a *fait accompli* by the time it got to parliament. The seat belonged to the party and there was no role for any independent thinking by an individual member of parliament.

What was your focus once you had left parliament?
Johnny - In the mid-nineties I felt that if the working class were to act, it could become the major beneficiary of the new largesse that resulted from the racial transformation.

There seemed to me to be the opportunity for the trade union movement to build a substantial capital base for its members by becoming involved in several major business developments in the country. This base could transform the lives of its members and dramatically increase the range of things the union could do for them once it had the financial means.

Our union is called SACTWU – Southern African Clothing & Textile Workers' Union. It has about a hundred thousand members, which together with their families, amounts to about half a million people. I started an investment company for the union members and their families. It is owned by a trust, controlled by the current union leadership, the purpose of which is to provide social benefits to the union members and their dependents. Over time, this trust was able to become the major shareholder in a company called HCI which is a private equity corporation listed on the Johannesburg Stock Exchange. I was appointed the CEO of this company. The board is mainly made up of people who served long terms in the union's leadership together with me.

Over the last twelve years, we have managed to build this trust into a multi-billion rand base for the social program of the union.

In the last couple of years, we have started a new philanthropic foundation extending our work beyond union members generally into disadvantaged communities. This too has built up a sizable capital base of several hundred million rand and has allowed HCI to operate its own social programs at a level matched only by the top twenty corporations in the country.

How does money filter back to the workers?
Johnny - In our union, for example, every child of a trade union member is entitled to a bursary if he gets to a tertiary education institution. We have some three thousand such children. We are involved in huge medical programs centered around AIDS and HIV education, home care programs, tying them into antiretroviral programs, etc.

Are you concerned about the criticism you have been getting in the press lately?
Johnny - There are two different levels of this matter. One is the work I am doing, which essentially is managing businesses. People decry the work as unbecoming for a social activist. I hear this, but I am very excited by what I am doing. It is incredibly creative and allows me to paint on a scale not previously imagined. Over the last twelve years we have built a really significant group. Its businesses employ over thirty thousand workers.

I feel the work we do is really a good contribution despite the fact that it engenders some politically-correct whining

The second criticism is about the about the fact that I became personally wealthy out of the success of our business. In truth, that is how capitalism works, for better or for worse. If you build successful businesses, you become wealthy. It's not a strong suit for me, but rather an area of considerable embarrassment. I guess for me the key is not to lose a sense of personal humility and to recognize wealth is a social responsibility while you have it and that it doesn't always remain with you.

What are the main challenges facing South Africa today?
Johnny – It's a place that might go belly-up like Zimbabwe but I feel the challenge is to prevent it from going like that. It will only go that way if people who could make a difference don't put their backs to it.

Do you think that people here believe that things can change for the better?
Johnny – My daughter studied medicine in Sydney. She decided to come back after she finished her housemanship. If she wanted a safe life, she should have stayed in Sydney. If she wants a challenging life, there is more to do here.

My son has come back after being in London for the last ten years. He is working for an NGO and is very fired up with fixing everything.

I was incredibly lucky in that my own personal growth matched the country's growth. I came along at the right time. Many people hit a brick wall in the trade union movement. When I came along, the wall crumbled and shot me through it.

I hope my kids will have their dreams fulfilled here. You never know, do you, unless you are a good communist. Life is about engaging with problems. It's not about being sure you can solve them. I'm happy that they have dreams.

Dennis Davis

Cape Town
24/09/07

Dennis was educated at Herzlia School and the Universities of Cape Town (UCT), and Cambridge. He began teaching at UCT in 1977 and was appointed to a personal chair of Commercial Law, in 1989. He held joint appointments at Witwatersrand University and UCT 1995 – 1997. He was appointed a Judge of the High Court in 1998 and as President of the Competition Appeal Court in 2000.

Dennis is a member of the Commission of Enquiry into Tax Structure of South Africa and was a Technical Advisor to the Constitutional Assembly where the negotiations for South Africa's interim and final constitutions were formulated and concluded. He hosted, Future Imperfect, an award winning current affairs program, between 1993-1998.

He has been a visiting lecturer/professor at the Universities of Cambridge, Florida, Toronto, and Harvard.

Dennis has co-authored nine books, contributed various chapters in others, and written more than 100 articles in academic journals in the fields of constitutional law, tax law, insurance law, and South African political history.

Throughout his professional life Dennis has been active in the Jewish community and writes regularly for the South African Jewish newspaper (SAJR).

Where did your sense of disaffection with things in South Africa come from?
Dennis - When I went to Israel in 1966, at the age of fifteen, I had a sense of freedom that did not exist in South Africa. It seemed to me to be a far more convivial place to be as a Jew than here. When I got back, I had a real desire to go and live in Israel. That is when I got involved in *Habonim. Aliyah* continued to be my major aspiration for years.

I don't think I made a conscious ideological decision not to go to Israel. I am just not a risk-taker. I have simply meandered through life. I came from a family where my father was a motor mechanic and my mother was a legal typist. There was no money in our house, so I had no sense of taking risks, of being entrepreneurial. It was not there. So it seemed quite an awesome risk to go off to Israel when here it seemed easier to … Once I got towards my final year I began to radicalize quite quickly.

In the mid-seventies in South Africa, it became clear to me that there was a major moral drama playing out here, which seemed worth doing something about - getting involved in the trade union movement, (not in the heroic way of Johnny Copelyn), but thinking, "This is a place to be." It seemed that law was a place where there was a terrain of struggle. Those two influences were quite significant.

Once I decided I was going to stay in South Africa there were only two places you could go to in those days. There were no legal centers or public-interest law firms. You could either go to the trade union movement or the academic community. And I chose the latter. I was offered a job at UCT and took it immediately in early 1977. Once I was at the university there was something I could do – teach students. The university could be used as a base for some sort of political activity.

Although I still considered going to Israel and even wrote the Israel bar exam, my own difficulty in taking risks and the unfolding moral drama here, just kept me in South Africa.

Was there an anti-apartheid struggle going on in academia that you were part of?
Dennis - Absolutely. In 1979 the university arranged for me to go on sabbatical to Cambridge. It was the tail-end of the Marxist academic highpoint. I was very influenced by that. That is when I moved from a liberal to a Marxist position. When I got back, there was a huge fight on the campus between Marxist and liberal academics: those who saw things in class terms and those who saw them in race terms - would the economy naturally purge the excesses of racism, etc?

Were you free to think and write what you wanted?
Dennis - Yes. It was utterly bizarre. I must have been mad but in 1980
I wrote a piece in the South African Law Journal – a Marxist critique of
human rights – and to the editor's credit, he published it.

You defined yourself as not being a risk-taker…
Dennis - I was a risk-taker in that sense. To a large degree one was pro-
tected by the academic community. There was talk of banning a few
of us but they never did. For reasons I will never understand. We were
reasonably free and it was an enormously exciting time in academic
life. There was a community out there, a community across academic
disciplines who were fighting the same fight.

What is amazing about South Africa is that there was more debate,
contestation of views and discourse in the late seventies and early eighties than there is now. Figure that out. There is a real deadening hand
from the top on this democracy of ours, which has certainly stultified
all of that.

Were people actively involved in recruiting, etc.?
Dennis - There was a lot of that but I was not involved. My involvement was in an ideological fight rather than a physical one. Once or
twice people tried to recruit me. But I was a maverick and somewhat
distrustful of the ANC and the Communist Party.

In the mid-eighties I wrote a book with a colleague from England
called *Beyond Apartheid*, which was a significant critique of the ANC
and how they had let down the masses. However, even if you were a
maverick in relation to the academic community, you ran the same
dangers. I landed up in the townships in the dead of night advising
various student groups on aspects of the emergency, despite not being
a risk-taker.

I was probably ignored by the security police because they had bigger fish to fry than some white Jew. I am not sure whether, as distinct
from the sixties and Rivonia, the Jewish part had some protective quality. I know there were Jews like Raymond Suttner who were detained
for long periods but I was on the fringes of the Jewish establishment.

I was a Jew who recognized his Judaism. It was important to me. For twenty years I gave sermons in the student synagogues. The community knew me. I was partially informed by my Marxism and partially by my Jewish ethos.

Where did this leave you in the debate with the Jewish Board of Deputies?
Dennis - As students, we saw the BOD as a bunch of sell-outs. Right through the seventies and into the eighties I was one of the people who were very critical of the Board.

That was the difference between me and other lefties. I was the only one who was a regular *shul*-goer, actually giving sermons on the liturgy on the high holidays, and its relevance to South Africa. I often wondered whether that might have helped me because the Jewish community was so up the bum of the government at that time. If I had been carted off they would have had to do something because I was one of them, in a different way to Raymond Suttner.

In retrospect do you think the BOD could have taken a different line?
Dennis - I disagree with Giddy Shimoni's argument. There was much more leverage. When we were kids, we were naïve and the community judged correctly that they were dealing with real fascists and there was a limit to what they could do. Where I part company with him is that by the late seventies, every other community in the country was shouting the odds, quite courageously. For the Jews to have joined in would not have jeopardized them in the slightest. The government had far more problematic issues than to pick a fight with the Jewish community, particularly now that Israel was on its side. The last thing it was going to do in those years was round on the Jewish community. I understand perfectly that at the time that Israel was on the side of the African states, in the sixties, the Jewish community was limited in what it could do. After that we were pretty dismal. I think that dismal nature has cost us dearly because it has meant that we do not have independence any longer. The establishment is uncritical of the ANC in the

same way it was uncritical of the National Party.

It seems unusual for a judge to be so open on political matters...
Dennis - One had to be careful. As a judge there is a limit to what you can say publicly and I have got myself into trouble more than once. But by and large, you promote the constitution. In other words, what you do is to argue to the effect that the government is not committing itself to constitutional guarantees. Your defensive point is to say, "I am here to promote the constitution, no matter who is in power."

Do you see crime as a societal problem or one that has to be treated from the top down?
Dennis - It is a basic problem but it has to be treated all ways. It has to be treated from the top by policing, but also upwards. You have to build community. If you go out to the Cape Flats now you will see it is not all that different from when you left. That is the breeding ground—kids have nowhere to play, no movie houses to go to, nothing. It is amazing how the spatial geography of apartheid has remained pretty constant in Cape Town and the nature of the townships has remained pretty constant throughout South Africa.

Do you think your generation of people who resisted apartheid was 'starry eyed' in terms of what the post-apartheid reality would be like?
Dennis - I think that for the people involved, aged fifty to eighty-five, there is a huge level of exhaustion. Besides saying, "It has not gone the way we wanted it to," do they really have the energy to carry on the fight to put things right?

Can you pinpoint areas where it has not gone the way you wanted it to?
Dennis - Firstly, the economy. The so-called 'historically disadvantaged' are still disadvantaged. Related to that, the incredible amount of greed. I am not against black people making money but BEE seems to be nothing more than a few making vast sums of money. As a result, corruption has been dire. For all Mbeki's achievements on the

economy, which have been considerable, the government has created an environment in which there is very little public discourse, in which populism and racist slurs have become the dominant feature of our society. That is hugely worrying. We are far more a racial society than one would have thought thirteen years in. We got off to a good start under Mandela and we have gone backwards quite rapidly.

I suppose it was naïve to believe we were just going to elide over three hundred years of racist rule. But the fact is you would have hoped for some incremental movement. Mbeki has taken us back. You only have to read his weekly column on the ANC website. It is bizarre.

There are still a lot of whites who are very mean-spirited. Some are saying, "Let's forget the past and move on." That is ridiculous. You cannot forget three hundred years of racist rule and say there is no need for affirmative action or remedial steps. But affirmative action must also take account of the values candidates espouse.

We must be careful that populist racial politics does not subsume everything including commitment to what is best for the disadvantaged.

Has the character of the Jewish community changed significantly in recent years?
Dennis - It is hard to know how religious the community has become. The fissures are more acute. When we were young, most people considered themselves orthodox. Today there are a few religious people and the vast majority is disaffected from almost anything. I do accept there is a move to the right amongst the hardcore which never was there.

On the fringes, people are organizing their own notions of Jewish identity in protest against the grinding conformity that orthodoxy has imposed. The right-wing rabbis have become the public face of the community and we handed leadership to them. And by the way, the leadership of *Habonim* is quite radical.

Habonim has got involved with social issues. I think that how Israel pans out is going to be crucial for Jewish communities around the world. I have little doubt that if Israel were to reach some meaningful settlement with the Palestinians this grinding conformity of orthodoxy would change. Rabbi David Rosen has always said you are going to have to wait for things to change in Israel before they change here.

Do you think Israel can learn anything from the South African experience?
Dennis - I think it can, but a lot is untranslatable. What is important for the Palestinians is that the ANC had a Freedom Charter. You have to have a vision of what you want. You have to have something that convinces the other side that life will not be terrible after the change. One of the key differences between where you live and where I live is that the ANC had a profound commitment to democracy of a bill of rights type. When the ANC and the National Party sat down to negotiate, they each had their competing bill of rights. They were debating under quite narrow terms, which is very different from when you want a divorce from a marriage. The fact that both sides had a prefigured vision was very important.

We also learnt that at some stage in the negotiations you can no longer put the genie back in the bottle. De Klerk desperately wanted to do that, but it was too late. Had he or Mandela been killed in the way Rabin was, I suspect we would have had the same chaos. De Klerk's one moment of greatness was his understanding that you had to make the big move in a decisive fashion. An Israeli prime minister would have to get the backing of the EU and the Americans and say, "I am going to make a major move and I need your support." Those are the major lessons we learnt.

People in the streets were stunned by what De Klerk did. They could not believe it. You cannot do these things incrementally. It is not as if De Klerk came up with a new idea. A lot of things occurred. The economy was in a tailspin. South Africa had got a bad knock in Angola from the Cubans, our *intifada* would not go away, communism had collapsed, and the military establishment was weakened by Angola. It took somebody to grasp the nettle in that situation.

The desire for change gained momentum, helped by the wish to be part of the world again, particularly in the area of sport.

How optimistic are your children about the future of South Africa?
Dennis - I have a daughter of twenty and a son of seventeen. I suspect I might lose my kids. They may leave. It is a risk I take.

How active have you been in trying to shape their outlook on life?
Dennis - Like every parent. Every Friday night I have read to them the Jonathan Sacks commentary on the Talmud. We sit there for twenty minutes and read it and then talk about it. I think, "Maybe something is going to rub off, maybe they will return," but at this stage they are going through a very rebellious phase.

Do you want them to return?
Dennis - Yes. I do. I said to them, "There seems to be a tradition worth preserving. Are you going to take it on yourselves to stop it?" My son is very skeptical of what Judaism has to offer. They are grateful we came back to South Africa. They like being here. If this country holds firm they will do what so many other people do - they will go away for a couple of years and then come home.

Do you think your children have the fire in the belly that you had, to fight for causes close to their hearts?
Dennis - I think they have less. My kids say to me, "You were confronted with great moral dilemmas. What have we got?" I teach at the university and there is no doubt that today's students do not have the fire in the belly which it takes to construct a new society.

Mickey Korzennik

Muldersdrift
28/05/08

Mickey Korzennik was born in Cape Town in 1930. After living in the Hashomer Hatzair bayit and working in their offices for five years, Mickey made aliyah to kibbutz Barkai .

He returned to South Africa in1957 and began a career in art that has spanned five decades.

Mickey's graphics have been used extensively by South African interior decorators and have also found international recognition in galleries in New York, London, Paris, and Israel. Often pioneering new techniques in the mural field, he uses a wide variety of materials.

His commissions include corporate buildings banks, offices, and places of worship. His sculptures can be seen in corporate and private collections locally and worldwide.

Mickey lives in a well equipped country studio/workshop outside Johannesburg.

Can you tell us about your outlook on life as a young man in Hashomer Hatzair?

Mickey - Why rely on my failing memory when I have written it down? Let me read you what I wrote in my book *The Journey is the Teacher* (1998). (Reads aloud) "The struggle for a place in the sun and social justice which dominated and still dominates my *weltanschauung* can easily be transposed from the milieu of my Jewish background and those historical times, to the struggle of the previously disenfranchised people in South Africa." (p.5)

Life until age six was in the environs of the "Jewish ghetto which evolved around the Gardens in Cape Town, Vredehoek and

Muizenberg. Family ties were close… Yiddish was the language of the home… a tight tribal fortress. 1936 saw a move to Johannesburg, and again it was the ghetto, this time Doornfontein. By the age of twelve, little wonder that the Zionist movement and Palestine captured (my) imagination." (p.158/9)

Joining *Hashomer* was purely accidental. Although I told them I was not interested in going to Palestine they managed to get me interested in meeting other Jewish kids, hiking, playing games, etc. without any particular ideological angle. I went to summer *machane* and I was impressed that these people were different. The women for instance - bloomer shorts and red kerchiefs. Conditions were really rough. A lot of kids went home early. The toilet holes filled up and had to be emptied. Seeing Jewish kids, up to their bootlaces in s… surprised but impressed me. I was caught up by the spirit of the thing and ended up going to thirteen *machanot*.

Hashomer Hatzair had a lot of brainy guys running things. People were pulling in different directions. There were the Trotskyites, people like Baruch Hirson. The "sexual guys" (Reichians) like Vivian Rakoff put up a contraption the called an orgone accumulator, where you got supercharged sexually. Our *madrichim* and *shlichim* pulled the movement back to what we saw were its essential values of Zionism, socialism, and *chalutziut*. We considered ourselves the "unintellectuals", down to earth.

Chayim Shur came as a *shaliach* at the right time. He focused on *aliyah* to a kibbutz. He wasn't weak on socialist theory but he was a far cry from where Hirson and his thinking were going. Our activities were Jewish-centered, (Jewish) identification, with the simple aim of going to Israel and working the land.

You say "simple", yet Hashomer Hatzair in contrast to Habonim at that time had the image as of being very serious …
Mickey - It was, it was heavy stuff. A number of people left *Habonim* because it was not serious enough. Our *madrichim* used to bring us leaflets and send us off to the Zionist Federation library to read books

about Jewish history and Zionism.

But in the eyes of the parents we were an unknown entity. They wanted to know two things when we tried to get their kids to go to camp: 1. Were we communists? 2. Did we believe in free love?

What we had was not free love in any promiscuous sense. When a relationship was serious then, you took the woman to bed. Being in love was the criterion, however, and you were expected to adhere to this absolutely. If I walked in on a girl showering at the movement *bayit*, I was not to look at her as a sexual object (laughs). It was a little far fetched but it worked for us. I lived in a *bayit* for five years and never touched a lady inappropriately, though it got pretty hot at times I can tell you. That was the value system that was passed on to us. Sexuality was rife but for us it had to be governed by your head and your values.

What made you decide to go on aliyah?
Mickey - It was a natural progression. I became a *madrich*, lived in the movement *bayit* and worked for the movement. I was accepted at Wits for architecture but the movement was against careers. If you spent five years at university, the chance of your going to pick up stones and shovel manure on a kibbutz was very remote. I worked in the movement office for five years. That was my tour of duty before going to a combined *Habonim-Hashomer Hatzair hachshara* in Israel. Aki Lopert from *Habonim* was actually responsible for weaning me from some of the *meshugassim* of *Hashomer Hatzair* . He taught me that it is possible to be a *halutz* and have fun. By the time I got to kibbutz, I was already partially spoilt in the sense that my *Hashomer Hatzair* dogmatism was less extreme.

Would you describe your connection to Israel and Zionism as ideological?
Mickey – There was an aspect of that but it was far more complex. In my book, I describe some of what would go through my mind sitting alone on guard duty in the haunting quiet of a moonlit night on kibbutz Barkai. "… in a historical cauldron, armies marched to and fro in a procession spanning thousands of years - and the land speaks …

from Father Abraham to glorious wencher, fighter and sweet singer of psalms David, have trodden this same soil… and I feel a rootedness that defies description." (p.166/7)

Was art a part of your kibbutz life?
Mickey - On Barkai's fifth anniversary I did the story of the kibbutz in graphic form. As a result I was given permission to study art once a week after work. Of the fifty-two possible days, I used seven. Despite what I said about my dogmatism being less extreme, when you are a good *halutz*, if the insects are eating your grapes, you don't leave your work to study art. The next year I was given a day a week but had to do an early morning work shift first and then hitch a ride to the *Galil*. The result was that I gave it up. It was just too heavy a *shlep*. The next year I was given a full day a week. I had had only three classes when the 1956 war began. That was the end of that.

Are you saying that the needs of the group always won out?
Mickey – Perhaps, but you have to remember that the kibbutz was only five years old. Your position on the kibbutz was determined by your ability to put in a long, hard day's work and not by the beautiful decorations that you could do for a festival or a play. I was due to become *merakez* of the vineyards. Who knows? I might have become a great agriculturalist and sublimated other needs that way. It's an imponderable.

Were there other things that troubled you about kibbutz life?
Mickey - You start getting bothered by things. There were the hard workers but there were also a number of loafers, even parasites. It was all so equal that it became unequal. The first radios were not given to the guys working sixteen hours a day in the bananas, but according to who came to the kibbutz first. There were things that didn't seem right to me. I loved the concept of equality but it was a utopian idea. People aren't equal. In reality people were jockeying for positions and all sorts of inequalities became apparent.

Why did you leave kibbutz?
Mickey - I was very much a *kibbutznik*. I would never have left. But I

married a woman who was sick for three years while we were on kibbutz. Conditions and nutrition were just not giving her a chance. It was to take care of her health that we eventually went back to South Africa in 1957. The kibbutz supported our going unanimously bar one exception. The *gizbar* asked me to write home for the ticket. I can't tell you how that broke my heart. When I was working in the movement, I used to pop up to my mom's flat on the way to the office. She would offer me something I loved like peaches and cream. I would say, "No" because the other *chaverim* didn't have peaches and cream. That is how seriously we took our *chaverut*. And now this… to be thrown out, as it were. Had I not done enough to earn those two bloody tickets? They also suggested that while my wife was being treated I should study art seriously in Cape Town. Who was going to pay for it all? Nobody bothered to figure that out at all.

At about the same time, I was losing faith in communism and the Russian model. Khrushchev got up at the twentieth congress of the Communist Party and said that whatever the West said about Stalin was true and worse. At that stage, the ships were bringing arms from the Eastern bloc to Alexandria. They were gearing up to wipe us off the map. Every fishwife in Tel Aviv knew that the Russians were a crowd of bastards, and *Hashomer Hatzair* were still debating it. Now where was I placed in this whole bloody shambles? I had been brainwashed, no doubt.

In short, by the time we got back to South Africa my ideological ardor was seriously dented. I discovered that the capitalist system wasn't all that bad. If you picked up your bag, went downtown and pitted yourself against the system, you could start earning a living. My Israel and kibbutz days crumbled like a pack of cards. I started reading and studying art. My whole life moved in another direction.

Was it difficult re-adjusting to South Africa?
Mickey - What happened to me is very strange. I was born here but I am a split personality -the Jew and the South African. I married twice into Afrikaans families. Part of me lived in an Afrikaans milieu with

ouma en oupa. I had an affinity with the Afrikaner, with his struggle for a place in the sun. The average Afrikaner was cast in a place similar to the Jew in Israel, into a place that was too big to handle, an impossible situation. The physical country has a special place in my heart. I can cry for the Afrikaner as I can cry for the Jew. Part of me thinks the Afrikaners got a raw deal. In my own experience I never saw them as the monsters some of them undoubtedly were.

Now take the Jews. Many of my friends in Israel say they have nothing in common with the religious settlers on the West Bank. There is something parallel here. Many of the Afrikaners I know had nothing in common with the racism and the ugliness of apartheid.

Sport is the greatest thing in this country for me at the moment. When you see black and white and colored all going down in the scrum together... My son has picked up my liberal outlook. He is actually married to an Indian lady.

What role has Israel played in your life over the years?
Mickey – There have been letters to and fro from Israel and old friends that go back to those halcyon days when I lived on Barkai and I have carefully followed everything that has happened there. My memories of the songs we sang around the campfires for the reborn homeland and the ecstasy of the dances as we linked arms in a circle of oneness, are with me all the time. The assumption in these letters was that I was basically a *kibbutznik* in exile. The values of earning your bread by the sweat of your brow and A.D. Gordon's 'religion of labor' have remained deeply ingrained. My identification with the shock and loss caused by Rabin's murder was deeper than you can imagine.

I am going to be cremated. At first, I thought of asking for my ashes to be spread on Barkai but that is unfair. I haven't been there for donkey's years.

Michael Kuper

Johannesburg
17/10/07

Michael Kuper was born and educated in Johannesburg where he has prac-
ticed as a leading Senior Counsel since1984.

In his youth Michael was active in Bnei Zion and Habonim. His accom-
plished rhetorical style made him a well-known figure as chairman of the Zion-
ist Youth Council.

He was called to the bar in 1969 and lectured at Witwatersrand University
between 1966-69. Between 2002-05 he was Honorary Professor in the Depart-
ment of Procedural Law, at the University of Pretoria.

Michael was chairman of the Johannesburg Bar Council in 1987,1988,
and 1995. He has served as Acting Judge of the High Court of South Africa on
various occasions. Michael has been the chairman of the Arbitration Founda-
tion of Southern Africa (AFSA) since 1996. He has participated both as coun-
sel and arbitrator in South Africa as well as abroad. Recent activities include
Chairman – Steering Committee of Africa A.D.R. (African Dispute Resolu-
tion).

Michael is currently the Disciplinary Commissioner for Cricket South Af-
rica.

Which influences would you note as playing a significant role in the
way you came to see the world?
Michael - Well, clearly typical influences, family etc. I was involved
in the youth movement in a concentrated way from mid to late high
school and through my university days. So Zionist ideology, which was
my father's ideology was a dominant initial influence on me. I always
remember my university years, though, as being years of liberation, as
it were, after school. I think my views were helped along by academics,

my lecturers, and my professors in the arts and in the law. In particular, people like Julius Lewin, Godfrey Le May, and Bobby Hahlo. I read and I listened to the radio and I suppose I was subject to all these influences.

Were there particular books or people that had an impact?
Michael – People, rather than books, as I recollect. My father was an early formative influence but he had died by the time I was eighteen. The balance of people who influenced me would have been the university people. Prof. Le May offered me an Oxford University access and I had to make up my mind whether I wanted it or not. In the end I refused. I remember him telling me that the road to Jerusalem could be through Oxford. In the end I took neither road. I did an honors degree in African Government in a class which consisted of three people. The one was Essop Pahad (Minister in the Presidency 1999-2008), the other was Marius Schoon, and myself. Only one person finished the course and that was me. Essop went into exile during the course. Marius tried to blow up the Hillbrow police station during that year and was jailed for twelve years. So it was quite an interesting class of three.

And then I did law and was exposed to very fine legal academics who found the study of law a matter of absorbing interest.

Many of your youth movement contemporaries remember you as a youth leader passionately and articulately debating Zionist and other ideological issues. Can you tell us where you went with this?
Michael - I went nowhere with it. I did not make *aliyah*. I suppose I had the wrong qualifications for Israel, but far more important were personal and family reasons. I guess there's a window of opportunity to make *aliyah* and if that passes then your roots are established elsewhere. I would have taken an interest in the South African Zionist movement but I had a bad experience with the then Chairman of the Federation and I drifted away.

What replaced the strong ties and experiences that characterized the social structure of the youth movement?
Michael - Well, a wife and family, children, and then grandchildren. And then of course I had entered the legal community and that is a world of its own.

My recollection is that while you may talk of my having a passionate ideology, having moved over from *Bnei Zion* I was always in opposition in *Habonim*, always clashing with the established leadership. My take on that at the time was that very narrow-minded people were in control. They were teenage ideologues dedicated to *"chalutzik* Zionism" as they saw it. They saw the whole world through that particular prism. My feeling was, perhaps unjustly, that they closed their minds to other views. You always knew what they would say, you always knew what they would think. And these were the people who were running the movement. So I never saw *Habonim* ideologically as a comfortable place.

I felt within the movement there was far too much involvement with a particular narrow strain of Zionist thought and that what we should have been doing was exploring all aspects. I thought that training South African youth who had a privileged upbringing and education to live on a farm was wasteful. This was a glorification of an agricultural way of life laced with a heady mix of romanticism and idealism. Why wasn't the movement open to urban Zionism? Anyway it's all long past and what remains with me is the warmth of good companionship and the company of friends.

What were the ramifications of your decision to stay in South Africa?
Michael – I settled down to a busy profession and family life. So far as politics were concerned, I thought liberal and voted Progressive and got on with my life. I certainly wasn't a political activist. At work, there was a choice either to get involved with "political trials" or not. Members of the Bar would either take them or try to avoid them. I was involved in a few of these political trials and I learnt a lot about the reality of the situation from them. When I was offered a brief in a political

trial, I took it. It was a matter of duty, not choice. There were others at the Bar much more involved than I was.

I became involved with government policy in another capacity when later I became vice-chairman and then chairman of the Bar. It was our obligation to deal with government and try to get it to alter its stance on repressive political issues. I must say that government ministers received us and sought to interact with us, but ultimately were not going to be persuaded for a moment by anything we said. But they were interested in not antagonizing the legal profession.

Can you give us some sense of what the legal community was like during the 1970's?
Michael - The influence of the Bar Council which governed your professional life was pervasive. In my day the people who would be at the top of that hierarchy were people like Issy Maisels and Sydney Kentridge. I came just after Bram Fischer had been arrested.

My first political case was wonderful for me because my leader was Sydney Kentridge. George Bizos was in the team. It was a trial in which the government had prosecuted twenty-four members of the ANC, starting with Winnie Mandela, under the charges of the Suppression of Communism Act. The State hadn't proved their case and they were acquitted.

As the accused were walking out of the court having been acquitted under the old Act, so were they arrested again under the new Act. I was called in (I was probably about twenty-seven years old at the time) by George Bizos who said that I should research whether this duplication of charges was legal or not. There was one other accused, who wasn't part of my group of accused who had been kidnapped and brought back across the border. So in his case the question was whether he was subject to the Court's jurisdiction at all. The two trials were held together and he was convicted. When the acquittal of the twenty-one was read, so too was that single guilt-finding announced. But his wife didn't understand. She thought her husband had been acquitted and came running down with their little child only to find her husband being taken away in the Black Maria. He was a very strong man and when they came down he stood there shaking the wire shouting "*amandla my son amandla*" (Xhosa and Zulu word meaning 'power'. A popular rallying cry in the days of resistance against apartheid). It was a sobering reminder of the realities. I made occasional forays outside of my usual practice, which was essentially a practice in commercial law and litigation and was pretty typical lawyer's work as you would find anywhere in the world.

What about the stuff that happened around rather than inside the courtroom?
Michael - Well the Biko case had a dramatic effect on the Bar. It was seen as murder, known to be murder. It was freely spoken of. The Bar was fiercely independent, even though its members had all sorts of different views. Shortly before my time we had two members of note: John Vorster and Bram Fischer. They were in the same bar at the same time in the same community. All my life there the dominant thinking was liberal. The Johannesburg Bar was always in opposition.

I think if you had said to anyone at the time, "What will happen with majority rule?" They would have answered you by saying, "Well it's going to be a bloodbath." I think that fear of a bloodbath overshadowed a lot of the thinking. People said there was just no solution to South Africa's position. And of course there were things happening that made one less sympathetic to the liberation movement. There was a period in which the ANC and other groups embarked on a violent path. I remember driving into Johannesburg to work and hearing explosions.

Sydney Kentridge, Jules Browde and I were involved in a long commercial matter. A limpet mine was placed in the robing room immediately below the court room. If it hadn't been for some old janitor identifying it in time and getting it removed... that is the only reason we and others didn't get blown up. That didn't give me a good feeling about the ANC or what the ANC would bring with it. Remember that at that time it was an avowed communist movement and although many would have said their communism was skin deep, one just didn't know. And remember that we were also cut off from world knowledge of what they were.

But generally there was huge dislike for the government. Fear, I suppose, in the time of Verwoerd and Vorster, contempt, in the days of PW Botha and then bewilderment in the days of FW de Klerk.

What was life like for white liberals? How did thinking people maintain their equilibrium in the face of the day-to-day reality of privilege based to such a large extent on oppression?
Michael – Well, there were liberal activists and they were subject to government bullying. I wasn't in that category at all. First thing I did was to live my personal life with all its ups and downs, to the full. And that absorbs a lot of energy. You try to make your way in a profession which is not easy. Law is a difficult profession. The notion that politics was dominant in my day-to-day life is hugely exaggerated. For me there would be the constant dismay at the poverty, there would be constant irritation and hostility to the broadcasts that you would hear. There would be outrage at what the government was doing. But much of it was, as they used to say, "the table talk of the northern suburbs." There were those I suppose who found it was just too difficult to reconcile their daily lives with the realities, and they left. But for those that didn't, it was a given part of life. You just dealt each day with that day. I did nothing at all which would have brought the government to an end by violent or illegal means. I knew very few people who did that.

Was the proportion of fellow professionals who left high?
Michael – Yes, quite high. There was a continual drain over the years and then spurts of emigration after 1976 and at various times after that. South African lost a great many good people. But the Bar was more insulated and I felt that one was doing meaningful work at the Bar.

I must say that during transformation, questions were asked about the Bar's record. Whether it had been too self-satisfied? I never thought so. I thought that the Bar had done a good job in maintaining legal standards and ensuring fair trials during the darkest days.

But the trend of your questions highlights the apartheid issues. We all lived our lives day-to-day absorbed in our personal lives. Apartheid was an intractable issue but it did not dominate everything. I suppose the Palestinian issue is the same kind of thing. It seems to be intractable but everyone lives their own lives nonetheless.

Since transformation, there have, of course, been different problems and challenges. Rampant crime is most obvious but there are also very great rewards in living in a society which is transforming itself, as best it can. I do not know whether we will establish and maintain a truly democratic society. But there is so much good work to be done in trying to improve ourselves as a country and as a more united people.

By and large, I do not regret the decisions I took or the life I chose to lead. I would guess that those who emigrated and found their feet in other countries feel exactly the same. There is no right or wrong about it.

Leon and Lorna Levy

Cape Town
25/09/07

Lorna Levy started her working life as a trade unionist in Johannesburg in the late 50's. While attending conferences abroad, her husband, Leon was arrested in Johannesburg and she did not return to South Africa. With Leon she established a home in London, where they were forced to live in exile from the 1960s.

Lorna was active in the British Labour Party as a Councillor but returned to her 'political home', the ANC, for the final years of exile in the UK. She returned to Cape Town in 1997, taking up a life of political activism.

In 2009 she published her memoirs, Radical Engagements, a Life in Exile. She has been politically involved throughout her life in numerous issues, presently concentrating on environmental ones.

Born in Johannesburg in 1929, Leon Levy began work at the age of 16 and became an active trade unionist. He was a founder member of the South African Congress of Trade Unions (SACTU), serving as its first national president. He was a member of the South African Peace Council in the mid-1950s and a defendant in the Treason Trial from 1956 until 1961. Leon was the first person to be detained for 90-days without trial. Banned in 1957, he was detained for five months during the 1960 state of emergency. He left South Africa on an exit permit in 1963.

Leon returned to Cape Town in 1994 and got a position as a commissioner in the Conciliation, Mediation and Arbitration Commission. He is also the chairman of the Center for Conflict Resolution.

Can you start us off by giving us some personal background…
Leon - I was about fifteen when I started getting interested in the liberation movement in this country. I taught at a night school that was organized by the Communist Party for illiterate Africans. Neither they

nor the teachers had to be communists. It was run by Myrtle Berman, who was all of nineteen or twenty. I taught at the school and I was also a member of *Hashomer Hatzair*, as were Joe Slovo and Baruch Hirson. In around 1946, at the age of eleven, I got interested in *Hashomer Hatzair*. It was rather radical and I liked it. We were introduced to Marxism in an interesting way. We discussed all sorts of unconventional ideas, like relationships with parents and sex. That all intrigued me at that age.

Later on, still as a member of *Hashomer Hatzair* I used to attend Young Communist meetings. When I matriculated, I went to work in an ordinary commercial place. I did not go to university then but later I went to Ruskin College, Oxford when I was in exile. Very soon I switched to the trade union movement and I became the general secretary of two secondary industry unions and eventually was a co-founder of the South Africa Congress of Trade Unions, the forerunner of CO-SATU. I became the president of that organization for nine years.

Round the age of twenty-five I was arrested on a charge of high treason and was on the treason trial for five years. I was detained a number of times during that period. After I was acquitted in the treason trial I continued in the trade union movement, was banned several times over, a common saga. Eventually, at the age of thirty-three, I was detained under the ninety-day detention law. When I was released, I went to London, where I continued my anti-apartheid activities but became interested in trade union and wider labor matters. At Ruskin, I studied industrial relations, labor economics and the economics of social development. That interested me a lot and I worked in that sphere for a long time.

Lorna – My background is very different. I was never in a Jewish youth movement, which is significant because so many people seem to have been influenced by being in a youth movement. I had a pretty conventional childhood in Johannesburg - white, middle class. But when I went to university at the age of about eighteen, probably because there were African students at Wits at the time, almost overnight I suddenly became aware of this crazy place I was living in. Nobody influenced me to change my whole perspective. It seemed to be something that came from within. It would have been from reading Father Huddleston's book *Naught for Your Comfort* or Alan Paton's *Cry the Beloved Country* but also because it was where I found myself. There was a point at which I changed absolutely radically and from then onwards I questioned everything that happened around me, which made me very unhappy about things in South Africa.

I began to fall out with my friends and I questioned them about how people who seemed to share my views were indifferent to their surroundings. Then I drifted towards more radical people and I looked around for different options, different groups. Was it to be the Liberal party or Helen Suzman's new Progressive party? I took part in demonstrations against segregation, then called Extension of the Universities Act. At one, I was standing with a banner and this man in a post office van drove straight at me and I thought I was going to be mowed down.

When I finished my degree, I wanted to do something useful. I got a job in the Shop Worker's Union, an all-white union. And I hardly knew what a trade union was. It was there that I met Leon. We eventually got married and as a result I also found myself in exile. I was never a member of the Communist Party. I had a passport and I did have the opportunity to leave the country to attend conferences. Leon was detained while I was in England and I did not go back to South Africa. This was a catastrophic thing to happen. One minute I was thinking this is a lovely place for a holiday, and the next I realized I was going to be living there for the rest of my life. At that point, we started life together in England.

Leon, how did you get interested in Marxism so early in life.
Leon – I was very poor. My father died when I was five and my mother worked very hard to bring up four children. Both my parents were *yiddishists*, not Zionists. I understood poor people, what it meant to have no money, and not to be able to buy school uniforms and pay your school fees on time. I was very interested in solutions for poor people, having been exposed to *Hashomer Hatzair* and the Young Communist

League. My sister took me quite regularly to the Left Club, which was a multi-racial club where members enjoyed singing, dancing, and lectures. So from an early age I grew up among those sorts of people.

I did not go the Israeli route because I did not think it was the solution to the problems I had. I was more influenced by communist and socialist ideas. To me, becoming part of the collective on kibbutz was a damn good way of not having to work. They were not very interesting people, they did not have radical ideas. They were staunch Zionists and really believed in *Hashomer Hatzair* and Israel.

What accusation was brought against you at the treason trial?
Leon – Trying to overthrow the state by force of violence and trying to establish a communist state. Twenty thousand documents were produced at the trial and thousands of pieces of evidence which showed how I was involved in the peace movement, political movements, the trade union movements, and the Congress of Democrats. All that activity was supposed to lead to the conclusion that I was part of a conspiracy to bring about the aims and objects of the Freedom Charter, which was deemed by the prosecution, not the judges eventually, to be subversive, treasonable.

Did you consider not leaving after you were released from ninety-day arrest?
Leon – There was no question. There was nothing you could do in South Africa. People who stayed went to jail and I was in jail. I decided not to stay. Good people did stay here, some went to jail, some were thrown out of windows, and some carried on and did magnificent things.

From the early sixties until the Soweto riots in 1976 there was no question of working underground. Bram Fischer tried it and did not succeed. We all knew that before he went underground, otherwise he would have had many more people with him. It was a valiant thing to do but it was not successful. If I had stayed and met with other people I would only have exposed them to the police. There was nothing more you could do and I had come to that conclusion before I went to jail.

I was not going to leave before I went to jail but while there I changed my mind. I don't regret it.

Was there a feeling in the trade unions in the early sixties that you could really achieve something and bring about change?
Leon – Absolutely. We were on a rising tide of activity and involvement by more and more people. In the trade union movement we developed with the liberation movement a relationship that had not existed before, took part in campaigns and won victories in terms of better wages and working conditions for people. There was a great deal of interest in the liberation movement. We were hideously optimistic but we really believed in the cause. There was not a single person who sat in the treason trial who thought we would not win this struggle, even if it took a very long time. We did think we were going to win. We were enthusiastic about the responses we got to our campaigns. Unfortunately the state was too strong for us and destroyed whatever we built up, right into the eighties.

How did your parents and the community relate to your activities?
Lorna – Interestingly enough, they supported me. My father was an attorney and he had a big African clientele. I pulled him along and he took Defense and Aid cases, political cases which he didn't charge for. I did not have a problem with my parents. They had a problem with their friends. I feel bitter about that.

The Jewish community behaved appallingly. My family was just a microcosm of something wider. When we went into exile, my parents were ostracized. The reasons were twofold: one was fear, the other was that they really didn't approve. This was something that continued over the years.
Leon – The Jewish community was awful. They were not interested in us. I was in solitary confinement in the Pretoria for five months. All the prisoners received their clergymen who came to give them encouragement, advice, etc. A rabbi came along and said to me, "I really don't want to see you and the congregation is not interested in you." He did not ask me how I was or if he could take any message to my mother.

I was incredibly young. I said to him, "I don't mind if I never see you again. I would much rather be in solitary confinement than have you next to me." He left. And he was the representative of the Jewish community! The Jewish community was not sympathetic to any of the Jewish political prisoners. There were individuals from time to time, like Benny Isaacson, who were very decent.

Did this affect your attitude to being Jewish?
Leon – No. I would not want to disown being Jewish or not be regarded as a Jew in any way. There were so many Jews that surrounded me in the treason trial, twenty-six in all. Many of the whites in political movements were Jewish. I never felt antagonistic to Jews. I was not a self-hating Jew.
Lorna – What has always interested me is that the Jews never saw the parallels between Nazi race laws and South African race laws, or if they did see them they never took them on board. They had been the victims of racism and here they were doing to others what had been done to them. I have never been able to understand that.

Did you continue the struggle in England?
Lorna – For the first couple of years in England we were very deeply committed to the South African struggle. We worked in it and for it, traveled and worked in the anti-apartheid movement and stayed very close to the South African struggle. As time went on things got very quiet on the South African front and we all had to make a new life and fit into a new country. After a period of about twenty years, in which I got involved in British politics, as a councilor, I moved back into South African politics in the eighties.

After the 1976 uprising it suddenly looked as if something was happening. With my deep-seated feeling about South Africa I became active again and joined the underground ANC. I devoted myself to working for the organization right up until 1994. In that period I was trained by the ANC to go into foreign affairs. We organized all kinds of activities for Mandela when he came to England after being released.

It was a most exciting time. The embassy, a symbol of apartheid, was taken over. Suddenly it changed and became our building.

Leon - Our sympathies never wavered from the cause of the overthrow of apartheid. We followed developments in South Africa closely as the day of liberation arrived. I was interested in the development of the labor movement and labor relations as well as mediation and arbitration.

How did you experience things when you got back after 1994?

Leon – Everybody's experience is different. I felt I had done the right thing by increasing my skills in labor relations, economics and legislation – all extremely useful here. I got a position as a commissioner in the Conciliation, Mediation, and Arbitration Commission and have fulfilled myself and realized the aims I set out as a twenty-four year old, wanting to organize farm workers, mine and domestic workers. I found myself sitting with the workers together with the farm owner and discussing a whole range of issues. I returned to the canning industry, where I had helped to organize strikes in my young days; squared the circle.

I am the chairman of the Center for Conflict Resolution, with a staff of thirty-five people. It is a remarkably good civic organization and is interested in a pan-African vision. There are lots of very interesting societies of this sort.

How do you see other aspects of the new situation?

Leon – I was never starry-eyed about the possibility of great, remarkable transformations. I think the changes brought about from apartheid to democracy in thirteen years are impressive. Civil society is incredibly strong.

There is a lot of corruption and incompetence. I think that affirmative action has been positive in that it created positions of importance for black and disadvantaged people. It has caused some problems in that it has denuded local government etc. of the skills they need.

I am not uncomfortable about the progress. There are people in government and local government who are not very competent but I do not feel I have been let down or disillusioned. You go through life and you become a little more hard-boiled, you see warts where you never saw them before.

Lorna – For me the main thing was the collapsing of apartheid. However, I am disappointed not just because of the amount of corruption, but poverty alleviation was one of our main tools as an organization before we were in power. We have not addressed it as strongly as we could have. We have not improved education and housing as quickly as we could have done.

At the same time, we have had three peaceful elections and people who did not appear able to, have been able to share the country, which is more than happens in Israel. I think we have made significant progress and there are lots of things one can be positive about.

I would like to see people (Jewish) make some contribution to upgrading, helping, making good, showing some generosity.

Alan Lipman

Johannesburg
03/10/07

A veteran of the ANC, the Communist Party, and a self-confessed anarchist, Alan Lipman, now 83 years of age, is able to look back on a life of satisfying activities, though one of disappointed ideological expectations.

Alan holds an Emeritus professorship from the University of Wales, two honorary doctorates, a Medal of Distinction in architecture, and is a Fellow of the British Society of Gerontologists.

Now retired, Alan has also written on architecture and other subjects for the newspapers Frei Weekblad and the Sunday Independent. Alan is an adoring grandfather of his three grandchildren and describes himself as an 'unhesitating non-Zionist.'

Alan – I was brought up to be a nice Jewish bourgeois boy. At the age of about eleven, I realized that my father and I did not share views of the world. We had no books in our house besides the Reader's Digest and some spines of books that you could buy by the yard. I started going to the public library and I lost myself in books.

My uncle gave me a copy of Shaw's book *The Intelligent Woman's Guide to Socialism and Capitalism* and his allegory *The Black Girl in Search of God*. My mind was blown. To this day, the Guide sticks in my mind, with the passion for universal freedom that Shaw conveyed. He claimed we did not need God any longer, that the world was getting better all the time. He was wrong on that.

I changed. I started reading more and more and spent more time in the library than anywhere else. I had been a member of *Habonim*, which my father was pleased about. I was a member of *Gedud* Trumpeldor, a fascist pig if ever there was one.

In 1948 I had been to Israel, where I served in the army for eight months. I had recently qualified as an aircraft navigator. The people I was with were magnificent. We, the crack troops, were socialists. We were trained by Orde Wingate but we had no weapons besides sticks. We used to walk the *Negev* walk in Tel Aviv to impress the women. There were three Super Fortresses that had been stolen and I was to serve on one as a navigator. While they were being refitted, I lived a sybaritic life in Tel Aviv. The Super Forts were not ready so they put me onto another aircraft, Boston, I think. We flew to Gaza, over the target and dropped our load of bombs. Only rifle fire was returned to us.

Back at the mess I said to the chaps I wanted to talk about our mission. "We have just bombed a civilian population," I said. "I don't like it. I didn't come here for that." We had been invited to help the motherland and received special treatment. I was very upset and I decided I was not going to go on with this. It was not in me. I had read Bernard Shaw.

A few days later I passed a café in Tel Aviv and I heard the sounds of a Bach fugue coming from inside it. I was stunned, so I went inside and saw the place was full of left-wing literature. I started talking to the people there and I realized they were my sort of people. We chatted and they told me they were fed up doing what they had been doing up north – forcing villagers out of their homes.

Four of us decided to join the *Palmach* and for me it was bliss; men and women serving together, no officers. We beat the shit out of the *fellahin* in Be'er Sheva. We found them chained together in the trenches, bearing the marks of their (foreign) officers' whips on their backs. That sickened me. We were fighting guys who did not want to fight. What did they know about the concentration camps?

I found myself and my *chaverim* walking the streets triumphal, the super race. I went to the *Machal* offices to say I was fed up but before I could complain, they told me that they wanted me to go back and finish my studies. I had an out and I came back to South Africa.

In my head I had a mixture of Shaw, Heinrich Buhl, a German who advocated non-achievement, Bakunin, and Kropotkin, all anarchists. I

continued my architectural studies and did well because I was motivated. I became a professor at Wits.

We were very active politically and the police were after us. I was in
the Springbok legion. We joined the Communist Party because it was
the only party where there was no racial distinction. I became a great
friend of Nelson Mandela. He hid in our house at various times, once
dressed as our garden boy while Winnie dressed as our maid.

I was working at home one day when there was a knock at the door.
Detective sergeant Coetzee and two black policemen had come with a
search warrant to look for illegal literature. He went through my books,
shaking each one out, until he came to the section on Afrikaans poetry.
He asked me if I read this stuff. I said I did. He came across a passage of
beautiful poetry by Eugene Marais. "Do you like this stuff?" he asked.
I said "Yes." "So do I," he replied. I was thinking: he is a bloody strange
cop. He reads poetry and what is more, he understands it. And he was
probably thinking: what a smart Jewish communist this is, reading our
poetry. He looked at me then at the other cops and said, "We are going."

About a year later this man Coetzee saved my skin. He called me to
his office and said, "If you want to go you had better go quickly because
your name is on a list and there is going to be a big sweep." I went to
see him to say thank you and to tell him we were going on such and
such a date. He said: "You're going, not your wife and kids. They are
staying here until you prove to me that while you are in Britain you are
not going to take part in anti-apartheid activities." I said, "How will you
know?" He said, "I'll know." My wife and I discussed this backwards
and forwards and eventually decided I had better go. He did not say
how long. It could have been eight years but it turned out to be eight
months.

In Britain I was a frustrated political animal. I could not meet my
South African friends, who were having *braai's* in the drizzle of south
London. I did get involved in CND and became a fairly senior person
in the organization. We stayed in Britain for almost thirty years.

For a long time I was on the committee of Anti-Apartheid Wales. We had members all over Wales and speakers would come to talk to us. Neil Kinnock became a great friend of ours. He warned me off going into politics.

We spent a year in the US and then we came back to South Africa in 1990. I was surprised they let me in, because when I left I was considered one of the hundred most dangerous people in the country.

I gradually became more and more disillusioned with the corruption, the self-seeking actions and notions of many of my comrades. I stood for election for the ANC in a local election but did not stand a chance of getting elected in a white area.

We have been here ever since. My wife is deliriously happy here. I am reasonably happy here but not completely settled.

What troubles you here?
Alan – There are people starving now who were starving seventeen years ago. Schools have not been built and if they have they are not properly staffed. The hospitals are in a terrible state. I did not expect miracles but I also did not expect that Mbeki would talk about the 'wild left', meaning people like me. If Chris Hani had been president I would not have felt that, though it does not depend on one man.

I still have the guilt feelings of white South Africans, even though I am part of the 'southern aristocracy'. We have state pensions because we were part of the struggle and we live reasonably well. I am settled. I'll die here.

You seem very critical of your past actions and decisions...
Alan – I am. I am ashamed to have been part of the Israeli expropriation of land and removal of people in 1948. I feel like saying *mea culpa*. I am appalled about what the Israelis are doing now. I was invited to come over for the fiftieth anniversary and I refused.

Do you feel there is a country you would have felt good in?
Alan – I felt tremendously at home for those months in the *Palmach* with people who I thought were admirable. I remember going to say

goodbye to them and hugging them and weeping. I remember one guy picking up desert sand and saying, "Ilan help us turn this into a garden." I could cry now for that. They were fine guys. I crawled through a minefield to give blood to someone who had been badly wounded and I thought to myself, "You are f…ing mad." Then I thought to myself: "You have got to do it. He is a comrade." They all came from *kibbutzim* and they were marvelous people.

Are you not saying that no place is perfect?
Alan - I am permanently dissatisfied, out of kilter with the world, a dissident. I would probably be happy (for a few months) in Venezuela under Chavez. I would have been happy with the Zapatistas in Mexico – small groups, small countries. In the Spanish Civil War. I was brought up reading Hemingway. That is where I cut my teeth. The world has gone global-capitalist and I am opposed to that. I am opposed to the whole bloody world. I have a few like-minded friends in various parts of the world and fortunately I have traveled a lot. I loved New Zealand. So, I am not entirely a sore thumb but I have got to confess "That thumb hurts." I haven't mellowed.

Ronnie Miller

Durban
10/10/2007

*Born in Durban in 1943, Ronnie Miller lived in Israel and studied in the
United States before returning to South Africa.*

*Ronnie started his academic career at Witwatersrand University, where he
obtained honors, masters and doctoral degrees. He worked at a Research Institute in Jerusalem for three years and spent an academic year at the University
of Michigan.*

*Since 1982 he has worked in the School of Psychology at the University of
KwaZulu-Natal in the broad field of Cognitive Psychology with a special interest in learning, development, and change. During this time he served as Head
of School, Dean of Faculty, and Deputy Vice-Chancellor.*

Ronnie has two sons and three grandchildren.

What do you remember about Habonim in Durban?
Ronnie - I joined *Habonim* when I was six. You weren't allowed to but
I used to go with my older brother. My entire life was dominated by
Habonim. There was a group of about ten of us that went to *machane*
and seminar every single year.

Was it your peer group that influenced you or was it the madrichim?
Ronnie - Both. What made Durban *Habonim* very strong was that
there was no other youth movement. There was no competition. The
Jewish youth of Durban were divided, you were either in *Habonim* or
you were not, and the two groups had virtually nothing to do with each
other. And of course the *Habonim* kids felt much superior.

Were you still in the movement when Leib Golan came on shlichut?
Ronnie - Yes. I was very close to Leib. We lived in the *bayit* together.

I was very close to Hermona (Leib's wife). They were almost surrogate parents for me.

Leib's *shlichut* was characterized by a very powerful emotional tone. How did this jell with your more intellectual approach?
Ronnie - I had already made intellectual decisions long before Leib arrived. I was always very drawn to the socialist ideology, like most young kids. Youth are attracted to socialist ideas.

There is another side to all of this that was unusual for me. I lived and went to school in Durban North which was quite unusual. At school, I really did experience anti-Semitism, not in a horrific way. I did not get beaten up every day but I was regularly singled out and called a "Jew boy" and there were very few Jews in the school. That, I am sure, had a major impact on my strong Jewish identity and the whole Zionist story – it was a kind of personal thing for me. No one had to tell me the Jewish people were at risk.

Your Jewish identity was obviously very strong...
Ronnie - It was not very strange because I came from a very, very Jewish family - not religious. My father was an atheist. My grandfather was a very well-known figure in the religious community in Johannesburg and that trickled through to my mother and her brother who also lived here in Durban. He was a key figure in the Jewish community serving as chairman of the *shul* and so on. So I had these very strong Jewish connections but they were never religious, which is fairly unusual. I always had a kind of anti-religious streak.

Habonim ideology conformed to some extent to the utopian aspects of the Zionist narrative. At that time, did you suspect any dissonance between the two?
Ronnie - No. I must say, it really took me years and it was quite painful … years … to come to grips with some of the myths that I followed. It's only in the last fifteen years or so that I had to start coming to terms with the fact that it was not quite as simple as that and that an injustice has been done to the Palestinians. I had actually been fed misinformation.

I really did believe that the Arabs all ran away because they wanted to join the other side and fight. But I was always convinced, and remain to this day convinced that you actually need a Jewish State.

I trace that belief to my experience at school. I always felt the reason you needed to have an Israel was so that you could be an ordinary person like all the other kids at school and not the odd guy out. And I was always very convinced and remain to this day convinced that you can't escape anti-Semitism. You can't escape it either by assimilating or by trying to be a good guy. Jews are Jews because other people make you Jewish. That is the lesson of the Holocaust. The Holocaust was a huge influence in my youth as well. For all sorts of reasons the existence of Israel ensures that it will not happen again. This is stuff we all grew up with.

How did you get onto the path of socialism?
Ronnie - Straight from a very good brain-washing in *Habonim*. Giddy (Shimoni) and Foggy (Yehuda Peleg) come to mind among others. My passion was around the socialist issue. I came very close … the year before I went to Johannesburg to becoming involved with the Communist Party in Durban through Rowley Arenstein. If I had remained in Durban I may well have landed up in the same jail as David Ernst, Steven Friedland, and Dave Barkham

Are you saying that the circumstances of moving to Johannesburg to study medicine determined your path, rather than a conscious decision not to be an activist?
Ronnie - I would not put it that strongly. I know that I was drifting in that direction. You can't turn the clock back, so you don't know what would have happened.

Socialism could have led you to be active in the South African struggle but you chose the kibbutz option…
Ronnie - I just soaked all this stuff up. There was such a nice mix of the two – the Zionist and the socialist. Even historically we know that the two ideologies came together.

What was it about the movement dynamic that enabled people like you to make the choices you made?

Ronnie - My parents were appalled when I gave up university and my mother raised the issue with me of spending my life as a farm laborer. There are two answers to the question. At some point, I did think I could do some of the agricultural work. I could have worked, as I did, in the orchards and in the dairy. But I also thought that there were other options. There were people who were teachers on the kibbutz. Teaching was what I was hoping I would move into.

What happened in terms of your commitment to kibbutz? Was the decision to leave something sudden or was it a slow process of disenchantment?

Ronnie - It is difficult to know. These things are always more complicated than they seem. I wasn't alone on the kibbutz. I was married. The decision to leave the kibbutz involved us both. I am not clear exactly what led to what. I did think I was going to get the chance to teach and then that did not happen and so I was bitter about that. I also sensed I was kind of disillusioned. There were little things. One of the things that triggered this will sound so utterly trivial but I remember being in despair over it. Every afternoon someone had to drive to the bus stop at the main road to transport colleagues who had been away back to the kibbutz. It was my day on duty and I couldn't get any one to give me a vehicle. I remember going home and wondering what is this all about. Why have I got to beg people so that I can go and fetch colleagues from the bus stop and why do they act as if they privately own these vehicles? This is a kibbutz. After forty years I remember this so clearly and it was one of the little things that pushed me to think that this was not quite what I expected.

Having said that, if other things were going well, that would not have been the big issue it was. But I do have regrets, especially when I think now what has happened to the kibbutz. I often think that it was pity that it didn't work out for me.

After leaving kibbutz did you look for a way to incorporate the values that were important to you?
Ronnie - After we left the kibbutz we got involved in a group that was going to set up a village on the Syrian border. It turned out that the American who was leading this group was a member of the Mafia. The whole scheme collapsed but what I am saying is my idea of doing something did not go away. But like others who do not live on a kibbutz, you end up voting for a left-leaning party if you have left leanings.

One thing that did happen though, which is the reverse of what you are asking me, and that has stayed with me for a long, long time is a feeling that never again would I become a member of anything. I have lived in Durban now for a long time and I am not part of any club or community and I am not a member of anything. I never again wanted to be in a position where I had influence on somebody else's life and then it turns out that I am the one who doesn't live up to expectations.

Have you ever missed the group experience?
Ronnie - It is impossible to say that you don't... I think we had the most incredible youth. It would not have been possible to have had a better youth than the one that we all had. When my kids were at school here, they went to *Habonim* and they went to camp but it was not the same thing. It had become a social club.

What led to your decision to return to South Africa?
Ronnie - My idea was never to return permanently to South Africa. The idea was to come here, get some professional training and to go back. I became an academic and I then needed to get my Masters. The usual story.

But at no point were we setting down roots, thinking this is where we wanted to live our lives, in apartheid South Africa. My break came after I finished my doctorate and was due for a sabbatical, which I did in Jerusalem in 1978. I then got a job with a psychologist in Jerusalem.

My connections with Israel seem to have been very unfortunate. I worked at an institute in Jerusalem for a few years but fell out with the director over academic issues and this led to my resignation. Once again I was without a job and with very few prospects of finding an academic position in Israel. At a certain point, a job became available in South Africa and this is the job I have now.

How difficult was it to be back in South Africa?
Ronnie - Immensely difficult. There was another added thing that was even worse. For me to come back to Durban represented utter failure. If I had gone back to Wits/Johannesburg it would have been different. To come back to Durban ... a place I had put behind me, I had left Durban. Coming back to Durban was the full circle and I came very close to a breakdown during the first six months we were here.

Professionally, was it better than you expected?
Ronnie - In a very real sense I was a huge apartheid beneficiary. I came back at a time when there was a boycott. I got an appointment at the age of thirty-eight that you would never get now. There was nobody else. There is no way I could have got that sort of a position at that age with my qualifications.

In the academic community in the eighties was there any ferment you wanted to get involved in?
Ronnie - Every day there were protests and police arrests. There were very brave people who joined the underground. I just did what most white South Africans who were opposed to the government did. I did not do anything very brave, did not go to jail. Voted against. But it was all hot air.

Did you have any prescient ideas about how things were going to change in South Africa? In Habonim we claimed that change would only come about via a revolution...
Ronnie - I was always optimistic about South Africa. I did not believe there was going to be a revolution. The one thing the resistance movements did not achieve was a revolution and they were not close to having one. I think that today the consequence of that is the ghastly levels of crime that we have. Because there was never a victory. The one thing that black people don't have is a victory. They got a settlement.

They did not win anything.

Black people are still poor and look at how whites live and there is no indication it is going to be otherwise. What did they win? "Those white bastards managed to cleverly negotiate a situation where they carry on exploiting us. The reason I don't have a job is because of those white bastards." Whereas, if there had been a revolution I think that anger would have dissipated. We have had all this peace and reconciliation. I think the violence is partly explained by the unresolved anger.

How do you view the way the country is being run?
Ronnie - I think the government is remarkably competent. Everybody seems to forget how appallingly bad the white government was for all those years. They were useless.

Compared to other developing countries we are doing quite well. South Africa has excellent relations with India, China and Brazil. I think our judicial system and our constitutional court work well. There are lots of scandals but the fact they are exposed and not hidden means the system is working. Our politicians are politicians. I don't have a negative view. Thousands of new houses have been built. Clinics have been built. I don't think it is negative at all.

The disparities here are huge and still connected to race. Do you see South Africa being able to sort out its problems without violence?
Ronnie - A black middle class is developing rapidly. If you look at the numbers, a relatively small black middle class will outnumber the whites. There is often more bitterness expressed towards the *nouveau riche* blacks than towards the whites. I think the race issue is going to disappear. It is a class issue and it is a matter of time.

Most young people I have seen are optimistic. I am not talking about the rural poor, but in the townships, most black people think they do have a future.

Even though they are living no better than they used to...
Ronnie - I have a colleague who runs a program with township kids. They are remarkably optimistic. I think we are heading into a world

that none of us can comprehend, where the world powers are going to be China and India and the world we are familiar with, dominated by America and Europe is not going to be. I don't know the answer to 'the haves and the have-nots'.

What is your impression of the students you have had contact with?
Ronnie - They are hugely positive about the country and are proud of South Africa. The other fascinating thing is that we are now seeing black kids who did not know apartheid and when you tell them about it they look at you, "When was that, three hundred years ago?" They don't have a concept that it was 'yesterday'.

Do you think there is room for idealism, like there was in our generation? Has the age of idealism passed?
Ronnie - That is a big question. I think it is tied up with the new world order, the neo-capitalist ethos, and an ideology that won. Socialism lost.

Are you bothered by what you see as apathy regarding the disparities in the society?
Ronnie - I am. There are things I am puzzled by. For example, why don't we have a special tax to provide housing for everyone? Who is looking after the AIDS orphans? I have often thought it is a pity that there are such bad relations between Israel and South Africa. Israel pioneered children's homes and that know-how could have been used here. Instead, in villages a kid of twelve is looking after a kid of eight.

In Johannesburg the Jews defend Israel, for fear of being seen as traitors...
Ronnie - That is also wrong. In any country, if a shell is fired onto a beach and kills three innocent people that is clearly not okay. On the other hand, there are other kinds of Jews, like our cabinet minister, who is a classic Jewish-hater, a Jewish anti-Semite. He literally believes that Israel should not exist and should be wiped off the map. There is also a group of Jewish intellectuals – "Not In Our Name" who seem to need to make public statements that they are the "good guys" and not

like other Jews. I find it interesting that they feel the need to tell the world that the actions of the present Israeli government are not carried out "in their name."

Habonim is having a hard time finding a raison d'etre...
Ronnie - I didn't even know it still existed.

How comfortable do you feel with your life and the decisions you have made?
Ronnie - Those are two different issues, feeling comfortable and decisions. You never know if you had turned left and not right. In a way, I think I have had some bad luck. I have also had a huge amount of good luck. Very few people thought South Africa was going to resolve itself the way it has. There are lots of things I really like about South Africa. I like the multi-cultural mix. When I go overseas, I miss it. There is something very liberating about having grown up with apartheid and then experienced the democratic changes. It is an exciting country. We have all lived through an incredible period in history. I never thought I would see the Soviet Union collapse. The only thing that remains is Israel. We'll see what is going to happen there. It looked as though South Africa and Israel were sorting themselves out at the same time and then things seemed to go wrong in Israel.

Ilona Tip

Johannesburg
3/10/07

Ilona Tip is Operations Director for EISA, a continental organisation working in the field of elections, governance and democracy. Ilona was formerly employed by the Independent Mediation Service of South Africa, firstly in the community mediation department where her work involved the establishment of Peace Committees in Gauteng and facilitating and chairing two local Peace Committees. Thereafter she worked in the Elections and Balloting Department, conducting elections for trade unions, civil society organisations, and industry. She was also responsible for a national voter education in preparation for the 1994 South African elections and training, deploying and co-coordinating 9000 counting station monitors.

From 1977 to 1992, Ilona was office manager and para-legal assistant for the human and civil rights practice of Shun Chetty, and afterwards for Priscilla Jana, representing anti-apartheid activists as well as being the instructing attorney for most of the civil liberties court cases.

To what extent was your decision to stay in South Africa an ideological one?
Ilona - I think I am going to disappoint you, I really do believe that whatever I did was circumstantial. I happened to be at a particular place at a particular time in history, rather than sitting down and actually making well thought-out decisions. I always thought I'd go to Israel but I got involved in things here, so I just ended up staying. For many years I didn't have a passport. So when I might have travelled I didn't.

You didn't have a passport because...
Ilona - Because of my involvement in a range of anti-apartheid

activities. I didn't have a passport for fifteen to twenty years.

What elements in your background influenced what you did later on?

Ilona - I think for us all *Habonim* was a major influence in our lives. I came from a small town (Bloemfontein) where going to the movement was like going to the movies, everybody does everything together. It gave us an opportunity to discuss a lot of interesting ideas that we might not have been exposed to. I was at an impressionable age (around fourteen), when Benny Isaacson came to Bloemfontein as the Rabbi. He had a great influence on all of us.

My parents weren't radical. My father probably voted Nat if anything, but we grew up believing that whoever the person is, you treat them properly. I think my parents taught us basic values.

You said earlier that your actions were largely the function of being in particular places at particular times. Tell us about the particular places and times that led to your involvement in anti-apartheid activities.

Ilona - I went to teachers' college and later to Wits. I landed up living in a residence where for the first time I was interacting with people who were not Jewish. I found that we actually got on quite nicely. When you bring people of different racial, ethnic, and cultural backgrounds together, you find that as human beings you share common humanities. I think that kind of also changed my world view.

Although I still had my Jewish friends from before, I got involved with a guy who not only wasn't Jewish but came from a German background. I remember when he asked me out I said, "I am sorry but I can't go out with you because you are not Jewish." He called me a racist and I was absolutely dumbstruck. I said I was quite happy to meet with black people. His calling me a racist opened my eyes. I agreed to have coffee with him but you know my mother and grandmother proved to be right - it doesn't stop at a cup of coffee. I actually ended up marrying him. He was involved in politics and I became involved in student politics as well.

How radical were the people you were involved with?
Ilona - Very radical, very active, though not all of them of course. I was having discussions with these people like I used to have in *Habonim*. We were debating the same issues. Through my involvement with NU-SAS, I became quite active. There were meetings, conferences, and a whole range of contacts across the color bar. It did expose me to a whole range of other people who were involved in politics beyond the student movement. A number of them joined the ANC.

What was your feeling at that time? Did you believe you were moving towards a real change in South Africa?
Ilona - No, I didn't think that at all. We thought we were making a contribution to a change at some point. But to be quite honest, I think very few people in South Africa thought they would see it in their lifetime. This doesn't mean you don't stay involved. I certainly didn't think I would live to see a new society.

Your husband was deeply involved. How radical were you prepared to be?
Ilona - You know, I didn't draw a line. Things just happened and I went along with them. I suppose it was because I was young but I never stopped at any point and thought, "this is dangerous." Every day was another event so I just kept going. Once I was on the treadmill one event just led to another.

People who I was working with made all sorts of recommendations for post-apartheid society. The recommended changes were not illegal.

I was friendly with Rick Turner, a Marxist philosopher and a lecturer at the University of Natal. He was a very radical thinker, who I think influenced a lot of people. He was assassinated, we thought by the security police. In other places and at other times his Marxist ideas would not have evoked that kind of response but then they did. In the middle of the night he was shot dead in front of his two little girls.

That must have really frightened you?
Ilona - No, I don't know why, but it didn't. Each event or each

intervention I had would broaden my horizons.

I chose not to be drawn into anything too radical because I felt that to be effective I needed to be able to have room to move. And also I'm not a very good person at joining anything. I can't even join the library. I hate feeling restricted. If someone tells me what to do I will react against it. Though I might have had empathy for a particular ideology and work for similar goals, I preferred to work outside of a very formalized structure.

What about your husband?
Ilona - He eventually left the country after spending a long time in detention.

While he was married to you?
Ilona - Ja, ja

And what did that do to you?
Ilona - Well so many people we knew were being detained, everybody was detained.

But you were a nice Jewish girl from Bloemfontein...
Ilona - Remember there were a lot of Jewish people in that whole framework. It was almost like *Habonim*. It was a very tight- knit community under siege in a way. So people were very warm, helpful and responsive, like one big family.

With people around you being detained was there no sense that perhaps this was all too much and that this was in fact a non-winnable battle?
Ilona - You know, I never stopped and thought that I can't get there or that this is dangerous. I mean of course it was a shock when my husband was detained but lots of people we knew got detained. I remember that day. It was *Rosh Hashanah*. At about twelve o'clock there was a knock on my door. My cousins, half hysterical, were on the doorstep, lovely chocolate cake and herring and what not because they'd heard. In my family, no matter what, the family was always there to support you.

You had children by then...
Ilona - One little girl. She was nine months old at the time.

How did you cope with all this?
Ilona - I think it was the network, a strong network of people. The thinking was that if it wasn't you today, it would be somebody else tomorrow. You stood by each other. That was your community.

You have told us that you worked with Steve Biko. What was he like?
Ilona - He was remarkable. Memories of Biko are not exaggerated. They are not because he is no longer alive. He was charismatic beyond belief. I was very, very fortunate in that I was able to meet, work, and interact with the most remarkable people.

In some ways like all countries that have gone through this kind of thing, many people died in the process to which they could have contributed so much. You had Rabin, here they talk of Biko and Chris Hani. They may have made an impact, they may not, one doesn't know. They died so young. But Steve was totally charming.

How did people relate to your parents?
Ilona - I think it was hard for my parents. I spent three months in jail for refusing to give evidence against Winnie Mandela. My mother had to handle people who said, "Is your daughter mad?" She was great - she'd come visit me in prison. She was looking after my five year old daughter because I was on my own then. My husband had left the country so she stepped in. My father had just died but even when he was alive, I think he thought we were crazy but he never ever said, "Don't do it"...

When my father died, Winnie Mandela couldn't come because she was banned so she sent her daughter Zindzi with some friends to pay condolences. Now can you imagine it? - Lots of people at my mother's flat in Bloemfontein where we were 'sitting *shiva*' and there they arrived. On the one hand, they were all fascinated, on the other they were horrified. She came in gave me a big hug and a kiss to say, "Mommy (Winnie) sends her sympathies", and proceeded to give my mother a big hug and kiss as well. My mother nearly fainted.

How difficult was your detainment?
Ilona - It was easy in a way because I knew the sentence was three months. There were many instances of being detained again immediately on release but that isn't what happened with me. A friend and I refused to give evidence and at first were sentenced to a year's imprisonment. That would have been horrific. That I wouldn't have handled.

What were the conditions like for a white woman prisoner at that time?
Ilona - It was okay because I wasn't under section six (the Terrorism Act which meant being held incommunicado). I was a political prisoner, allowed one visit a month and I couldn't study or read anything. Eventually they gave me books from the library, God alone knows what. Thanks to the intervention of Helen Suzman, my friend and I were able to spend some of the time together. But we sat in teeny weeny little cells all day, apart from an hour a day when we could walk around the courtyard.

It was only three months, but that is when I did sit back and think, "What is a nice Jewish girl like me doing over here?"

At that point did you still not consider leaving the country?
Ilona - No, I didn't even have a passport. I suppose I could have left illegally, but I just couldn't imagine making a life elsewhere then. I'd never been to Israel, I'd been to Europe once in the winter and I hated it. I couldn't go and live in the English climate to be honest even though exiles were given support.

But you could handle the climate of Pretoria prison …
Ilona - That was in summer. And don't forget, my whole community was here.

What did you do once the prison period was behind you?
Ilona - I carried on. I went back to my job with the lawyer and carried on with my life, Ja.

Where were the security police at this time? Did you feel their presence at all?

Ilona - We were definitely not very popular in those circles. We had paint thrown at our house and calls with death threats. We felt the threat of the security police all the time. They would follow us and do all sorts of unpleasant things.

All around you there were people who were in trouble with the authorities and there were those who were leaving...

Ilona - Oh absolutely, all the time they were being arrested as well. There was a wonderful guy called Neil Aggett, a trade unionist. I remember him coming to see us. The next day he was in prison and a week later he was dead. There was David Webster, a lecturer. We were friends. One Sunday morning a phone call: "David has been shot." But you know what? I never thought I was important enough to warrant that kind of thing.

How optimistic do you feel are you about the situation in South Africa today?

Ilona - I am a realist. People are not nice. Thinking people are honest, will never cheat, won't become corrupt or want to be rich and have a big house is unrealistic. They want to live the comfortable life so temptation is always there. People say they never thought corruption would come to this, etc. How can they think this way? People are people.

I do think South Africa has a positive future. There is no doubt that South Africa is a miracle and I think it says something about the people in this country, black and white, that have enabled this to happen. I don't think that the numbers of white people are going to grow or that whites are necessarily going to feel comfortable in fifty years time. I think we have a contribution to make, but I think we have to accept that we have to play that role in the background.

How do you respond to those South Africans today who are throwing in the towel and choosing the Australian option?

Ilona - I actually don't think about these things. I just take each day as it comes. I don't have any anger or resentment. That is the way the world goes. If you are going to sit here and say, "Woe is me, I expected something different." No!

Do your children share your way of looking at the world?
Ilona - My son is in computers. But I think he'd much rather do this kind of work (election observation and research). But as I said to him, "Absolutely not, there's no money in it, it's long hours, first you make your millions and if you have time after you have made your millions you can do some nice humanitarian work."

That's very different to what you heard when you were their age isn't it?
Ilona - I'm sorry nobody said that to me. I didn't have a pension or anything because we were "socialists" and the state was going to look after us one day.

I think it is wonderful to do good work and to work for the society and for people who are in need if you can afford to, but it's hard. So it's fine to go ahead and do it once you know your house is paid for, you have an income coming in, etc. You don't have to be a millionaire, but you have to know you can put food on the table.

Are you still a member of a community of people who were part of the history you have described?
Ilona – Yes, although a lot of the people with whom we are still friendly have gone into business. Many of them are making megabucks but we are still linked to each other. It is not an ideological thing.

Israel

Alan Apter
Steven Aschheim
Moshe Ben-Ami
Louise Bethlehem
Arnie Friedman
Aryeh Gilat
Merle Guttman
Alan Hoffmann
Harry Hurwitz
Meir Jaffe
Janina Kahn-Horwitz
Hertzel Katz
Jerrold Kessel
David Kretzmer
Ron Lapid
Zeev Mankowitz
Raphael Melmed
Tzvi Pantanowitz
Benjamin Pogrund
Gideon Shimoni
Itz Stein
Meir Winokur

Alan Apter

Beilinson Hospital, Petah Tikva.
29/12/07

Alan Apter is currently the Director of the Child and Adolescent Division, at the Schneider Children's Medical Center of Israel. He has devoted his professional life to research and clinical work in the field of child psychiatry.

Originally from Johannesburg, he went to King David School and subsequently studied medicine at Witwatersrand University. A leading member of Betar, Alan made aliyah in 1969. Later he graduated in Psychiatry at the University of Tel Aviv.

Alan is a professor of psychiatry at the Sackler School of Medicine University of Tel Aviv, where he has served as senior lecturer and department chairman. He has been on the editorial boards of a number of journals, including: Israel Journal of Psychiatry & Allied Sciences and the European Journal of Child and Adolescent Psychiatry.

Alan has been a visiting professor at Albert Einstein College of Medicine, Yale School of Medicine, Child Study Center, University of Pittsburgh School of Medicine and the Child Study Center Karolinska Institute, Stockholm Sweden.

He has received academic and professional awards from numerous international institutions. His recent research, "Saving Young Lives in Europe, a study of suicide prevention for young people," received recognition from the European Union.

Alan is married and has three children.

How would you describe your affiliation to Betar?
Alan - I was somewhat on the left of the mainstream in *Betar*. As a result, I was never very popular ideologically with the Revisionist establishment. There was a strong group of us in *Betar*. Our thinking was

that we represented the true spirit of *Betar* and Jabotinsky, which of course is not how most people in the movement saw us. We were a big thorn in their sides but I enjoyed being provocative, I think. Jabotinsky's writings do in fact have a lot of very left, very liberal ideas.

I never really identified with *Herut* as a party and in fact, since I came to Israel, I have become more left if you can call voting *Meretz*, left. I think that probably most of the people in our group have gone the same way.

What was it that attracted you to Betar and Jabotinsky when you were young?
Alan - Psychology would suggest that it had mostly to do with wanting to belong to something. Growing up in South Africa meant that identity was not a simple thing. There were so many identities with everybody hating everybody else. You had to belong to something. Looking back, I think I tried to rationalize a more liberal way of thinking and it is actually not difficult when you look at some of Jabotinsky's writings. There is a big emphasis on liberalism and the importance of the individual.

Did Betar's emphasis on ceremony and uniforms etc. have any special appeal to you?
Alan - Not really. I went along with it but it was not a big deal. It might in fact have made sense to have joined *Habonim* at one time but you know how these things work. You have a certain sense of power and prestige and an identity with which you feel good.

It was more for morale, identity, and so on. It was a kind of pseudo-military thing. I don't think it was negative or really different to the uniforms and ceremonies in *Habonim*. Perhaps I am seeing it as I want it to be. I did see that sort of thing amongst *Betarim* from France and other places who I met on a youth leadership course. That was horrifying, but I don't think we were like that in South Africa.

How did Betar relate to the situation in South Africa at the time you were active?

Alan - *Betar* never really saw South Africa as its problem. When we did try to introduce the issues in some way into the *Betar* structure, we were always told to forget about it.

In medical school I was quite friendly with a couple of Indian people. They made it quite clear that they were anti–Jewish and the Afrikaners weren't very different. We (the Jewish students) were a big group and actually felt quite powerful. It never really entered my mind to stay on in South Africa. There were times when I tried to become politically active but I never felt that it could make any difference. If you were white you were white. I always felt an outsider.

How would you characterize the Jewish part of your identity?

Alan - In South Africa I was not ashamed of being Jewish but I didn't feel particularly Jewish in any way. It was just part of the group to which I naturally belonged. If you ask me how I feel now, I feel much more Jewish than Israeli. I might be influenced by an article I was asked to write about Judaism and psychiatry. Is psychoanalysis a Jewish profession and was Freud Jewish or not? Freud was anti–Jewish and anti–Zionist but he knew he was Jewish. Psychoanalysis has been called a kind of "godless Judaism".

In retrospect and from your professional perspective how do you see education in Betar during your time?

Alan - Most of it was pretty good. I was in charge of programs at one time and wrote some of the books. We took it very seriously. We also had some very good *shlichim*.

Manipulation and propaganda were used in all the youth movements. But it was enlightened propaganda in the sense that you could argue about it. And I did. I wasn't thrown out even though some people might have wanted to do that. We would quote or show a source to show that Jabotinsky supported our view. Then they could do nothing.

How close was the image of the Israel you envisaged to what you found when you came on aliyah?
Alan - It was not very different then. I am more worried at what it has become than what it was. In many ways the *Betar* vision of what Israel should become is closer to reality today than to the vision held by *Habonim* or *Hashomer Hatzair*.

Did you come on aliyah on your own?
Alan – No. A big group of about thirty doctors came at around the same time, mostly to *Tel Hashomer*. I think I may be the only one left in Israel.

How do you understand the low profile of South African olim in Israeli politics or social justice movements?
Alan - I am pretty involved in academic politics and know how difficult that is. We are very different from a cultural point of view. It is hard for me to raise my voice.

What changes have there been in Israel that trouble you today?
Alan - Remember that professionally I often deal with the seamy side of society. We used to have very few problems with drugs or alcohol. We never used to deal with single parent families. We have teenage violence, a lot of bullying. We see terrible child and sexual abuse. Patients are much more violent.

I never realized to what extent money would become a status factor in Israeli society. The whole mental health system here is completely bankrupt. I never thought that in my Jewish State, the treatment of mental illness would not be reimbursed. Psychological help has long waiting lists so we might suggest medication that is available for nothing even if this is not the preferred treatment. I tell parents who are wealthy that it might be better to get private help. I say it outright but I am ashamed of it.

There is also extreme nationalism and toleration of racial prejudice. The one area in which I am active has to do with Palestinians and Israeli Arabs. I have been involved in the center we have here for Arab children. We collaborate with Al-Quds University. It is generally very difficult for an Arab psychologist to get a position. Here at Schneider (children's hospital) we give them preference. I have no illusions that this work is going to change the face of the Middle East. I am interested in scientific collaboration with the "enemy" as a possible bridge to peace. I am interested in what Palestinians think and their reactions.

Does ideology still have a place in Israel?
Alan - I have actually become less and less impressed with ideology. I am happy that my children are not ideological. Ideology has often caused more harm than good.

Ideologists seem to be able to suspend their social consciences. The ideology becomes more important than the people. I think you should be a decent person, try to help others as much as possible, be honest and so on. The minute people start saying that for socialism, for religion, or for the land of Greater Israel they have to do one thing or another, that is when people start killing one another. Ideologies are dangerous.

In some way it sounds as though you might regret having chosen a Zionist path?
Alan - I don't think it was a terrible mistake. But I work a lot internationally and when I see the salaries and the opportunities ...

So what is it that keeps you here?
Alan - That's a good question. A lot of guilt...

Now we understood what you meant when you talked about feeling so Jewish (laughter)...
Alan - I have invested a lot in Israel. Take the army. I still do *miluim*. I persuaded so many people to come to Israel. I have invested so much in Zionism that to leave now, I'd feel very guilty.

Towards others or yourself?
Alan - The mythical figures, the *shlichim* I admired, people I admired in the army... It is completely illogical. And to tell you the truth I don't

have a bad life in Israel. I have a profession, nice house, nice family, enough money to travel. I am very well respected so we can't really complain.

So how would you sum up where you are today? How well do you live with yourself?
Alan - When we talk about these things, uncomfortable

That makes us feel uncomfortable. People who come to see you here are usually coming for you to make them feel better, not for them to make you feel bad.
Alan - No, it is good that these questions are raised. I suppose I do as much as ninety-nine percent of what people do. But it is not enough.

What I can do is set up a center for Arab children. I can meet and collaborate with Palestinians and I do it, but it is nothing. I should demonstrate at the separation fence etc. but just don't have the energy. I feel ashamed about that. But I know that if I had stayed in South Africa I would have done nothing. I tried a little, but each time it got a bit rough I got scared. When, however, I faced dangerous things in Israel and the army, I felt okay. I was brave enough when it was in the right context. That is what made Israel seem the right choice.

I don't really believe in nationalism and Zionism is about nationalism. It becomes complicated.

Steven Aschheim

Jerusalem
30/12/07

Steven E. Aschheim holds the Vigevani Chair of European Studies and is the Director of the Franz Rosenzweig Research Centre for German Literature and Cultural History at the Hebrew University, Jerusalem, where he has taught Cultural and Intellectual History in the Department of History since 1982.

He has spent sabbaticals in Berkeley and Princeton and was the first Mosse Exchange Professor at the University of Wisconsin. He has taught at Columbia University, the University of Maryland, the Free University in Berlin, and the Central European University in Budapest. He has also taught at the University of Toronto and at the University of Michigan, Ann Arbor.

Steven has recently been appointed a Research Fellow at the Institut fuer Sozialforschung, Hamburg, and will serve as the Diller Visiting Israeli Professor at the University of California, Berkeley.

Steven is the author of six books, several of which have been translated into German and Hebrew. His latest book, which appeared in 2007, is entitled Beyond the Border: The German-Jewish Intellectual Legacy Abroad (Princeton University Press). He is the editor of the conference volume, Hannah Arendt in Jerusalem (Berkeley: University of California Press, 2001), also translated into Hebrew.

Steven is married and has three children and two granddaughters.

What can you remember about the development of your thinking during your childhood?
Steve – One of the earliest experiences that comes to mind occurred when I was about seven or eight. It did not really evoke "thinking" but rather something that was intuited, that happened at the threshold of consciousness. We were living in Lower Houghton, not in poverty-

stricken circumstances. My parents wanted to spruce up the servant quarters, not that they were exactly major activists in the anti-apartheid struggle. They hired an Afrikaner contractor to do the job. I was walking past where they were building and I overheard this guy say, "These bloody Jews want everything for the bloody blacks and for themselves." I was shocked. I knew what he was saying: "I have to get money from the Jews to build for the blacks. What could be worse than that?" I remember crawling away, quite scared. That is the first quasi-political memory I have, although I doubt that at the time I could have articulated it this way.

My Jewish self-awareness and the fact of not really feeling at home had to do, in addition to the general fact of growing up Jewish in South Africa, with the fact that my parents were German and had German accents and were clearly not *drommies*. One somehow knew about Nazis even though, like David Grossman's Momik, the subject was never directly or overtly addressed. It had to do with an awareness of difference, and also the fact that in some way my parents were refugees, which, as I grew older, tied into stories I heard about the *Shoah*. Not that they were in the *Shoah* or ever even presented themselves as refugees, let alone survivors.

Then of course there was school. The fact of being Jewish was a kind of natural given. Even though I was not persecuted, though there were some clearly anti-Semitic teachers, the distinction between being Jewish and non-Jewish was absolutely clear. I do not recall a non-Jewish guest ever coming into our house, not one. Being Jewish was fundamental, constitutive. It meant that you were not like the non-Jews. This was simply the way things and groups were organized in South Africa.

Were there messages, direct or indirect that came down to you from your parents?
Steve – There was no conscious story-telling. What was transmitted was a sensibility. In speeches at celebrations, such as my *barmitzvah* - my father spoke about being a good Jew and a good citizen. He did not object to me being in *Bnei Zion* but he said, "You are being suckered in,

they are playing on your innocence. You do not realize but that is what is being done to you." There was some truth in what he was saying but only partially so because, basically, we were as much the creators of our own culture and myths as were the *shlichim*. It was this that provided the excitement and authenticity of it all.

My father, I suppose, was worried that I would never make a living and wondered: "What on earth is my son going to do with his life?" When I answered that I was going to live in Israel, he said that moving to another country was not a profession.

What does being Jewish mean to you?
Steve – Over the years, its meaning and significance have changed. Because I was raised in South Africa and because life was so tightly organized around communal and group belonging, a reflection too of the racial and ethnic bases of the wider society, I was always utterly aware of that identification. To this day, when I am not in Jewish company, there is an acute awareness of this Jewishness, as a kind of psychological quality resistant to any clear definition or content. Avoiding conspicuousness was an important activity and vulnerability, a constant feeling there, which made, or still makes me a Woody Allen kind of Jew.

But, of course, this acute awareness of vulnerable difference went together with a kind of pride in who I was. I think this tribal component goes deep. I still look for Jews and identify with them, at least the kind I like and am more embarrassed by those I dislike precisely because of the identification. If I am in London or in America I act differently, I am more polite, conciliatory, apologetic, self-protective.

This has nothing to do with Judaism, whose content and rituals mean increasingly very little indeed to me, as opposed to the study of Jewish, and now especially Israeli history. The more pious, traditional, and nationalist and thus self-referential Israel becomes, the more my distance from and distaste for these things increases. In fact, my Zionism, if there is such a thing, consists in living in this country because it is the only country in the world where I don't have to be Jewish in the negative sense of being self-conscious, although this is becoming increasingly difficult.

So, despite everything else, Israel is still the only place where I can function without this burden. It raises all sorts of other issues yet relieves me of that negative kind of self-consciousness. But I certainly can't identify with Judaism or any kind of organized ideological Zionism any more. Being in Israel, the need for communal identification seems to be far less. It may be true that "the family that prays together stays together," but here there are various other kinds of glue making for solidarity, pleasant, and less pleasant. And as I observe the attitudes of many people who define themselves as essentially religious in this country, my disinclination grows. But here again I must add a qualification. As I said before, my life is full of contradictions. On Friday nights, partly because my son Daniel thinks I am entirely Hellenized, we light candles, say *Kiddush* and so on.

Where do you see the roots of your intellectual thirst and curiosity?
Steve – The only place I was allowed to think about things that mattered to me was in *Bnei Zion/Habonim*. The youth movement provided an answer to the deadliness of school where any semblance of thought and intellectual activity – anyone who knows the South African school system at that time will confirm this - had to be immediately repressed. I remember going to the Zionist Federation library at the age of twelve and taking out Alex Bein's biography of Herzl. Why did I do that? Obviously I was looking for answers to existential matters that the world was not supplying, that was being repressed. That is when I started my reading life. That was a kind of liberation, as against the imprisonment of school.

Certainly when I started going to university, ideas fired me up. But being in the movement, these were always tempered by having fun with the *chevre*, the importance of friendship, singing, skits, and so on. Even now, I find it difficult to have intellectual discussions with my closest friends lest I be considered pretentious.

What was the significance of growing up in South Africa?
Steve – Well, growing up in a very conventional home there, with servants, and with a kind of inbred, taken-for-granted (rather than overtly ideological) racism, that arrangement seemed to be part of the natural order of things. When you are kid, that's the way the world was presented to you. I am sure that if one grew up in a politically liberal or radical home one would have taken in the injustices of apartheid with mother's milk. Some of my friends did. But my home was not that way inclined. I remember the day, perhaps I was ten or twelve years old, when I became tacitly aware that this racist status quo was not really a natural but rather a historically constructed, and thus changeable, matter. Of course I didn't articulate it this way but I do remember being in one of the large, luscious green playing fields at school, and seeing these vague, usually invisible, gardeners at the edge of the field, and suddenly realizing that these were actually people and not part of nature. The power of apartheid, like other functioning regimes, was to persuade people, perhaps the blacks too, that this was really part of the natural rather than the politically created order of things.

From that time on, the dehumanization and humiliation of blacks profoundly disturbed me but already then, as indeed now, I was guilty of the sin of inaction, of grave omission. Apart from little, completely token, things, I never actively or politically opposed all of this. My approach, nay my character, closely resembles that of Mel Brooks' *Two Thousand Year Old Man*. When the old man was asked: "Two thousand years ago, what was your main form of transportation?" he answered, "Fear, mainly fear." That was, and remains, me.

Apartheid was clearly intolerable, but if that had been my thing, I would have said, "Be like the Rusty Bernsteins, the Baruch Hirsons, the Wolpes, and the Goldreichs. Do something serious." But I am the two thousand year old man. I was not going to risk my neck. So there was never a question of my joining a militantly active, anti-apartheid organization. And this dove-tailed very nicely with my Zionism. It was not anti-apartheid alone that drove me out of South Africa, as I think is true for most of us.

To this day, the two thousand year old man's transport problem is still with me. I am still not really able to reconcile my actions or non-actions with my conscience. Actually, if I feel guilty of anything, it is not that I did not participate in South Africa but rather, having argued that Israel is the place where my involvement belongs, it is my non-involvement here.

This defect is only very partially excused by the fact that most South African middle-class kids were raised in an authoritarian fashion and most of us still docilely obey authority and certainly have immense difficulty questioning, let alone defying, it. My actions were pretty puerile. I thought I was really radical because I sang *N'kosi Sikalele* – the ANC and later South African national anthem - in the kitchen with the servants. My parents too thought this was verging on the subversive. We often had arguments on South African issues but we were able, as I am with my sons, to distinguish the political from the familial, so it did not affect our relationship in any deep way, which shows that my commitment was really a shallow one.

In your view, was there something unique about South African Zionism?
Steve – Unique in my experience was the ecstasy of the youth movement - complete, collectively self-enclosed ecstasy, and a depth of bonding. To this day, these friendships endure and these are people whom one most trusts and who instinctively understand what you think, say, your jokes etc. In our case, youth is not a matter of age but a state of mind. I recognize now that our self-righteous sense of morality, our ideological fervor, was quite often rationalization of all kinds of other needs and satisfactions.

How do you explain the fact that there were so many bright people in the movement who were uncritical when it came to what they were educating about?
Steve – I'll give you two reasons. Number one is because Zionism in South Africa satisfied, deep, authentic needs of our own. It gave us a sense of ourselves, it distinguished us from our elders, it made our

position with regard to South Africa clear, it gave us a utopia in which to believe, it solved our self-consciousness as Jews. Also, it helped that we were actually not in Israel so we didn't really know what was going on. Number two, in the history of Zionism generally, not just in South Africa, in the *yishuv*, blindness to the (Palestinian) problem was a precondition for implementing Zionism. I was no exception in this respect. You could argue that this myopia was a necessary condition for pursuing the Zionist project. Openly acknowledging the price this was exacting on the indigenous population – essentially dispossession and a kind of humiliation - was and is an extremely difficult thing to do. Even if such displacement was not intended, it was bound to come to that, and to this day, most Israelis are unable to face this head-on. They cling to the traditional narrative. If this was a necessary myopia, it is no less myopic for that.

I know how difficult such recognition is. Even as a historian who is trained to view matters from above and from a variety of perspectives. It took a long time for me to face this head-on. What I do about this recognition, given all my two thousand year old man characteristics, is another question.

Have you ever given any thought to the different choices you and your sister have made?
Steve – In a sense, we resembled German-Jewish youth at the beginning of the twentieth century. There were those bourgeois kids who accepted things as they were and then those who participated in a kind of youth revolt. At that time, sensitive and intellectually inclined "anti-bourgeois" Jewish youth, all of whom, like us, were entirely bourgeois, basically had the choice of a kind of radical anti-apartheid activism, often tied in with some kind of Marxism or Zionism. Some linked the two. We shouldn't forget that at that stage, and even in our time in the movement, Zionism appeared to be an authentically radical choice, the participation in a kind of revolutionary adventure, a proposition quite difficult to maintain today. Youth in my time in South Africa all divided on similar lines: the anti-apartheid left, the *kugel*-socialites and

the Zionists. *Bnei Akiva* did exist then, but it was marginal and the religious, almost fundamentalist, turn was light years away in the 1960's. The genesis of these commitments was hardly intellectual, of course. I went to *Bnei Zion* by chance. There was a soccer game at Oxford *shul*. I could just as easily have gone to play soccer with the *Betarim*. Once *Bnei Zion* essentially collapsed and merged with *Habonim*, I was so hooked into youth movement life, that the difference between a more liberal and socialist ideology really possessed only the most peripheral significance.

You did, however, engage in serious debate about chalutzik aliyah…
Steve – It had nothing to do with what I really believed in and everything to do with my competition with Wolfie Mankowitz. It was a personal rivalry based on my very real admiration – jealousy is probably the better word - for him. The most telling example that I can recall of my entirely non-ideological motivation was when I resigned from the movement on grounds of principle. I have no recollection at all what those principles were! This happened at the same time that there was a seminar at Olifantskloof. It was an idiotic act of self-exclusion. I remember walking around my home lonely as a cloud, forlorn, crying in the wilderness, and asking myself: why on earth am I depriving myself of the thing I most enjoy? The *chevre* are having a great time and I am suffering for principles that I myself could not enunciate, never mind believe in. So I got into the car and went to the seminar saying (meekly), "I have changed my mind" - and had a fantastic time.

So it is clear how you would characterize that time in your life…
Steve – Excitement, involvement, even ecstasy. Fun and a sense of passionate experience which went together with openness to intellectual and artistic discovery. We listened joyously to the black choir singing *The Messiah* with a white orchestra, rapturously watched *West Side Story*, read and admired Isaiah Berlin. All of these things went together with the sing-songs, the skits, the laughing, and of course the girls. Or were they women? I don't think we had a clue, some still don't, just how male chauvinist we were, incidentally a characteristic

of most youth movements.

The South African youth movements created their own cultures in a very powerful way. In crucial ways we ran them, even if there were some *shlichim* and others who were "above". We created a kind of youth culture which was all-embracing. And many of us have not grown out of it yet. To some degree we were part of the sixties generation and we sung Dylan and Joan Baez, but we distinguished ourselves from the Woodstock phenomenon. We filtered those messages. We were far more puritan than that American equivalent. I suppose that I am still puritan.

How do you look on all that now? Do you think you were manipulated in any way?
Steve – I would go through it again. I don't think the *shlichim* were manipulating, conniving people. I don't think they pulled the wool over my eyes. So, despite all the very serious criticisms, I suppose I am happy here. I really can't be proud of narrow ethnic nationalism any more so what does this say about me who always seems to be more comfortable in homogenous, tribal contexts?

Can you tell us something about the evolution of your thinking since coming to Israel?
Steve – This is a very complicated, convoluted matter. It's hard to talk or write about partly because it relates to much broader aspects of the ways in which one's self matures, develops, is transformed. At the same time, these are intertwined with the old self and thus at base remains the same. So the story is one of unresolved, perhaps irresolvable, inner emotional-intellectual needs, tensions, and conflicts. I'm not only the two thousand year old man, but also the subject of the ditty that goes: "Roses are red, violets are blue, I'm schizophrenic, and so am I." I just have to live and wrestle with these tensions that pull me in different directions.

What are some of these? I keep on saying that I am more comfortable and happy here. The reasons for this are not hard to find. My self-consciousness and sense of vulnerability in the Diaspora were obviously the product of belonging to a (not very admired) minority. Zionism meant sovereignty, normalcy, rendering oneself the majority. Apart from everything else, it profoundly changed the psychological grounds of comfort.

At the same time, I have come to understand that rendering ourselves a majority was based upon a forceful displacement of the overwhelming majority that was here before and rendering them into a similar, if not entirely exact, situation that we sought to escape. I only came to understand much later, that this tension is probably inherent in ethnic nationalisms. It took me years to understand what Ernst Simon, who advocated a bi-nationalist arrangement, declared already in 1943: "The Jewish State means domination over the Arabs, just as an Arab State means domination over the Jews." Some kind of shared sovereignty would, of course, be ideal. I know all the historical and practical problems surrounding such federal or bi-nationalist directions – the lack of successful examples, the refusal of the Arab side to even discuss this possibility etc., the radical antipathy of the majority to even countenance the idea. But all this does not invalidate the insights and warnings its advocates brought to the table. Ethnic sovereignty in this regard is both the solution and the problem. If I can't find an acceptable solution to this conflict, let me at least have the honesty to admit its existence and face it frankly.

Let me give you another example. If I accuse the Zionists (and myself) of myopia, my children, who look at me as the kind of *yefei nefesh*, bleeding heart liberal who can't even take his own side in an argument, also make me aware of another myopia of mine: the implicit presuppositions I make about the Arab side. I have become so critical of our side and so moralistic, they say, that I don't take into account many of the problematic realities of Arab society which, they keep reminding me, is hardly based upon the premises of liberal Enlightenment humanism. These are only two instances of the endless paradoxes, ironies, tensions, and contradictions in my position.

That is the intellectual angle but what was the process?
Steve – First of all, in 1967, very early, many of us said that there was something essentially wrong with the occupation. That seemed painfully obvious very early on – the nationalist and religious triumphalism, the talk of enlightened occupation, seemed both distasteful and dangerous to me. But that position assumed a kind of purity before 1967, as if prior to that we were angels and now we were demons. But I began to intellectually question this convenient dichotomy when I was in Madison, Wisconsin doing my PhD in 1978, I think it was. I picked up an article by Edward Said, a name I had never heard before. I even remember the details of its publication, *Social Text, Vol.1, No.1.* because it was so shocking and threatening to me. The article was entitled *Zionism from the Standpoint of its Victims.* Given my movement background and the inculcated belief in the universal goodness of my own national movement, the idea that Zionism, not from 1967 but from much earlier on, could actually have victims seemed positively outlandish. But as I read on there came the realization that this was indeed the case. This hit me like a bolt. It shook me to the core. You can say that Said is wrong on this or that point but the overall insight remains.

Why do you think that shook you so much? Was it related to your South African experience?
Steve – Not completely, but in many ways, yes. We presented ourselves as being completely against racism, utterly for political and social justice in South Africa, and our Zionist self-representation consisted of regarding Israel as the epitome of progress, equality and so on - the very opposite of the South African experience. The shock was the realization about our own narcissistic myopia, our empathy with the victims of apartheid and our inability to empathize with those who were dispossessed by our own project. I am not suggesting that apartheid and Zionism are one, nor do I want to elide the tragic complexities of the Israel-Arab conflict. I have stressed before, the Zionist case was based on urgent and authentic inner needs. That is a long and complicated

story and not the point here. What is at issue here is the question of empathic recognition, the ability to step out of one's own skin and at least honestly face up to the consequences and everyday realities of our needs and actions on the people who also live (or lived) in this land. What was also shocking to me is the fact that I had for so long bought into the narrative without real questioning, and as shocking is the fact that so many don't even do this to this day.

All this is made even more problematic by my own ambivalences and understanding that I can say precisely because I stand on majoritarian, sovereign ground. I can make my universalist arguments because I live in a tribal way and because the army, police, and border police do the dirty work and protect me. It's the same contradiction I talked about before.

Can this situation be resolved?
Steve – First of all, there may be no solution at all and that's part of the tragedy. In principle, I have nothing against a unitary state in which all the people who live here would find a suitable arrangement in which to pursue their separate collective existences but also live together. I don't hold out much hope in any case for any of the commonly-proposed solutions. But then history is interesting precisely because it is largely so unpredictable. In our own time the most unexpected things have happened.

How do you understand the fact that people who seemed to be so critical of what was going on in South Africa and preached a humanistic creed have buckled under here and gone with the flow?
Steve – I have buckled under here and I buckled there, so I can't criticize. We all, the *Habonim* boys, buckled in South Africa. We all rationalized that that was not our struggle. Here I haven't got that rationalization. If there is a struggle, this is it. I remain an arm-chair critic. It's very comfortable this way but it doesn't come with too many moral credentials.

Academics would seem to be well placed to criticize, etc…

Steve – Their status has changed. They used to have a much more important role, say in the sixties: Leibovitz, Talmon, Arieli, Uri Avnery. They were the leading tone-setters of the critiques. Then, very rapidly there was another set of people who set the tone, the novelists. Amos Oz, A. B. Yehoshua, David Grossman. Even they no longer occupy that position to the same degree. There are no moral tone-setters. There are people in the media like Gideon Levy, Amira Haas, and maybe Akiva Eldar but they don't have the same status that the academics or the authors had. Who are the moral tone-setters? The intellectuals have lost status precipitously. I think that applies world-wide. There is nobody in France today like Sartre was. There is Chomsky in America but he is seen as being 'off the wall'. Maybe in an era of mass media, they are less likely to have influence throughout the world. In any case the problem and loss of moral authority goes much deeper than merely the role of intellectuals. Moreover, their influence has, as often as not, been as pernicious as it has been beneficial.

In South Africa many people speak about 'uncertain times'. Perhaps this applies more generally?

Steve – A cynical friend of mine says we don't have to worry about the end of the State of Israel because the world is going to collapse beforehand. Well, whatever, it remains true that living here the existential edge is sharper than anywhere else I know. People in Iowa or Wisconsin don't know this kind of intensity. We live on the edge almost by definition here.

So where does that leave you?

Steve – All the reservations notwithstanding, clearly living here still answers deep needs. I suppose I should be ashamed to say I am happy. I am fulfilled professionally, have a lovely family, good mates. But don't you dare publicize that.

Moshe Ben Ami

Kibbutz Shoval
12/11/07

Moshe Ben Ami was born in England in 1924 and at an early age moved to South Africa with his parents. He matriculated in Pretoria and studied chemical engineering at Witwatersrand University.

Moshe, the archetypal chalutz, was a role model for generations of Hashomer Hatzair members in South Africa. Deeply committed to kibbutz and Zionism, he left for Israel immediately on completion of his degree.

He became a member of kibbutz Shoval, a man of the soil who worked in agriculture and agricultural experimentation in the Negev until the age of 65.

In 1990, after retiring from agriculture, Moshe was approached by the kibbutz to manage their ulpan. He took on the job and has worked there tirelessly ever since. He developed a unique method of recruiting students that involves his interviewing individual students in their home country.

Can you give us the general setting to the young Moshe Ben Ami?
Moshe – I was born in England in 1924. That means my age at the moment is eighty-three. I have stopped counting. At an early age, my parents moved from England to South Africa.

After matriculating, I went to Wits to study chemical engineering. I was not very interested in my university studies because my parents were very pro-Zionist and that definitely had an influence on me. I was very active in *Habonim* in Pretoria for a number of years. The movement took up more of my time than the university did, but I managed both.

I was very attracted to left-wing ideas, like those of the Communist Party, which was not such an easy thing in South Africa in those days. What interested me most was a Zionist-socialist group in Pretoria. I gave a number of lectures there and I became part of a group that was very important in forming my approach. Very soon I came to the conclusion that talking about Zionism was not the same as being an active Zionist. This was the early forties.

When I moved to Johannesburg, I met up with people from *Hashomer Hatzair*. Many of them had come from Europe and did not know English. When a number of young Jewish intellectuals joined the movement, they made an impact. The Europeans were very Marxist; the South African intellectuals were more psychologically oriented who looked to see to what extent the movement could help people express their personality through *chalutziut*. Their ideas, based on Reichian theory were quite a shock for us in *Hashomer Hatzair*. We were quite free about sexual activity but to make that the dominant idea above Marxism was very difficult to accept. There was competition between the two approaches.

With some people from Durban I decided to establish *Hechalutz* in *Habonim*. We started drawing in people to whom practical *halutziut* appealed. These things do not happen without clashes and at that period we found that *Habonim*, which was more like a scout movement, was against this young group coming in and taking over the ideological direction of the movement. Norman Lurie was the *Manhig* of *Habonim* and he was very much for the *Hechalutz* idea but eventually the movement laid down rules as to how we should behave. I felt that limited my ideas, so I went over to *Hashomer Hatzair*. That was just what they wanted. After I went across a number of people from *Habonim* came across as well.

I was in no way interested in being an armchair Zionist. I started learning Hebrew on my own and then I went to a rabbi in town who helped me for free. In that way I started speaking Hebrew. I could not wait for *Habonim*, I needed a different pace.

Why kibbutz? What was the big attraction?
Moshe – The peak of individual expression was the kibbutz. An individual who wanted to make a maximum contribution to Israel went

to kibbutz. I saw my own personal development only through Zionist socialism. Otherwise I would have concentrated on my professional education. After completing my chemical engineering degree, I never practiced it. I went straight off to Israel.

I had no arguments with the *Hashomer Hatzair* people who chose Trotskyism. But my Zionism did not allow me to leave the movement and remain in South Africa and fight against apartheid. Besides learning Hebrew, I changed my name from Morris Grupel, which had no meaning for me. Moshe Ben Ami was very appealing.

What were the influences on your Zionist thinking?
Moshe – I think it was my home background. My parents always talked about going to Israel. In 1933 my mother tried to settle in Israel with us but we could not manage economically and we went back to South Africa. The family made its mark. I did not have a lot of quandaries about going. I was always looking for something that would be a challenge for me. Zionism, the idea of *chalutziut,* certainly presented me with that challenge.

Did you have any doubts about not taking up the South African struggle?
Moshe – Now and again, perhaps at a time of crisis I might have thought about changing direction. I had a lot of talks with Baruch Hirson and I could accept his arguments intellectually but I could not accept them emotionally. I met up with him and with his wife quite often since then but there was no basis for ideological discussion. We were sensible enough to understand that there is a period when you stop arguing about which ideological path is the correct one.

When *Hashomer Hatzair* opened a *hachshara* near Cape Town, I moved there. Then we waited for the moment we could move to Israel. That was the period of the White Paper and things were very difficult. The Fed arranged for the Hebrew University to give bursaries for between ten and fifteen young people to come to study. The idea was to move to England and from there to Israel. There were a couple of South African girls in *Hashomer Hatzair* who were not South African citizens so we had to get married to them. We were formally married in a South African court and then we traveled to England. It was 1947. In England they explained to us that we would be taken to France and from there we would be sent directly to Israel.

In Marseilles there were a number of camps around the city for refugees who came from all over Europe. All were looking for a way to get to Israel. Most of them were sent via *Aliyah Bet* – illegal immigration. The possibilities were very limited because the British had found out all the routes that were being used. Those of us who had visas had to wait until there was a ship going across and in the meantime we lived in the camps. We met up with all the refugees and the only language connection we had was Yiddish.

I started working with the refugees and realized that this was very important work. This is what Zionism was at that particular period - to bring these people across and to make the transition to Israel as easy as possible. It gave you the feeling of being part of everything.

I agreed for those who were running the organization to use my passport to help people who had difficulty getting in. I still have that passport and it is full of stamps, at least ten. I was without any identification document but at that age I didn't care. We managed.

All my Zionism underwent a transformation from the day I started working with these people. What Zionism meant was to get people to Israel and to go there yourself. I found this work so fascinating that I was prepared to delay my personal arrival in Israel. I remained in the camps until February 1948.

Finally my turn came and off we moved. This was the most exhilarating experience I have ever had. We had a tiny ship with six hundred people on board. The conditions were terrible. We were approaching Crete when three British cruisers ordered us to stop. We understood there was no choice, so we put the engines out of action. We asked all the people to come out. It was a heartbreaking moment. We put up the Israeli flag and sang *Hatikva*. For two days they dragged us to Haifa.

We could see Haifa in front of us when then they ordered us to move across to one of their big transport ships to take us to Cyprus. We had a five hour struggle with them until they dragged each one of us across to the *Ocean Vigor*. From there they took us to Cyprus, where I made contact with the *Haganah* groups. There were about thirty thousand refugees in ten camps, surrounded by high barbed-wire fences, all very well organized by the British.

Three days before I was due to escape, the British found the tunnel I was supposed to use and they blew it up. Eventually, by marrying my second wife we were allowed as a family to leave for Israel. I arrived in Tel Aviv exactly two hours before Ben Gurion declared the establishment of the State of Israel. I ran to the museum in Rothschild Blvd. to hear him.

Shoval was one of the eleven settlements set up in the Negev one night before the state. I went down the next day. That move determined everything for me afterwards. The kibbutz was the next stage of my Zionism.

I wanted to be a member of a kibbutz, but not one that was well-established. Shoval was just the answer to that. There was nothing here. Of my group of about twenty South Africans I am the only one who has remained. All the rest found that kibbutz life was not exactly what they expected. I found it was what I wanted and I stayed.

How do you understand the fact that so many people did not stay?
Moshe – Being young and being far away you build up this dream of what the kibbutz is. It is very romantic and when you come to the kibbutz you are brought down to earth quickly - daily monotonous work. You have very little communication in the beginning because of language problems. My big advantage was that I could talk, even argue with everybody in Hebrew.

Secondly, I had prepared myself ideologically for the fact that I would have to do difficult physical work. Many of the South Africans were university graduates who wanted their life to revolve around interesting political and philosophical discussions. These take place in the kibbutz but not just for the sake of discussion. They are connected with daily decisions. The Anglo-Saxons could not cope with this so they moved across to other aspects of Israeli life.

How was socialism expressed on Shoval at that time?
Moshe – For me, things started to move through agriculture. There was a very practical democracy on the kibbutz. Then it functioned better than anywhere else. Afterwards we realized it was limited and had to be changed.

At that time, we had *shituf alef* – you didn't wear your shirt for more than one week. The next week you got somebody else's. It was not important what you wore; the ideology behind it was important. It was important to be modest, to live on a minimum and give the maximum to the society. There were not many questions whether what we were doing was correct. The questions only arose when people did not fit in individually. I was lucky. They said I was more like the Israelis than the South Africans.

Then I met up with Hadassah (my wife), who is originally from Berea. We have four children.

Tell us about the early days with the children.
Moshe – The arrangement of the children sleeping in the children's houses was very good because it helped you organize your day. Your day was packed with work and meetings, so you had to have things well organized. We did not feel any lack of contact with the children. Our youngest child had difficulty settling down and I did something which the kibbutz didn't agree to: I took her out of the children's house and brought her home. When she felt better, she went back to the children's house. I never felt I had to accept everything that the kibbutz demanded of me. If you wanted to be a bit different, you could be. The kibbutz does not have an argument with somebody who is working well.

Have your children stayed on the kibbutz?
Moshe – Only one has stayed and I am very pleased. The other three are in Israel. At one time, it was obvious that the children would remain

forever. As time moved on we saw that these things didn't work out as we planned.

Would it be true to stay that however ideological you were you always had a very strong pragmatic side?
Moshe – For me the kibbutz was a very good framework to live in. The fact that my work gave me a terrific amount of satisfaction helped a lot. I could remain on the kibbutz and maintain my outside contacts. To the contrary, I had much more freedom than if I had I lived off the kibbutz. I got what was important to me. For instance, I ate less when I was off the kibbutz and used my allowance to buy a book or a record instead. That was against the regulations of the kibbutz – creating private property. But for me that was ridiculous and I did what I did. Nobody came to complain.

What about political issues?
Moshe – I never went in for political activity because I had so much other activity which kept me active. If I do something I have to do it totally. I was totally involved in the agricultural expansion of the Negev. At various times, I was also kibbutz secretary and treasurer. I was head of committees.

How do you feel about the present state of affairs in the country?
Moshe – I am very worried about many things. But I have a practical approach to most of these things. And I see that certain things are the result of things we could or could not change. You don't have very much control of a change like the change from a socialistic to a private structure. You have to see how you can function within that framework. I accept the process of privatization of the kibbutz. The kibbutz was not functioning as it should so you have to change.

In South Africa we were concerned about the absence of social justice, etc. Are you not bothered about the lack of social justice, disregard for human rights and so on in Israel today?
Moshe - I do not do soul-searching about how I relate to Israel. I see many of the things here as the result of the change in the reality. Nobody

knows if we had not occupied the West Bank whether we would be facing a more friendly Arab population or not. I was always in favor of not going into the West Bank but that happened.

I accept Zionism and I have no question about the fact that Israel is the home of the Jewish people. If the reality becomes more difficult it just means we have to cope with a more difficult situation. I have never felt that I made a mistake in coming to Israel. I do not have to investigate the Zionist basis of being here. I have the same attitudes I had sixty years ago.

If the first stage was the movement and *Aliyah Bet*, the second stage was agriculture on the kibbutz, the third stage is the one I am in at the moment. I worked in agriculture in daily work in the fields, until the age of sixty-five. I needed my contact with the soil. Zionism for me meant physical work as well as theoretical work.

In 1990 the kibbutz asked me to set up an *ulpan* for Russians. I agreed to manage one *ulpan* to give the kibbutz time to find somebody else. I was only prepared to do the job because I saw it as a Zionist effort. To me it was a continuation of the work I had done in 1947 in *Aliyah Bet*.

The Jewish Agency was very pleased with our results and I stayed on. I have done eighteen years now. Our reputation has spread. Each year we finish with forty to fifty students who give me the motivation to continue. How many years I still have to do it I don't know.

Louise Bethlehem

Jerusalem
10/03/08

Born in 1964, Louise Bethlehem left South Africa for Israel in 1985. She holds a Ph.D. from Tel Aviv University and is currently a senior lecturer in the Department of English at the Hebrew University of Jerusalem where she heads the Program in Cultural Studies. She has published widely on J.M. Coetzee as well as on South African literary history more generally, including the recent volume Skin Tight: Apartheid Literary Culture and its Aftermath *(Brill/Unisa, 2006).*

You left South Africa in 1985...
Louise – It was about a month after the proclamation of the first State of Emergency. I had been in a Zionist youth movement, *Netzer Maginim*, for many years, as a *madricha* and later in a *garin aliyah*.

I then did an MA at Tel Aviv University and subsequently did a PhD and graduated in 1998. I began at the Hebrew University of Jerusalem that year and am now a senior lecturer. I divide my time between English and Cultural Studies.

Tell us about your family background.
Louise – My immediate family was not at all Zionist. We had strong connections to the Reform movement. My mother was always prominent in community circles, for instance she was head of the Jewish Women's Benevolent Society and later Chair of the South African Jewish Board of Deputies. My grandmother was also a life-time member of the Jewish Women's Benevolent Society. My father had a brief period in activist politics and had his passport removed for transporting black women to the townships during the big bus boycott.

The sense was that we were very rooted in South Africa. Unlike the Orthodox communities of the time, the Reform community was radicalized politically. That happened by virtue of the interventions of two rabbis: Ben Isaacson and Richard Lampert, who was the rabbi of my immediate community and who left South Africa after a particularly fiery sermon in which he denounced apartheid. He found himself undesired by forces in the community and by the state in general.

So, my coming into consciousness as a political activist was routed through the social commitments of the Reform movement – a sort of prophetic Judaism that sought justice. A formative experience for us through the *shul* would be, for instance, on *Shavuot* and *Sukkot* we would take fruit to a school in Alexandra township, named for Rabbi Moses Cyrus Weiler, who was one of the founders of the movement in South Africa. I still have a permit from the local police station allowing us into Alex.

In a sense, my coming to Zionism was unexpected although I went to a Jewish day-school for my high school career. Despite the ideological constellation of the school, which was always officially supportive of Zionism, only a tiny fragment of the school ever made *aliyah*. There were fairly influential people in the life of the school community who did end up in Israel.

As I became socialized into the youth movement and came under the influence of various *shlichim*, a social group formed around the idea of a non-traditional *garin aliyah*, that would not necessarily go to kibbutz but that would have some sort of communal ties and perhaps set up an urban kibbutz. We were very vague as to what we would actually do. Many of us were prospective professionals. I was probably most socialist in terms of my leanings and my reading. I read the Zionist classics and I valued the idea of re-establishing Jewish labor. But I could not quite make the stretch to seeing myself in a kibbutz setting.

At the same time, I was active in the youth movement, I was politically conscious. I elected to study African literature at Wits in 1983, which was a very political choice. It was the first time that a department of African literature had been established in any university and it had a clear political purpose. But in disciplinary terms it was a re-action against the conservatism of English departments in which you could complete an entire degree without, for instance, hearing Nadine Gordimer's name mentioned once. And you certainly wouldn't hear Es'kia Mphahlele or Steven Biko or any other black writers and think-ers. So my decision to be in the very first group of students was partly motivated by personal interest and commitment to those components of my identity which were South African and which had been fiercely politicized from the movement.

Politicization happened for me really early. In standard seven, aged fourteen, I wrote an article to the King David magazine denouncing apartheid. That was not the norm. I grew up in the immediate after-math of the Soweto Revolt of June 1976 and those of us who were politically conscious were aware of our privilege, perched on the top of the hill compared to the events happening just kilometers away in Alex. The key moments of my adolescence were June 16th, 1976 and then Biko's death a year later. Those events influenced the more socially re-sponsive members of my community, whether in the youth movement or at school.

What do you think made the difference between the way you re-sponded to those events and the way the girls and boys sitting next to you in class responded?
Louise – I think it is a matter of having been exposed to the politi-cal interventions of the Reform movement from the age of eleven on. When I was studying for my *batmitzvah*, I would sit in *shul* week after week and at some point in the sermon Rabbi Lampert would turn his gaze onto what was happening. There was open discussion in my fam-ily around the controversial interventions that the Reform movement was making at a time of political quietude that resonated very deeply with me.

My parents were classic South African liberals, which meant hu-mane treatment of servants. They prided themselves on knowing the surnames of the people who worked for us, which wasn't a given. I guess my father, through his professional life as a doctor and his train-ing at Baragwanath, was aware of what the structural violence of apart-heid did to people. We were not a radical household at all but there was a deep commitment to a liberalism rooted in a sense of social justice that the Reform movement at the time promoted.

I also had a strong experience of being an outsider, of being exiled as a child. At some point, we went to live in England and we ended up in Wimbledon, where I went to the local grammar school. The school was mixed ethnically and I found common cause with the Jamaicans and Nigerians against the working class English kids, who could smell my privilege and made my life miserable. So, I was an African. I was also the only Jew in the school. This was the time the *Yom Kippur* War broke out. I was about nine and already the question arose: With whom does one affiliate? The friendship I had with children from the Carib-bean normalized race relations for me in a way that I was later able to articulate.

During your time at university, were you torn between South African activism and Zionism?
Louise – It was a very fraught time for me, especially in my last year. The commitments I had made to the African literature program had radicalized me politically. I was taught by the late Es'kia (Ezekiel) Mphahlele, a celebrated author who had been in exile for many years.

That was a moment of enormous intellectual flowering. There was an enormous amount of ideological work by intellectuals that went into making the categories of Althusserian Marxism suitable for radical work. Intellectuals were going out into the field and conducting inter-views and were organizing trade unions. There was a very strong sense of the committed intellectual that began to seep through the insula-tion with which I had previously viewed my profession, my identity as a reader of texts. All of a sudden I realized what the political stakes of my choices were.

At the same time, I was still active in the youth movement and was shuttling backwards and forwards between South Africa and Israel. I had committed myself to my Jewish identity, obsessively perhaps in retrospect.

Previously, I had been sent to Israel as part of a combined school and youth movement delegation to the first gathering of Holocaust survivors. That was a very formative exposure to the historical trauma of the Holocaust. My grandfather on my mother's side was a German refugee, who came to South Africa in the 1930's. Many of his brothers came to Palestine. The sister who did not leave Germany we assume perished in Auschwitz. So there was this subterranean commitment to this post-Holocaust historical identity as a Jew, alongside the Reform movement with its ambiguous message about being Jewish and also being committed to South Africa, alongside a political radicalism that was becoming more and more explosive for me and harder and harder to handle.

I was very conscious of what we called 'dual identity'. At some point during that last year I was at Wits, it seemed to me that I had the choice of leaving the country and emigrating to Australia, San Diego, or London, as most of my contemporaries were doing. It seemed to me that that was an escapist option and not one that I could consider ideologically relevant to myself. In essence, what was left was to determine which nationalism would win out: a South African nationalism or a Jewish nationalism, which I was still naïve enough to believe contained traces of socialism and traces of a program for social justice, despite the fact of the Lebanon War and an occupation that was well into its second decade.

I was unsettled by this but I refused to look too deeply at it. I was still an apologist. At the time of the Sabra and Shatilla massacres, I was active in the South African Union of Jewish Students (SAUJS) where predictably my move was to overturn the discrimination that prevented Reform rabbis from speaking on campuses in South Africa. My friends on the left would challenge me often about Israeli politics. There were a number of very radical Jews who were virulently anti-Zionist. They asked me to render account for my Zionism because they knew I was also deeply involved, certainly intellectually, with the life of South

Africa. My PhD thesis would eventually treat the role of South African literary culture in the struggle against apartheid.

Everything about my socialization as a teenager in the Jewish community meant that I opted for the route of Jewish nationalism. I think that this had as much to do with an exaggerated belief in the power of the South Africa state to harm me. The first year I was on campus, Neil Aggett died in detention. I remember my parent's outrage and fear when I came home one day and announced that I had signed a petition for the freeing of Nelson Mandela. Immediately they had visions of me being cast into prison, as they had for the fact that I was keeping banned literature.

I think I collapsed the distance between the options that might have been available to me. I saw my choice as either coming to live in Israel, committing myself to this cause, or going underground. What did I imagine that might be? I could not quite see myself as a member of the ANC underground, but I had this image of the mythical trade-unionist who was going to get thrown in jail and tortured to death like Neil Aggett. My sense of the political was not astute enough and my sense of being in a community with activists was not strong enough for me to realize that I could have played a role in South Africa that need not have brought me immediately into confrontation with the state security apparatus.

You are saying that there was an alternative to either doing nothing or going 'all the way'.
Louise – Yes. My sister took that alternative. (See interview with Lael Bethlehem). We bifurcated. We had the exact same social formation. Like myself, she was in the youth movement, she visited Israel and then she came into contact with exiled black South Africans and when she went back to South Africa she could see that there were legitimate paths open. But it did eventually bring her to the attention of the security police. Her car was smashed up as a warning that she was treading on dangerous ground. Her phone was bugged.

As I saw it, I had two mythological options. One was being an underground resistance person in the heroic mould. The other was the struggle for social justice in Israel for the Jewish people under the rubric of some kind of socialism. I did not have the courage to go underground but I might have had a very productive life as an activist intellectual in student circles, in groups that were looking at how structures would look at the end of apartheid. However I blinded myself to those options because I was committed to the idea of transforming my life through making *aliyah*.

In 1994 did you have thoughts of changing direction?
Louise – I felt in a way betrayed - betrayed by Zionism. I still do feel betrayed by Zionism. I was envious of the people who were living through the moment of transition in South Africa. In some respects my intellectual work was a bridging of that gap and because I had committed myself in my PhD to charting the course of intellectual history through literature and the growth of South African literary studies. I started to compensate for my strong sense of being exiled as a South African by turning in my PhD to South African topics, that would keep me current, that would keep me in the archive and that would allow pedagogy to give me a form of political intervention here that I felt I had deprived myself of there.

My work has been very political, not with facile, rhetorical analogies with the apartheid state but very cautious and intellectually driven, and indebted to the particularities of apartheid as a paradigm for thinking about how the occupation works and how structures of spatial containment, of capital, of segregation, of labor operate.

So there is a way in which my intellectual profile is a continuation of my commitments to South Africa. But it is one that has to come to grips with my own conflicted belonging here as an intellectual, as the mother of a child in the Israeli army. The structures of my belonging, the structures of my Jewishness, my identity have become slightly chaotic in the sense that I belong in each place and I belong in neither place.

I use my positions and my commitments to critique each other, even when this is uncomfortable and even when I realize I simply can't wash my hands of any of them. In that sense I am not an anti-Zionist, to the extent that I am the mother of Israeli children and I function critically in Zionist society. I am certainly anti-occupation. I am certainly anti- the deeply structural racism that characterizes Israeli society internally and externally. But at the same time, I sense the strong historical continuity in my own life in terms of how a very conflicted relation to Judaism, to the ethics, to how I was taught to identify with being Jewish remains strong and current.

In a sense you have to balance your South African identity with what you have encountered here...
Louise – I think categories are fluid and can be used strategically to disrupt one another. Our structures of belonging are performative. We belong differently at different times of the day. I am a mother. I am a motorist on a road built to facilitate the movement of Jewish people from the West Bank into Jerusalem, or I am activist in the *Zochrot* organization, or I am a teacher, or I just go to the grocery store in Hod Hasharon. Each of those moments in the day might reflect a different dominance of where in this fluid mixture of identities I happen to find myself.

So balance is not what it is about. It is a matter of holding in suspension different and not always compatible commitments to my own personal past and a kind of historical past that has placed me in Israel now, perhaps inextricably, in the sense that I have children in Israel in 2008.

Do you think that being an intellectual enables you to live more comfortably with all these inconsistencies than if you had not been an intellectual? Do you have the privilege of being in an ivory tower?
Louise – For me intellectual practice never occurs in an ivory tower. I am an activist intellectual. In the past, I served on the governing body of *Zochrot*, which has as its motto the task of narrating the *nakba* in Hebrew, so as to facilitate some kind of historical reckoning of the trauma of 1948 and the creation of Palestinian refugees and the nationaliza-

tion of their land. If we continue to repress this as a normal part of Israeli identity we will never get closer to addressing core issues and will we will perpetuate conflict with Palestinians for as long as we are not prepared to recognize that the conflict is also over prior rights of ownership. We are not going to unpack our national traumas very effectively until these taboos are lifted. So Israelis have to come to terms with the events of the *nakba* and Palestinians have to terms with the events of the *shoah*. I am not in any way suggesting a parallelism between the two. There is a historical process of reckoning with difficult pasts. They need to be spoken about.

I choose to look at facets of the society that many Israelis prefer not to confront: from unrecognized Bedouin villages in the Negev through to ongoing racism directed against Ethiopians plus the whole Palestinian issue. It is not always comfortable to confront such issues, particularly in light of my past and the commitments of that past. At the same time, there is always the danger that my not having been born here renders me suspect for Israeli society in terms of the validity of my critique, although after twenty something years into this process I think I have earned some credibility.

What are the lessons that we in Israel can learn from the South African case?
Louise – It is a question that has fascinated many of us for a long time. What I have learned is the fact of transformation in South Africa, where for so long we had thought that it was impossible, and the fact of its coming about, and then this astonishing phenomenon called the Truth and Reconciliation Commission (TRC), which I critique, but which I very much believe in – those two things: a set of contingent circumstances overturns a trajectory that looked certain; a number of factors coalesce unpredictably to bring about democracy in South Africa. The message coming out of South Africa is, "It happened for us so it can happen for you."

At the same time, there are very disturbing negative lessons to be learnt. If apartheid was a form of racialized capitalism, if it used structures of spatial control, of unequal access to resources in order to maintain its power, then we could do worse than ask how the (separation) wall, for instance, is a structure of spatial delimitation that produces certain forms of governance, certain forms of violation of human rights, certain forms of economic deprivation, which have deep structural parallels in the history of apartheid.

I am not interested in Israel being denounced as an apartheid state. I am interested in criticism being leveled at structures of government, at structures of thought, at the role of ideology in making discriminatory social apparatuses comfortable for those who are privileged in them. I want to talk to middle class Israelis and make them part of social transformation. I want to look at the position of Palestinians in Israel differently from the mainstream.

My affiliation to *Zochrot*, which has an inclusive policy of trying to promote the rights of refugees has something of the reconciliatory spirit of the anti-apartheid movements in the eighties.

Have you encountered any hostility from people as a result of your views and activities?
Louise – I have learnt from experience. I am effective ethically and politically when I speak in the right places to the right communities. I no longer allow myself to engage in dinner table denunciations, to allow myself to be the subject of often quite harsh personal attacks when people discover that my politics are left of consensus. Sometimes, for the sake of friendship, I choose not to cause a confrontation although I am aware of my own distance. That is a source of internal exile and I feel that living in Israel is a state of prolonged exile. At other times, I feel myself to be only residually South African, or South African with huge chunks cut out of what it might have been to live with the transition.

That brings us back to the category of my conflicting identities. At a given time, I can be perfectly in place in Johannesburg, as a South African intellectual. And at other times I can feel perfectly in place in Israel as an activist intellectual. And many times I feel imperfectly emplaced in each of those locations.

Are you tempted to return to South Africa?
Louise – As a woman who has taught gender studies I am extremely disturbed by the possible implications for woman across the board of a Zuma presidency. I don't like ethnic chauvinism of any kind – Jewish, Zulu or Palestinian. There is a lot of doubt and skepticism. I no longer believe in the idea of a return. In other words, going back to SA will not be the closing of the circle although for many years I felt that my life had been ruptured by Zionism, that I had been fatally displaced by the Zionist movement and that I had been actively misled by the agents of ideological policy, be they insufficiently critical teachers in the day schools or *aliyah shlichim*.

When I say I was actively misled, I don't mean only at the ideological level, of the big narrative of Zionism as an emancipatory movement for the Jews, or socialism at a time when the *shlichim* from kibbutzim knew that socialism was in its final gasping death throes. At a time when the *shlichim* were actively reckoning with their own displacement in South Africa - missing family back home, their employment of servants to do the dishes - in all my years in the youth movement, never once did anyone have the personal courage to open up the question for us as very young people of what the long-term consequences of living without one's family, bringing up children at a vast remove from their grandparents might mean. They chose to smooth over these things when talking to very impressionable youngsters about to make irrevocable life choices at extremely early ages. For me, in retrospect, that raises enormous ethical problems. The personal price was not elaborated in the *aliyah* discourse.

You have spoken passionately about your commitment to various ideologies. How do you feel now about the choices you made?
Louise – We need to look at these choices critically. I am aware that although my discourse here has been that of an alienated intellectual, in some respects living in Israel has made me more intellectually flexible,

more open to a range of options for being human, a range of ethnicities, a range of styles of life, of religious experiences than I would have had either as a member of an enclosed Jewish community in South Africa or had I taken the path taken by many people who stayed in South Africa, who retreated into a religious support network. Alongside trying to come to terms with some of the losses here I am aware that there have been unique benefits. For me, those benefits have been more a matter of personal choice than what the ideology promised me as a teenager. Perhaps that is always in the nature of ideology.

Arnie Friedman

Kibbutz Yizra'el
4/11/07

Arnie Friedman was born in Johannesburg in 1934. After the family moved to Cape Town, Arnie did his schooling at SACS. He went to Israel on the Machon Hachoref in 1952 as a member of Habonim, and returned to South Africa to work in the movement. With aliyah to kibbutz as his goal, he did a building course at the Technical College

Arnie left South Africa for Israel in 1956 and immediately joined the IDF. On completion of his army service he settled on Kibbutz Yizra'el, where he lives to this day.

In 1962 the Friedman family went on Shlichut to Cape Town Habonim where they endeared themselves to the local Zionist community.

Back on Yizra'el Arnie worked in the dairy and as a landscape gardener. Arnie is, however, best known as an organizer of Ulpnanim for olim and volunteers. His name has become synonymous with the traditional role that kibbutzim played in absorbing new olim.

Arnie is now semi- retired and he and his wife Peggy are enjoying their six grandchildren.

Can we start with a little bit of family background...
Arnie – I can't say anybody in my family introduced me to ideology or the idea of leaving South Africa, because my family were very Jewish South Africans, not very religious and not very traditional – the usual, warm South African family where Judaism was around the culinary arts. We were a very strong Jewish family. My sister was a jazz pianist and piano teacher.

They were not all that keen that I should go to *Habonim*, but I went, and they started to get upset when I started speaking about Israel.

I managed to persuade them to help me go to Israel on the *Machon Hahoref* in 1952. I came back with stars in my eyes, having spent a month on Tzora, which was a great influence on my life.

I actually joined *Habonim* properly at a later age, in *Shomrim*. My *madrich* was Moshe (Muzz) Hill. He was without a doubt a tremendous influence on everybody who was in that *chavura*. There are so many of us in Israel, it is unbelievable. He was an amazing guy. He introduced us to so many things. In those days *Habonim* produced booklets on Ahad Ha'am, Berl Katznelson Harav Kook and all the main Jewish and Zionist leaders. We used to read and talk and discuss, and he also had a wonderful approach to outdoor activities, with lots of hiking and camping, and climbing Table Mountain. He use to *shlep* us along and would not take no for an answer; weird caves on the way to Paarl. He encouraged us to organize our own cultural evenings, and took us to the classical concerts at the Cape Town City Hall every Sunday night and plays. I have the feeling that had I not been in *Habonim* with Muzz it might all have just passed over me.

Those years between the ages of fifteen to twenty, with a guy like Muzz around, were a tremendous force in shaping my particular approach and my Zionism. I am very thankful to the movement for introducing me to classical music and to my sister for introducing me to jazz.

You can imagine what Tzora was like in the middle of winter in 1952. It was an eye-opening experience. I can remember people like Foggy, Batya and Tzvi Jaspan, who had a great influence on us. When I came back from that trip, I got involved with *Habonim* a lot. I had finished school and I felt I did not want to burden my parents, who were not well off, with the expense of sending me to university, so I decided to work for a while and see later what to do. I managed to get a job in Woolworths, of all places, and eventually became the assistant branch manager of the Sea Point branch at the age of twenty.

After I went on the *Machon Hahoref*, I decided I must start preparing myself for *aliyah*. I decided to do a course in building. I went to the tech and did bricklaying. But it was not enough to learn, you had to do. There was a Mr. Burger who had a building company and I applied to him. He said it was fine but I would have to work with all the Coloreds and Malays because he did not have any white bricklayers. I said I would give it a try. "What can be?" So I went to learn bricklaying and it was bloody difficult because the bricks are heavy and you have to pick them up with one hand. Your hands get full of cement and I got cement burns. I suffered. It was a terrible half-year until I more or less got the hang of it.

Working with the coloreds and Malays was also very influential. We had discussions about South Africa and the apartheid regime. There were blacks too, who used to make *machawe*, this horrible beer, and they used to invite me. They were all very nice to me, very understanding.

After the first six months, when I was quite useless, I had a most interesting experience. At the time, I was a *Shomrim madrich* and one of the girls invited me to a school dance at Good Hope School. Shortly before that, Mr. Burger had taken on work at the school, so there was I with all my *chanichot* staring at me laying bricks. It became the talk of the movement. The head teacher, Ms. Tyfield, used to walk around the site to see how the building was progressing and she always said good morning to me. Then I pitched up at the school dance with Anne, wearing a tie and a suit, and the girls had to introduce their partners to Ms. Tyfield. She took one look at me and I could see what was written on her face, "One of the girls has brought along a builder!" It was the joke of *Habonim* for weeks afterwards.

I did not really enjoy the building work but I felt it was what I should be doing. I had the feeling that one can't just go to Israel without being able to do something useful there. At one stage, I applied to the Forestry Department, but my dad would not hear of it. And then I joined the *garin*, which was also a great influence. The *garin* (*Gimmel*) was about thirty strong. And before going on *aliyah* I went to work for the movement. We were planning to leave in 1957. The *garin* was actually formed on *hachshara* in the big tobacco barn. There was a big ideological argument about whether *Habonim* people should be growing tobacco, not for health reasons but because smoking was considered bourgeois, as was ballroom dancing. Some said, "If the kibbutzim can grow grapes for wine, why not tobacco?"

What was it that you latched onto on the Machon Hachoref and from Muzz Hill?
Arnie – The whole education was towards Zionist socialism, the kibbutz idea and kibbutz ideal, which was very attractive to us in those days. Not to everybody, of course. We even tried to live like on a kibbutz. We had a *kupah* and we used to camp out.We used to go to the Mirvish's farm in Durbanville and spend the weekends digging and planting things. It was all very intense and the discussions were all about the kibbutz movement, and in those days the kibbutz movement was a very influential force in Israel. We thought that if we were going to go to Israel the best thing we could do was strengthen the Zionist movement, which was the kibbutz idea.

We were also influenced by the *shlichim* – Yoav and Aliza Tivon and Reuven Rogalsky, who was a tremendously important influence on me. He was forty and the only *Habonim shaliach* in South Africa. He wanted to visit us in Cape Town but the (Zionist) Federation would not finance the trip, so he hitched down by himself. He was a hell of a charismatic guy. There were also a few of the *Hashomer Hatzair shlichim* who made an impression. All these people had a tremendous influence, and our big guru was Michael Cohen from (kibbutz) Kfar Hanassi. When my parents were arguing with me about Israel and the kibbutz, I decided to invite him over for Saturday lunch. He spoke to my parents and my dad said, "I think you people are crazy. Look how difficult things are there, such a difficult life." And my granny kept on saying (in Yiddish), "Is there anything to eat there?"

Then there was the big revolution in *Habonim*, when it was decided that the main aim of the movement was *halutzik aliyah*. Sam Piper, the *Manhig*, said that was against the principles of the movement and he interviewed all the *madrich*im and all those who supported the ideas of *halutzik aliyah* being the main aim were asked to leave the movement.

There was a counter-revolution where the movement asked Sam Piper to resign and Jules Browde took over. All this was very intense. You can imagine the arguments, the discussions and the shouting. One guy said he was going to leave *Habonim* anyway. Why? Because he was tired of wearing short pants.

Habonim was so important. I remember sitting in our little flat doing my homework, when I heard the *Habonim* whistle from outside. There were Ruby and Eli Shluzny going off to some meeting. I would say, "Ma, I am going to a meeting." She replied, "But you haven't finished your homework." And I would say, "Don't worry, I'll finish it when I come home." It was just that magnetic whistle. You stopped in your tracks.

I went to SACS and half the boys at the school were Jewish. I was at school with Albie Sacks and Benjy Pogrund and there were always tremendous ideological fights with them during the breaks. Albie used to say, "As Jews you should know that your place is not in Israel. That is running away from the realities and the problems of the blacks in this country. Your place is here to help the blacks fulfill their dreams and ambitions and not to run away to Israel." Tremendous arguments.

Perhaps you can tell us a little bit more about that argument. What convinced you that Albie was wrong?
Arnie – Nobody was one hundred percent sure that they were right. There seemed to be two rights here. People in *Habonim* had three choices: either to say the Zionist idea was the right one, or Albie was the one to follow, or to just let things slide, as many of our friends did. In our day there was a *chalutz* register and an *aliyah* register and all *madrich*im were expected to sign the register. You could not be a *Shomrim madrich* if you were not on the *chalutz* register. You had to sign: "I Arnie Friedman am a member of *Garin Gimmel* and I intend to settle in Israel on such and such a date". Muzz always used to say if you want people to believe what you believe in you have to lead. These things were very convincing. Many people refused to sign. Again, deep discussions into the middle of the night.

I remember once me, Ruby and Eli were sitting on the pavement at about half past one in the morning, after a *Habonim* meeting discussing all these matters, when Ruby suddenly said, "Oh my God. It's half past one. Our parents will be worried."

Things were much less complicated and also we were helluva naïve. There is no doubt about it. We used to accept things at face value very easily. It was a very black and white situation: either you were this or that. And it followed if you were this you had to do *x*. We had lots of people in the movement who were very bright but, on principle, did not go to university and did trades instead.

It wasn't common to be anti-apartheid at school. Did Albie and Benjy have a big following?
Arnie – One group was the youth movement crowd – *Habonim*, *Betar*, and *Bnei Akiva*. Three quarters were the social crowd, who were interested in parties and the girls. A very small minority gathered around Albie and Benjamin. But I remember the school debate when I was in standard nine, which was judged by university staff. Benjamin got up and said, "If someone who is concerned about the way the blacks are being oppressed in this country is a communist, then I declare that I, Benjamin Pogrund, am a communist." And the whole school went "Hooray".

In *Habonim* we also did things for people who needed help. Before Xmas we used to go to SHAWCO and collect gifts for the colored kids and we had to wrap them and decide who they were for. We also used to go and teach English at night schools for the African staff of the hotels in Sea Point. That was considered a very brave thing to do. We even used to sing (very quietly) *N'kosi Sikalele* at meetings! Nowadays the Springboks sing it. In our day nobody believed such a thing could possibly happen.

Were there people who moved over from Habonim camp to the Albie and Benjy camp?
Arnie – Oh yes. There were a couple of girls who spent time in jail and ran off. Becky Lan joined the ANC and Hosea Jaffe met his colored

wife at a Trotskyist meeting. The story goes that when Albie finally got out of jail in Roland Street, he ran all the way to Clifton fourth beach and jumped into the water with his clothes on. Since his return to the new South Africa that has become a tradition.

Did you have cordial relations with Hashomer Hatzair?
Arnie – We had good relations with them but they thought we were just playing games. They were extremely intense. However, it was safer to belong to *Habonim* than *Hashomer Hatzair* because they were being watched. Interestingly, many of them came to Israel but they did not stay. The real *verbrentes* did not stay. The same thing is happening in the kibbutz movement today – the most extreme were the first to privatize, without much argument. On Yizra'el, we have not got there yet.

How would you characterize that period of your life?
Arnie – The best period of my life, without a doubt. The age of fourteen till I came on *aliyah* was the most thought-provoking, creative period of my life.

You have not mentioned girls much. Was Habonim very chauvinistic?
Arnie – First of all, many of us came from SACS, which was a boys' school. We only started having social relationships with girls from *Shomrim* age. I did not know any girls until I joined *Habonim*. There were influential, charismatic girls in our group who we were all madly in love with. They were very outspoken and very active. The problem with the girls was that we had to walk them home after the Friday night meetings because we did not have cars. They were as active as we were and boy, were we active. When I think of the things that we did! I remember once we dressed up as poor coloreds and the *Bonim* had to find us. Two of us sat on the pavement talking Afrikaans and they walked right past us. We did crazy things with Muzz.

One Friday we took the train to Paarl, where we slept in the *shul* hall and the next day we climbed DuToit's Kloof and went to a cave that Muzz knew, called the Leopard's cave. We slept in this bloody

Leopard's cave and we forgot to bring essential foodstuffs so we all we had was tinned fruit. We sat in this dripping cave eating tinned fruit. These are things you don't forget. We organized camps and seminars and Muzz used to organize weekend seminars and we all had our little books on Ahad Ha'am and Jabotinsky. We studied them and learnt them and we had to prepare speeches as if we were those people. Perhaps we were over-serious and also naïve. For example, Ruby and Cecily were going out at that time and they did not come along a few times when the *chavura* went out on a Saturday night because it was frowned upon. It was such a relief when the Mormons came to Cape Town because they organized square dancing and that was allowed by the movement.

It seems that ideology went hand in hand with social activity...
Arnie - The *chavura* was a group of friends that got on well together and did fantastic things together. For example, we used to organize progressive suppers. We used to go along to movies and plays together. When we became *madrichim*, it left a big hole in our lives because we had to do things with our *chanichim* and not with the *chavura*. It is interesting that we still get together sometimes. We are still so close. The ideology and the social life were equally strong.

How do you relate to those people who were so close to you in those days and chose not to follow the path that you chose?
Arnie – At the beginning, it was disappointing and we were inclined to be cynical about them but as you get a bit older... Even people who came with us to Yizra'el and then left ... there was a kind of boycott. It took many years to realize that people must make their own choices. The same applies to our kids. We thought we were coming to kibbutz and our kids would remain here. That is not necessarily so. Of our four kids, three are not here today. That was a bit of a shock but then you think: we did not do what our parents wanted us to do. We cannot expect out kids to follow a life they don't want.

Now, when these people come to visit there is such a nice welcome for them and there isn't that feeling that they were deserters. It took time to get over that hurdle. But there are still some people who I would give my eye teeth to have back here.

Do you remember the first cracks in your expectations of what things were going to be like?
Arnie –The first couple of years were really very difficult because the combination of South Africans, Australians, and *sabras* did not go smoothly at the beginning.

We came with all our possessions and there was nothing here. The members had one radio for four rooms, which changed every week. And here we came with our records and record players and toasters. "Why do you need toasters?" they asked. "You eat toast only when you have diarrhea." And the blankets and the sheets… which were unknown things. People lived very frugally here and we received truckloads of goods from South Africa. It took a long time to get over those tensions.

And the language was also a problem. The *sabras* objected to hearing English spoken in the dining room and in the children's houses. Only Hebrew! We spoke to our kids only in Hebrew. Thank God my wife Peggy's parents came here and our kids learnt English from them, not from us. Gradually the social barriers started breaking down. And after a time, when we saw them (the *sabras*) getting inheritances, we realized that many of them came from much better-off homes that we all thought. Now many more Israelis have private money than Anglo-Saxons.

What about your expectations of equality, etc.?
Arnie – One of the Israeli ideologues here believes that it is the Anglo-Saxons who have kept the ideological flame burning here. It has always been an uphill battle, with a few exceptions. For example, children sleeping at home. The Anglos were always in favor but for the *sabras* it meant the end of the kibbutz, as did the idea of putting fridges in people's houses. Having TV was the final word. Telephones at home! That's it. It needed the Anglos to make people realize that there could be some sort of compromise on all these matters.

But we went through a period when people were leaving in droves and we were among the nineteen kibbutzim on the verge of collapse.

What do you think it was that distinguished those people who stayed from those who left?
Arnie – I don't think it was always ideology. It was also personal. There were quite a lot of work problems, especially for the Anglos who had professions and were not allowed to work in them in those days. Now things have changed completely. People could not handle the situation where they had degrees and found themselves working in the dairy or in the children's houses and many of them left. People were very upset with the financial situation generally especially when there was not enough money to make provision for the kids to sleep at home. They thought the kibbutz was going to collapse and decided to leave before that happened.

Maybe if they had belonged to the generation of people coming to kibbutz today it would have been a different story. To an extent people found the reality of kibbutz life very different from what they had imagined. When I think about how we used to live here, we can only laugh. When we came to the kibbutz, there was no personal allowance, there were points. Everybody was entitled to five points per month – one for soap, one for sugar, one for biscuits/cookies, one for coffee or tea, and one for toothpaste. For many people it was too much to bear. Others could not tolerate the children sleeping in the children's houses, for the women especially. Visits overseas were problematic. The kibbutz used to send a maximum of two families a year to visit their families and you could not go at your own expense.

Many people found it difficult to be away from their families in Australia and South Africa and went back. Interestingly, many more Australians left Yizra'el than South Africans because theirs was a very strong kibbutz ideology, whereas *Habonim* in South Africa was more flexible.

Is it not striking that there was an enormous gap between all the talk in the movement about Zionist socialism and the reality on kibbutzim?
Arnie – Correct. The realities of life were not what we thought. We had these romantic notions of dancing together and of equality but in reality there was lots of friction between members about a million and one things. As soon as the Anglos pitched up on Yizra'el a large number of *sabras* left, often to go and study.

I remember one incident when we were expecting visitors and Peggy asked me to ask the woman in charge of the store, a tiny room, whether we could get our biscuit ration earlier in the week than usual. I went along to her and she said that regretfully she only gave out biscuits on a Thursday. I quickly ran to the dining room to get some bread. Ridiculous. And we accepted these things. Either you accepted it and thought there was some hope for the future or you said, "This is not for me. I am off." Very often it was these petty little things that used to break people.

Would you agree that one of the big factors in people leaving kibbutz was the sense of 'not being master of your own destiny'?
Arnie – Without a doubt. In the movement we used to say, "A big fish in a little pond or a little fish in a big pond." For sure, there were people who felt they would not be able to succeed or fulfill themselves if they stayed. I am thinking about someone who worked with the sheep and you could see he was miserably unhappy. For a year he cut himself off from any of the activities on the kibbutz and barely had meals in the dining room. He sat at home every night and taught himself Hebrew. He studied solidly for a whole year because he knew that if he wanted to stay on in Israel and practice law he would need Hebrew. He left after a year and advanced fantastically well. He would not have been able to do this here at the time.

We had a few doctors here at one time. One of them was working in the hospital but he found it very hard to combine that with being a kibbutz member. It was cutting yourself in two, and eventually he also left. Now there are fewer problems of that kind. What young people are saying today is, "We are working much harder than the older people. Why shouldn't we get a bigger allowance?" That is the beginning of the feeling of privatization. Some people think we waste too much money on the dining room but the vast majority is happy with it as it is today.

I want to mention something else. When I was looking for a title for my book, my life story, I recalled a poem of Longfellow's I learnt at the age of eleven. One line goes: *"Footprints in the sands of time"*. And that is perhaps the secret of the kibbutz. Because it is the one kind of society where, if you want to, if you are strong and have got the know-how and the oomph, you can leave your footprint. In any other community, unless you are really tops, you will never be able to do so. I feel that Kibbutz Yizra'el would not have been the same without me, for better or for worse. There are very few people who can say, "I have left my footprints in London or in Johannesburg or in Tel Aviv." I think that is one of the good things about kibbutz society. People have left their mark in various spheres, like academia. Not many have left a mark on a community outside of kibbutz.

Is it money that has determined the way people feel about the kibbutz?
Arnie – Yes, but not always to the good. The feeling that there is money to play around with is not always good for the general atmosphere.

Do you think that Yizra'el would have kept its present structure without the wealth it has generated, or is there something special about the members here that would have kept it this way?
Arnie – Because there is a feeling of financial security it has helped the society to stabilize. As somebody said to me the other day, "In order to have a strong socialist framework you need a lot of capitalist funds." The money is there at the moment. We are on the stock-market and we have got shares but I don't understand a thing about it.

Going back a bit. What was the message you tried to get across when you were a shaliach?
Arnie – I think we were much too orthodox. Fortunately Itz Stein was

there at the same time and he could offer lots of things – about life in Israel, not necessarily on kibbutz - that we could not and there was a real thirst for them among the *chaverim* in Cape Town. I encouraged that. As time went by it became harder and harder to persuade people to choose kibbutz.

How do you cope with the dissonance that exists between the Israel we envisioned and the problems of social justice in Israel today.
Arnie – We try to live with it by forcing ourselves into all sorts of situations, but not always succeeding. For example, an issue came up to the *assefah:* Should we accept these refugees from Darfur or not? There was a huge discussion. Some people said, "As Jews we must do this kind of thing." Another issue concerned the question of whether we should let our kids do *hadracha* before going into the army, as a service to the country. The kibbutz encourages it.

There is a feeling that the kibbutz has taken a back seat, which is sad. We used to feel that the kibbutz was going to lead the country forever, but even in the sixties we realized that it was on the way out.

We find ourselves in the position where we have to help other kibbutzim. We are helping Hamadia and Givat Oz to get over their bad times. We try a little bit but it does seem like a drop in the ocean. It is disappointing, without a doubt.

What we can do other than that I really don't know because we find ourselves so pressurized with our own lives. People often can't think of themselves as giving any more than they are already. The younger generation does more but it is not enough.

Do you personally feel troubled by the reality of Israel today?
Arnie – Most of the members here feel very disappointed with the way the country has gone. People thought that things were starting to move until Rabin's assassination, which just took the wind out of everyone's sails. I don't think we have recovered, especially in the kibbutz movement. We are concerned about the influence of the religious right, who we always regarded as a quaint minority and they have proved to be a huge political force and it is very upsetting. Most

of us are very fearful of how the country is changing and what it is going to be like in say twenty years time.

Are you surprised by the low profile of South African olim in Israel?
Arnie – I had not thought about it but it does seem to be the case. Maybe it had to do with the language barrier. It seems that South Africans who have left the country have made tremendous progress compared to those who have stayed. Had some of the outstanding leaders of the movement remained in South Africa rather than come to Israel they might have made more of a mark than they have made here.

Perhaps the culture shock of aliyah knocks people backwards...
Arnie – I don't know about your kids, but as youngsters our kids often asked us in a rather critical way, "What made you come to Israel, to kibbutz? What made you do this?" They could not understand how we left the fleshpots of South Africa, especially when they saw for themselves how our families lived there. Yet recently I heard two of our sons telling a visitor that there is no place like Israel. They sounded like real Zionists. What has happened to them?

Aryeh Gilat

Kibbutz Hatzor
10/12/07

Aryeh was born in Poland in 1918. At the age of 14 he and his family moved to South Africa. Having been a member of Hashomer Hatzair in Poland, Aryeh founded the movement in South Africa. He made aliyah in 1939 and became a member of Kibbutz Hazor.

As a member of the kibbutz, Aryeh worked in agriculture and in the brick factory, where he served as secretary of the workers' committee.

Aryeh was sent as a shaliach to Hashomer Hatzair in South Africa in 1950. He returned to the kibbutz in 1953 and was elected treasurer in 1955. In 1958 he became the kibbutz truck driver and later became the manager of the factory. Afterwards he was politically active in Mapam.

On completing his studies in Behavioral Sciences at the age of 56, Aryeh took on the role of secretary of the educational institution Tzafit in Kfar Menahem.

He continued to be active in various public spheres until the age of 90, when he retired.

Aryeh has 11 grandchildren and 7 great-grandchildren.

You were not actually born in South Africa were you?
Aryeh – I was born in 1918. I came to South Africa at that age of fourteen and I had already been in *Hashomer Hatzair* in Poland. I was part of the group that founded *Hashomer Hatzair* in South Africa.

In Johannesburg I joined a group of people who came from Germany, Lithuania and Latvia. We decided to join the world movement of *Hashomer Hatzair*. We were all people who came from overseas. Alec Marcus was the first member who was born in South Africa.

Who were the dominant figures in that group?
Aryeh – There was Nahum Sneh, and Mendel who went to fight in the Spanish Civil War and was killed.

We had a lot of discussions with communists. Nahum was a Trotskyist but he was in the movement and we believed in our own socialism of kibbutz life.

Where did your Zionism originate?
Aryeh – For us it was obvious. As Jews we wanted to go to Israel and establish a kibbutz. In Poland every little village had a group of *Hashomer Hatzair*. When my father left for South Africa in 1929, he took me on his knee and he said, "There is one thing I want you not to do, don't join *Hashomer Hatzair*." And as soon as he went I joined *Hashomer Hatzair*. He was an orthodox Jew. I had to bring a signed paper from a parent allowing me to join *Hashomer Hatzair*. The first thing I falsified in my life was my mother's signature.

I worked as a printer before I went on *aliyah* because I wanted to choose a trade. I had read a book by Max Gorky which said that printing was a very revolutionary trade because they had to print illegally. In one year I collected enough money to go to Israel. I told my parents I was only going for a tour and that I would be coming back. I specially bought a return ticket to show them I would go and come back.

Were there people in your group who decided to fight injustice in South Africa?
Aryeh – Most of us believed that finally the black people would stage a revolution, that they would find a way to justice. We believed it was their struggle not ours. For us it was obvious that we must go to our place and they must fight their struggle. The communists were involved in their struggle but we did not want to be involved in it. From our point of view I think that was the right approach.

When did you go on aliyah?
Aryeh – In 1939. I was the first *oleh* from *Hashomer Hatzair*. There were three of us and we started to look around for the best kibbutz of

Hashomer Hatzair. We had some money and we had cigarettes. We didn't smoke but wherever we came to a kibbutz we offered a cigarette and if they took it, we said, "This kibbutz is no good." Then we came to kibbutz Gimmel, which was Hatzor before settlement, and they said, "We don't smoke." They also said there was a meeting that night so they did not have time for us. We decided that as the kibbutz for us. I knew Hebrew when I came here because I had been to Hebrew school in Poland. There were eighty people in the kibbutz at that time.

How did what you found compare to what you expected to find?
Aryeh – I liked it from the very beginning. And I worked very hard. I worked in the brick factory and in the orchard. You had to water the orchard by opening the furrows and let the water run. But I was so tired that I fell asleep and the water covered me. From that day I have had backache. I worked very hard with a *turriyah*.

What was appealing about the kibbutz?
Aryeh – I liked the communal life, the discussions we had. We used to come together in a warm place to talk. I enjoyed it immensely.

I was not disappointed in the kibbutz. There were very intelligent people here and you could discuss every problem. There were no other Anglo-Saxons and I soon became an Israeli. I am not disappointed till this moment – I have been here over sixty years. The kibbutz has changed but you must accept life. I would have liked it to continue as it was.

In 1950 I went as a *shaliach* to Johannesburg and we started a *ken* in Cape Town.

What is your view of South African Jews?
Aryeh – I liked the South African community because they were Zionistically-minded. We were accepted well there. We brought in the idea of *halutziut*.

Do you feel that halutziut was right for South African Jews?
Aryeh – South African Jewry is capitalistic-minded. The kibbutz was too socialistic for them. They liked to give money for Israel to clear

their conscience. I think it was a good idea to have *halutziut* because we saved the people by bringing them here.

Was there talk at that time of members staying in South Africa?
Aryeh – There was no split. Everyone had the idea of going to live in Israel.

When you chose kibbutz as a way of life, did you not think it was going to have a wider influence and not just remain a small community?
Aryeh – The job we did for Israel is enough. You can't deny the fact that thanks to the kibbutzim that spread all over, the boundaries of the country were determined. For instance, we were in Rishon le'Zion when I came. While we were there, we wanted to settle in the Galilee but the leaders of *Hashomer Hatzair* came to us and said we must settle in the Negev. A group of about ten of us went to Gevulot, which was beyond the area of Jewish settlements, for a year. Because of that other settlements sprang up around us.

Did you think the kibbutz would become more central in Israeli society?
Aryeh – We never thought the whole country could live a kibbutz way of life. It is for particular people, who want to live communally. But we did want to be the leading factor in different aspects of life, for instance in education and in settlement, absorbing people. We used to have *chevrot noar*. This was something we did for other people.

Have you been opposed to changes on the kibbutz?
Aryeh - You have not found the right character to ask that question. I adjust myself to the way of life but always look for the best, the most interesting way of life. If the majority changes, you go with the majority. I have never got into conflict with the society. It is not good always being angry and complaining and always criticizing. It won't help.

How important was it for you that your children become kibbutznikim?
Aryeh – This was important but what can you do? I have four children.

One is here, one is on kibbutz Yad Mordehai, one is in Rishon le'Zion, and my son married a volunteer and went to Holland. You love your children whatever happens.

How do you feel about the direction the country has taken?
Aryeh – It is disappointing that it has not worked according to the way I wanted it to.

In what way?
Aryeh – The country is capitalistic. There are so many hungry people in this country and so many rich people. This is something you tolerate but you can't accept it. However, if you run to another country you won't find anything better.

How do you view Israel's relations with the Palestinians?
Aryeh – Our stand is that we must talk with them. We must see what we can do to create two states. Actually everybody has accepted the basic principles of *Hashomer Hatzair*. In fact, Olmert now speaks like a member of *Hashomer Hatzair* in the past.

Since 1967 Israel has been on a path that Hashomer Hatzair does not approve of. Has this caused you problems?
Aryeh – Are they crazy – the whole of Israel belongs to us? I was not actively involved in opposing - just demonstrations here and there. I was the secretary of *Mapam* for one year.

Do you think the kibbutzim should have taken a firmer stand on this issue?
Aryeh – The kibbut*zim* are not a factor politically. It is the party they belong to, that counts.

If there were an election today, who would you vote for?
Aryeh - *Meretz*. There is nothing better than that. I am sorry it is so small.

Many South Africans came to kibbutz and left. Did you find that disappointing?
Aryeh – Of the South African kibbut*zim*, we had Nachshon, Barkai,

Shoval and a few on Hazor. It is a great achievement that we have been part of four kibbutz*im*. I don't mind if afterwards they went to settle somewhere else. So what? They didn't leave the country.

Overall, do your feel happy about your life choices?
Aryeh – Very much so.

Merle Guttmann

Tel Aviv
15/10/08

Born in Zimbabwe, Merle Guttmann is a well-known figure in Israeli-Anglo circles and in Israel's social and volunteer fields. A social planner, writer, editor and respected community leader, Merle has held tens of public and professional positions.

Merle is the founder and honorary life president of ESRA- English Speaking Residents Association, and has been editor of the ESRA Magazine since its inception in 1979. She holds an MA in Social Planning from Bar Ilan University.

She is also currently an Executive member of ETZA – the Israel Self Help Center, of which she was a founder and chairperson for the past seven years. Merle is the recipient of many awards for her community work including the Israel President's Award for Voluntarism (1992) and the Prime Minister's Award for Outstanding Volunteer Leadership (1999).

Did you have a conventional southern African education?
Merle – I grew up in Bulawayo and I did all my schooling at a convent. The nuns were amazing and very liberal towards the small Jewish population at the school.

Was your household a traditionally Jewish one?
Merle – We were not religious, but like many Jews in the Diaspora, we were observant. We used to go to *shul* on all the high holidays and there was a period I used to go with my father on a Saturday. We used to have these big family parties on *Rosh Hashana* and *Pesach*. We were very consciously Jewish and all my life I have felt that way.

It was a very Zionist home. I think it came from my mother, who became very conscious of anti-Semitism after a tour to Germany in the thirties. She became the driving force in WIZO Southern Rhodesia and later was internationally known.

She did not only work for Zionist causes. She helped set up a school for Africans and was on the International Women's Council. Her passion was Israel and women's causes.

It all sounds a bit like you...
Merle - I suppose I inherited her activism. I was in *Habonim* but never became a *madricha*. I never realized I had organizational capabilities until I started ESRA (English-Speaking Residents Association) in Israel.

Were you faced at all with deliberations about remaining in South Africa?
Merle – No, there was nothing like that. On the way back from a year at finishing school in Switzerland, I visited Israel. I was nearly seventeen and I just fell in love with the country. This was the early fifties, Israel was very young and I decided this was where I wanted to be.

Back in Cape Town, like a good Jewish girl, I did a BA in French and Anthropology. After getting married in Bulawayo we moved to Cape Town. We were very conscious of the hopelessness of the political situation but were probably scared of getting involved. We made up our minds to leave South Africa.

The only place I wanted to come to was Israel. My husband Gert would have preferred England or America but eventually became a lover of this country, an emotional Zionist. Our children grew up here and now our grandchildren are growing up here as well.

Would it be correct to say that ESRA's approach is to help people adapt to a given reality rather than to seek change?
Merle – Not at all. I'll tell you how ESRA started. In 1977, after I had been in Israel for about fourteen years I learnt that a lot of southern African Jews were emigrating. I believed in Israel and I wanted some of

them to come here and to stay here.

I wanted to do something and I had some vague idea to help English speakers. I was sure there was some way to make the English speakers feel better.

What was decided was that we would hold an evening in Herzlia of English speakers that I would chair. We were amazed at the turnout, about two hundred and fifty people.

And the answer to your question, in an indirect way, lies in the way the evening was divided up, based on a questionnaire I prepared. People were asked: a. What do you want? and b. What are you prepared to give? I took down the names and telephone numbers of everybody who spoke. The original few volunteers and I became the first committee of this English speaking group that was not yet ESRA.

What was it they wanted?
Merle – Various things. There were those who wanted social and cultural activities and there were those who said they were prepared to volunteer, to give. There were a whole lot of items that they wanted to talk about: getting phone lines, road safety, consumerism. We started forming sub-committees around the areas of interest.

I also called a woman who brought up the idea of a newsletter at the general meeting. I said, "What do you mean, how do you do it?" She said, "I'll show you and we'll do it together." I had never done anything like it. We did the first newsletter and while we were doing the second one she announced that she had no time. So the newsletter has been my baby to this day, thirty years later. I still love doing the magazine.

The whole of ESRA is built on bringing out confidence and enabling people to do what they want to do. ESRA is a very eclectic organization with two main thrusts, namely volunteering in the community and all sorts of activities which English speakers organize for themselves. This is totally a voluntary setup.

I think ESRA's greatness is in giving English speakers a place to volunteer, a channel to find themselves.

Do you think southern Africans are unique in respect of volunteering?
Merle – I include all English speakers. They definitely come from a culture of volunteering. In my first speech I said that volunteering is the common thread that runs through this group of people, whether in the Jewish community or otherwise. Almost every Jewish family volunteered in some way, for the *shul,* or for the poor.

How did you deal with the seeming contradiction between offering opportunities specifically to English-speaking *olim* in Israel and the need for them to integrate?
Merle – It was often thrown at us, "Is this a ghetto association?" What was important in keeping English-speakers in Israel was to have them feel good. I know that sounds simplistic but if you feel good then you stay. You start gaining confidence, start working and doing things and helping your community. You become an Israeli. I always saw it as a stepping stone for some and for others their life thread.

Ten years later when the mass immigration started we went into helping Russians and Ethiopians and others.

How did that pan out?
Merle – It was amazing really. We felt that we had something to contribute, and that we must contribute. This was a national effort to absorb a million Russians in a short time in this little country.

We got known very quickly. One thing happened after the other. Then the Ethiopians came and we developed all sorts of things for them.

Have you been salaried in ESRA?
Merle – No, never. For thirty years I have done it voluntarily.

How have you balanced the parallel lives that you run – work, ESRA, family. Has it been a strain?
Merle – Probably on my children when I was much younger. My youngest daughter had a lot to say about her mother not being home. I am sure my children resented it.

I run another organization, ETZA. That has been very hard, as opposed to ESRA, which was a natural growth. In fact, I am closing it down. I just can't go on. We can't find money.

What was the idea behind ETZA?
Merle – It is actually an organization that has been going for twenty-two years. It was a centre for self-help started in 1986.

It is an amazing service concept, a method of helping people to help themselves in groups. If you have any sort of problem, it can be social or health, there is a group to support you. There are some very esoteric themes, like women who lost their mothers at an early age, lesbians, parents of homosexuals, and so on.

Has Etza been involved with the Arab/Palestinian community in Israel?
Merle – Yes. We wanted to develop more. We have plans and I was trying to raise money for working with Arab groups in the north of the country. It is very much part of my philosophy. We are one nation. We have got to be equal, do things together, live together and flourish together. In our Haifa centre we have Druze groups, e.g. Druze women who are unmarried, Ethiopian women who want to be assertive. We are increasing the social capital of Israeli society and we are closing down…

What is your feeling about Israel today?
Merle – I am still an absolute Zionist. I still believe in this country and still love this country. I feel we have to have peace; it is an essential ingredient of Israel. We have just got to get there, to live with the Arabs. Certainly we shouldn't have a Greater Israel. I have never believed in a Greater Israel. I think we have created all our problems by believing in a Greater Israel. Within Israel we are one nation whether we like it or not.

Have people around you been supportive of your passion, your meshugas, or have they opposed you?
Merle – They say I am crazy. I have tremendous husband-support.

There have been times when I was advised to leave ETZA and my husband said, "How can you run away? You can't leave something you have taken on."

Looking back, would you have done things differently?
Merle – You know, I don't think like that. I just get on with my life and try to do things and move to futures and don't look back. Recently we sold our home of forty years with its beautiful garden and people ask if I miss it. I don't. I live in the present.

Do you not have any yearning for southern Africa?
Merle - I love Bulawayo. It was a wonderful life there but I don't yearn for it. I think Israel is wonderful.

Do you feel fulfilled?
Merle – I am not sure I know what that means. I am proud that I brought ESRA to a stage where it can go on without my everyday involvement.

Alan Hoffmann

Jerusalem
26/06/08 and 15/07/08

Having moved from the Federation of Synagogues, Alan Hoffmann became general secretary of Habonim in 1967 and made aliyah in 1968. He is the first oleh to hold the position of Director-General of the Jewish Agency.

After spending three years of doctoral study in educational policy at the Harvard School of Education, Alan's professional life has been dedicated to promoting Jewish Education. He has held numerous senior education positions in Israel and the Jewish world, including director of Hebrew University's Melton Center for Jewish Education in the Diaspora, executive director of New York's Council for Initiatives in Jewish Education and head of Hebrew University's Mandel Center for Jewish Continuity.

As director-general of the Education Department, Alan developed such groundbreaking initiatives as Masa, Israel Journey and Makom.

Alan lives in Jerusalem with his wife, Nadia. They have four children.

Were there any particular people or ideas that influenced your thinking?
Alan - I was one of the definite products of Louis Rabinowitz, who was Chief Rabbi of South Africa. My father was not religious though my mother was. She was a very powerful ideological force in our home. Rabbi Rabinowitz was not only charismatic and an example of modern orthodoxy, but extremely Zionist. He was the most powerful single figure in the history of South African Judaism. He was known primarily for his *drashot* on Friday night and he was extremely outspoken on the issue of South Africa. So by the time I went to university, I had already developed an attitude towards what was going on in South Africa, and then I studied political science, philosophy and African government.

Together with Benny Isaacson, the youth rabbi, Rabbi Rabinowitz created a new youth movement called The Federation of Synagogues. I was one of the very first members. It was just after my *barmitzvah* and one of the big debates in the FOS was about our stand towards Israel. I took a strong pro-Israel stand.

My father died after I had just started university and I went to *shul* with Mike Kuper to say *kaddish*. He persuaded me to come as a *madrich* to *Habonim* camp, where they had a *minyan*. That is how I joined *Habonim*. About a year later I was *mazkir hinuch*.

Now think about the context: South Africa, the steps of Wits, Bobby Kennedy, a basic political critique of South Africa, a Zionist ideology, a little bit of hormones, and fun. For all of us, ideology stems from coming from families that were reasonably strong on values, where a certain part of the Jewish community was extremely critical of the general society. A second factor was *Habonim's* version of Zionism and pre-1967 Israel, although the reality was probably very different from what we thought it was. We had a classical view of what Israel was about, the role of kibbutz, a just society, etc. All this was dynamite, which is why *Habonim* was such a successful organization.

Did orthodox religious thinking influence the direction you took?
Alan - I don't think it had to do with orthodoxy or the religious life in my home at all. If you look at Erikson's stages of development you'll see that adolescence is the time when people are interested in finding meaning. You are looking for a system that is going to put order into your questioning.

What *Habonim* did is absolutely clear to me. It took this inchoate energy and search and channeled it very clearly. I came to *Habonim* at the time when the big questions of ideology were in the air. There was this whole system that gave meaning, answers, a hugely powerful peer group, with a lot of debate and discussion, a way of life, and a future. South Africa was in ferment. What more do you want?

Was remaining in South Africa ever an option for you?
Alan - In 1959 I came with my family to Israel in my *barmitzvah* year.

We spent six weeks in Israel. We had a driver who I thought was a *Palmach* hero. He took us round the whole of Israel and in every place he told us the legendary stories of Nebi Yesha, Ramat Rahel, etc. I remember every single detail of that visit. It was hugely powerful in my life and it was not part of an intellectual/ideological biography, but it is definitely part of the affective material that this is connected to.

A few years later you are in this incredibly vibrant environment, you are a big critic of South Africa, and there are all these people who are going to Israel. The whole thing comes together and becomes part of one great personal, collective journey.

We knew very few people who were committed to the South African struggle and in our day it seemed that struggle had very little hope. It's true, we identified and we were worried about the security people censoring us. Also, we had such a pristine, adolescent view of Israel, which made it easy.

How did socialism fit into your ideological outlook?
Alan - I took it seriously but I don't think it was deep socialism. I don't think we ever tried to get into serious socialist theory. Socialism for us was about how to present the ideological rationalization for kibbutz. When I came with the *garin*, I thought I was going to live on kibbutz. And I think it could have easily gone that way but it didn't. Within a year I was already in what has taken the place of *Habonim* for me – Jewish education.

What was it that took you into Jewish education?
Alan - It would be great for me to claim that it was about consistency. It's more about protracted adolescence. A little bit about it was happenstance. I almost became an academic and then I was asked to teach on the Young Judea year course and within a year they asked me to run the program. Here, the notion of meaning, i.e. plausibility, structure, and identity all came together for me in this business which I have been involved in – institution building and world Jewry. My vocation became my profession.

Another part of my story is the return to *shmirat mitzvoth*, not religion. Although *Habonim* took me away from orthodoxy and a ten year break, I very easily went back to *shmirat shabbat* and *kashrut* after I married.

Are you saying that being Jewish is the core of your life and that your work is driven by being Jewish?
Alan - Definitely. But the question is: which is the chicken and which is the egg? From a psychological point of view it may be the need to feel part of a system that ties all the pieces together. I am now centrally involved in preserving the Jewish future. That is what I am interested in. It comes straight out of this biography.

Are there aspects of your work that clash with your value system?
Alan - I am definitely not a post-Zionist, like many of my friends. But I don't regard myself as a classical Zionist either. Even though we are part of the so-called Zionist establishment, we are working in a field that I would call Jewish peoplehood, which is about the survival of the Jewish people. When I first came to the Agency, we spent a lot of time trying to write a clear mission statement for our department. We deliberately took out of our mission statement reference to *aliyah*, self-realization, and the centrality of Israel. We say that our work focuses on how the connection to Israel is one of the core components of the identity of the next generation. In terms of a world-view, that is something I can live with.

On the level of principle issues, do you clash with the people in your organization and people you meet in the wider world?
Alan - I have been allowed to do more or less what I want. We know how to stand up for our views. We have taken a very clear stand on the issue of Israel's image. For instance, we are not part of the Israeli *hasbara* enterprise of the State of Israel. On the other hand, I definitely think I am part of the Zionist conspiracy. I am sure that Gideon Levy would see me as part of the infrastructure of the oppression of the Palestinian people. The Jewish Agency is fundamentally a vehicle of an

enterprise that believes that if Israel has to choose between Jewish and democratic, Jewish is a more important value. I have no doubt about that.

How do you deal with donors who insist on principles that you disagree with, e.g. not giving up on settlements?
Alan - I am ready to give them all back. Of course I have to watch what I say when talking to people. I am the 'parent' of a whole range of movements, including *Betar* and *Bnei Akiva*. We have *shlichim*, who, during the disengagement from Gaza wrote against it and came to demonstrations against the government of Israel. Do you send them home or not?

The donors are an interesting case. More and more of those who are interested in Israel are right-wing. Some of them are very rich and some of them are using their money to influence Jewish life in general.

How do you deal with people like this? Do you have to sell your soul?
Alan - Why do you have to sell your soul? You have to sell his soul. People are giving away huge sums to ensure the Jewish future. There are strings attached and you have to decide which piece of this you can live with. We laid down certain red lines. We made a decision to keep a firewall between the content and the donor. These issues come up all the time in real life with both right-wingers and left- wingers. If you are going to get into the pigsty, it's better not to have a sensitive nose. The important thing is that you set up mechanisms that make it clear that you can steer by your own compass.

How do you deal with government policy when governments change so often?
Alan - In an era when the Jewish people is less and less able and willing to look after its own future, the question is: what responsibility does the State of Israel have for the future of the Jewish people? This is a national issue and has nothing to do with who the current prime minister is.

I am an educational leader trying to make the governments of Israel understand that there is a responsibility to the broader Jewish people's agenda. It is not about Olmert's view of Israel versus Bibi's view of Israel. I don't see myself as a civil servant or as a politician. I see myself as somebody who is trying to build a world view.

What is identification with Israel based on today, when Jewish values are hardly different from universal human values?
Alan - My basic understanding of this is that all human beings need meaning. In that search for meaning, particularly in Judaism, there have always been two complementary forms of meaning: one is personal meaning (religious) and the other is collective. This goes all the way back to the heart of Judaism, where the fundamental narrative is the collective narrative. In modern times, the State of Israel is the collective glue that preserves the collective component of Jewish identity. It is not for nothing that Israel has become the collective project of the Jewish people, even for those who didn't come to live here. Israel will soon contain an absolute majority of the Jewish people; it already has a majority of those under eighteen.

For people looking for meaning, it is a basic tribal impulse. That is why almost a hundred thousand Birthright kids a year report that the most powerful single experience is going to the *Kotel*. This is for a non-observant group of people. I think it is about collective identity. The *Kotel* is a symbol of collective, historical memory. I think that is what Israel is about. These kids are not really interested in what is happening at the roadblocks (in the West Bank) or in the legitimate aspirations of the Palestinians.

Are you saying that Israel is no longer a focus for *aliyah* and has become a spiritual focus to keep the Jewish people alive?
Alan - I wouldn't say 'spiritual focus'. In many ways there is more interesting Jewish spiritually outside Israel. I am not sure that Israel needs *aliyah* anymore, as Anita Shapiro has said.

Has this not got something to do with the nature of present day Israel?
Alan - No, that is a narrow perspective. We came on *aliyah* at the tail-end of a heroic period of the State. We mouthed this platitude about creating a national home for the Jewish people without thinking seriously about what we meant by the 'Jewish people'. And certainly we didn't know what we meant by the Jewish part of the Jewish people. So, the State of Israel is a success beyond anybody's possible measure, but the dream was empty of a compelling vision of what it meant to be a Jewish State. And we have not done much to give it content. The emperor does not have enough clothes.

I think the South Africans are the earliest post-Zionists in Israel, the earliest cynics, because they had no background.

Maybe it's because of an anti-apartheid sensitivity.
Alan - I don't think so. That would have encouraged them to become social activists and they haven't. They have become cynical activists. I think nobody ever took what it means to create a Jewish state in *Eretz Yisrael* seriously. After all their passion and ideology, just look at how marginal the South Africans are.

How do you explain this?
Alan - My sense is that this is about the fact that the youth movement was a revolt and in South Africa apartheid gave you such an easy backdrop against which to build this intense so-called ideological life. So I am not sure that we ever really grappled with the real issues. Also, we were *chanichim* during the pre-1967 Israel, the founders of the country were still around, the core institutions still existed, the *shlichim* still seemed to be the embodiment of some real thing. We arrived in the country as much of this was crumbling. The occupation and post-1967 triumphalism is part of that story.

I believe that we in *Habonim* never grappled with the issues that are at the heart of the weakness of Israeli society, which is about where the real basis of values is. It is about what we meant by 'Jewish State'.

According to your analysis, Ben Gurion may not have known what a Jewish state was either!
Alan - The founders all knew it intuitively. Every breath and thought were impregnated with Jewish meaning. They came with the goods but they left the baggage outside the door. The reason I am so preoccupied with this is because I think this is one of the keys to unlocking the puzzle of what it means to have a Jewish people.

Is your conclusion that the level of ideological belief in Habonim in your time was questionable?
Alan - If you look at the early Zionist ideologues, they were people who were also involved in communism. They were really committed. I think we were dilettantes about South Africa. In our day we had a theory that you can't allow yourself to get involved because they will shut down the movement.

How do you feel when you see that many of your contemporaries are what you define as post-Zionists?
Alan - I cannot believe I am the last of the ideologists of our generation. I don't think of myself as the Last of the Mohicans. I am passionate about the Jewish people, not about Zionism as such.

Harry Hurwitz

Jerusalem
07/11/07

Harry Hurwitz was the founder and president of the Menachem Begin Heritage Foundation and the initiator and moving-force behind the Begin Heritage Center, as well as its first head.

Harry was born in Latvia in 1924 and at the age of 10 moved to South Africa with his family. He was an active leader of Betar, became the General Secretary and Chairman of the Zionist Revisionist Organization as well as the acting Chairman of the Zionist Federation. He was one of the pillars of the Johannesburg Jewish community and the long-time editor of the Jewish Herald.

When Begin became prime minister in 1977, he invited Harry to become his adviser. Harry and his wife Freda made aliyah in 1978. Harry served as advisor to Begin on External Information and World Jewry and as Minister of Information at Israel's Embassy in Washington, DC. He served as advisor on World Jewry under Prime Minister Shamir. He wrote a biography of Menachem Begin which is currently in its third edition (and has been translated into Chinese, Finnish, and Russian). At the age of 84 he was still working a full day every day.

Harry and Freda had one son, three grandchildren, and two great-grandsons.

This interview was carried out on the 7th of November 2007. Harry died on the 1st of October 2008, following a heart attack.

When did your involvement with Betar begin?
Harry – I was born in Latvia and was an active member there of the *Betar* from the age of about eight. My father had left Latvia to go to South Africa, as many Latvian families did. It was the *goldene medina*, where you picked up gold in the streets. Unfortunately he did not find

the gold, so he became a shopkeeper. He had a grocery store in Doorn-fontein. My mother was alone with two boys and struggling to exist. We stayed in Latvia for another eight years and then we came to South Africa. At the end of 1934, I joined *Betar*.

Do you remember Jabotinsky's visits having an influence on you even though you were young?
Harry – Oh yes. He came in 1937 and again in 1938. It was an unbe-lievable experience. I had seen him in Latvia and we knew he was the great leader of the Jewish people at that time.

I gradually became more active in *Betar* and when I was about eigh-teen I became a member of the leadership.

What was the emphasis for the young members?
Harry – We had scouting and songs and stories about the glorious past of the Jewish people, dating from the times of the Bible and Bar Kokhba and the Macabees, up till the beginning of Zionism and then Jabotinsky.

What was it that fired you up about Betar?
Harry – Frankly speaking, there were other youth movements that were active in my town in Latvia and none of them appealed to me. I had a cousin whose brother came on *aliyah* in 1926 so there was a fam-ily connection with Zionism. It was not an ideological impact on me. I was too young for that.

From about 1939 I used to go along after school, wearing my cadet uniform, to the offices of the *Jewish Herald* to help wrap the paper. I drew some cartoons that were published in the paper. So I became involved and then there was the week when there was a big picture of Jabotinsky on the front page – leader, teacher, friend, died Saturday August 4th. And then I was in.

In the early forties, very few people who were active in *Betar* went on *aliyah*. I became the guy who organized groups for young graduates of *Betar*. In Johannesburg and the Rand we had three to four thousand members of young *Tel Hai*. It was a major factor in Zionist life.

What made Revisionism attractive to you?
Harry – We liked the idea that the Jewish people were fighting for a Jewish State. That's all. In *Betar* ideology, there is a clause that speaks of monism – single-mindedness. We were not interested in -isms, like communism, socialism. We were interested in the path towards creating the Jewish State and that is where the main struggle was.

Do you recall any book or text in particular that influenced your thinking?
Harry – *The Rape of Palestine* by William B. Ziff, one of the powerhouses of New York Jewry, and other books like that.

Did you ever consider getting involved in South African affairs?
Harry – It never entered my mind. Up till the fifties-sixties it was not an issue. People lived in the country. We knew very few people who were communists. We lived a regular life as citizens of South Africa. Governments come, governments go; they change.

Was the nature of South African society not an issue when you were editor of the Herald?
Harry – Occasionally we made a reference to it but my own attitude was monism. We have a single-minded objective, which is the Jewish community, the Jewish people, the creation of the Jewish State. That's it. There are others who want to participate in the local struggle, let them do what they want and we will do what we need to do.

The focus was on Israel. As you know the South African Jewish community was one of the strongest pro-Zionist communities in the world. I would say that the role and prestige of Smuts had a great deal to do with it. Smuts, Steyn and Hofmeyer, who at one time were the heads of the South Africa government, were very pro-Zionist.

Was your organization campaigning for a particular type of Israeli state or were you happy with the one that was emerging?
Harry – We campaigned against, but what did it matter from South Africa. We were anti-partition. Jabotinsky was anti-partition, the *Irgun* was anti-partition. Then came the November 29th. Everybody was

celebrating and we were against dividing the Land of Israel.

In fact what King Abdallah now heads is eastern *Eretz Yisrael*, if you are serious about the whole concept. If not, you say we gave up three-quarters of our country in order to enable the creation of an Arab state. I am totally against the whole concept of the road map and the two-state idea. There is already an Arab state in *Eretz Yisrael*, its Jordan. But if we said that Jordan is the Palestinian state the king would go mad.

Where does Eretz Yisrael end?
Harry – (Goes to the bookshelf to fetch a map) The British made countries on a piece of paper, you know, with a ruler. This is *Eretz Yisrael*, the British Mandate. He already has this (points to Jordan) and now they want to take the inside of it away, have the two states here (area between the sea and the Jordan river), and a third state (Gaza) exists already over there. If anyone can justify that historically for a nation that did not exist ... can anyone show me in a biblical text that there is a thing called Jordan, Trans-Jordan, Eastern Palestine? There never was such a thing. It was an artificial British creation after WWI.

What was your stand at the time, in the sixties, when Israel was engaged in close relations with African countries and disregarding South Africa?
Harry – We did not deal with that sort of stuff. We dealt with South Africa - Israel relations but we said, "This is the government of South Africa, tomorrow there can be another government, this is Israel and that's it." In fact, I had something to do with normalizing relations between Israel and South Africa in the seventies.

Around *Rosh Hashana* in 1972 I wrote an article to say that the time has come to normalize relations between Israel and South Africa and it is impossible that Israel has representatives in South Africa but South Africa has no representation in Israel. I said the two countries should normalize relations and South Africa should send representatives to Israel up to ambassadorial level.

So I did have something to do with the fact that in 1973 South Africa sent a consul-general to Jerusalem. We have differences, Israel would never support South African apartheid, South Africa recognized Israel's special position in the Middle East, etc.

Were you ever involved in discussions as to what line should be taken on the government's concern about the high profile of Jewish dissenters?
Harry - The *Herald* did not take a stand on this issue. We took a stand on Verwoerd. When he cut the aid (money South African Jews could send to Israel), I was furious. He made a speech to the effect that the South African Jews would have to make up their minds where they stood. I wrote an editorial and put it on the front page of the paper. I said more or less that we had made up our minds long ago: we are pro-Israel, we are citizens of South Africa, we fulfill our duties as citizens of South Africa. We are not here on sufferance and will not be told what we may do and what we may not do. We resent the fact that the government has stopped the flow of our money, it's not your money, to the State of Israel which is in need of it.

What was your attitude to aliyah?
Harry - I wanted to go on *aliyah* very early on, in the fifties. This goes back to my relationship with Begin that began in 1946 when he was commander of the *Irgun*. In 1953 he came to South Africa for the first time and I told him we are thinking of *aliyah*. He replied, "Please don't talk about it. We need you here. When the time comes and I am prime minister, I will call on you to be on my team."

On May 18th 1977, the day after the Israeli elections, I got a phone call. "Harry, you remember what I said in Johannesburg? This is the time. Start preparing to come." Exactly a year later we arrived, on a Thursday night. On the following Sunday I was in the prime minister's office as his adviser on external information.

How do you explain the low profile of South Africans in politics in Israel?
Harry - First of all, politics in Israel is a very rough, not a very savory place to be in, and in politics generally, not always the best people

come to the top. South Africans had a problem with the language and did not have the high connections. They didn't want to get involved in the dirty game of politics.

Since Begin's death, where have you found yourself on the Israeli political map?
Harry - I always remained *Likud*. But now I don't talk about it because as president of the Begin Center I am supposed to be apolitical. We have done something here which is unique. It is modeled on the lines of an American presidential library. It has cost us twenty-one million dollars and it is all paid for. I raised about eighty percent of it. We have had, until this morning 337, 673 visitors in three years.

You could not have dreamt of a better fulfillment of your Zionist dream.
Harry - I created it. I dreamt of creating a memorial to Menahem Begin. A day or two after he passed away, I started this project.

Is your feeling about Israel today a good one or do you feel disappointed?
Harry - Not a good one. I am very proud of Israel for its unbelievable achievements in many fields.

When it comes to policy, I am deeply troubled. How long will we have to pay for our existence in Israel? So I am very worried from a political point of view. It is now the problem of my son, my grandchildren and great grandchildren and I think of it with trepidation. What is the future for them?

These are troubling times. But when you think in terms of sixty years, what it was and what it has become, it is unbelievable.

If you were to revisit the critical choices you made in public life, is there anything you would have done differently?
Harry - No. I started out as a poor boy in Doornfontein. I did not go to university for a serious degree because my family could not afford it. I go out at the end of my days as a poor man, but not as poor as I was then because I have worked hard all the years.

Yesterday we had a hundred and fifty Ethiopian kids here. I see hundreds of soldiers, sailors, airmen, police, and border police coming in here almost every day. I am happy when I look around me and see what we have created.

Meir Jaffe

Kibbutz Tzora
05/08/07

Meir Jaffe was born in Cape Town in 1932. He qualified as a diesel mechanic and then went to Johannesburg to work as general secretary of Habonim. He left for kibbutz Yizra'el in 1957.

Meir's professional life covers a wide spectrum, from mechanics to business marketing and management. He was a member of the Telfed Executive and on moving to kibbutz Tzora, became chairman of the Bet Shemesh youth football club.

Meir's abiding passion has always involved volunteering, fund-raising, and working for the large number of causes in which he believes. Special education, civil rights, animal welfare, and development town partnerships are some of the areas in which he has made a significant contribution.

Retirement has not changed much in Meir's life. During the last few years he has been committed to helping the residents of Bet Shemesh to deal with problems ranging from the needs of single parents to court injunctions.

Meir and his wife June have 4 sons and 7 grandchildren.

Do you have any early memories that might have shaped the way you see the world?
Meir - I remember my kindergarten teacher telling all the kids that Meir would be going home because his parents can't afford to pay for kindergarten. I got the shock of my life and ran home crying. That was a real trauma for me and probably part of the reason I became a socialist. There was this terrible feeling of haves and have-nots because I continued to play with the same kids from that kindergarten but only

after they came home.

My father was unemployed from 1936-42. I remember not understanding why he was taking me for walks around Cape Town once or twice a week.

Eventually I went to SACS where there were about sixty percent Jewish kids. I wasn't involved in any Jewish activities at that time. I was part a gang of Afrikaner and Jewish kids from our street that fought the English kids. This was a serious business. We used to fire arrows with the ends of razor blades fixed in them, as well as throwing massive stones at one another. It was a miracle nobody was killed. Later on when I was eleven or so, we moved and then again with Afrikaners we fought Italian kids. This was not a typical Jewish childhood.

At the age of eight, I was actually singing the *Internationale* with the red flag. My older brother was the leader of the Trotskyite party in Cape Town. I would go to conferences in the Cape Town city hall and listen to him speaking. He saw me as a future leader of the party and in 1942 he dedicated his first book to Meir Boy. It was a great disappointment for him when I moved towards Zionism and Israel. He eventually had to flee from South Africa.

In 1947 at the age of fifteen a friend took me to a *Habonim* meeting at the Jewish orphanage. At the end of the meeting, I went up to the *madrich* and told him that I wanted to buy the full uniform and to make a brick. He was amazed.

What was Habonim like at that time?
Meir - I was getting tired of being a street urchin. I became more and more interested and involved until I reached a stage when five nights a week were devoted to *Habonim*. Around 1948 the whole Jewish and Zionist world was very excited of course. We had a tremendous amount of activity - meetings, *tiyulim* weekend camping, *machanot* etc. I eventually moved to Johannesburg where I was *mazkir klali* for three years.

What picture of Israel do you recall getting from the early shlichim?
Meir - The picture given by Arye Ziv was not just a romantic one. He told us exactly how tough it was and you could see it on his face and his

hands. He was not a great ideologist but very practical. Reuven Rogal-sky was from a classical German youth movement tradition and could argue with anybody about anything.

Were there discussions about the indigenous Arab population and their rights?
Meir – No. In our day it was all about the British Mandate and establishing a state. If we had to fight the Arabs then we'd have to fight but two state solutions, etc. were not what things were about at all.

There was an ideological emphasis was on democratic socialism. The *shlichim* were all kibbutznikim and when I look back I think that for them kibbutz was Israel and Israel was kibbutz. Perhaps this is why so many *chevre* went straight back to South Africa if they left kibbutz.

What did you expect to find on kibbutz?
Meir - I did not believe in Israel being a kibbutz. I knew kibbutzim were very influential but they were only a tiny part of the country. By some miracle our *hachshara* was on a kibbutz where all the principles about kibbutz life that I believed in, existed – Ginegar. There was no hired labor whatsoever. I wasn't disillusioned at all. It was ideologically exactly what I wanted.

You then went to Yizra'el. That was a very different story to Ginegar wasn't it?
Meir - For ideological reasons we decided to settle on Yizra'el, which was in a terrible state, with only fifty members. They too, however, did not take hired workers. We thought that on Yizra'el we could have an influence. Remember that I was part of the group of people who did not go to university because we thought kibbutzim needed people with a trade. I gave up engineering and became an apprentice in diesel mechanics. I ended up as garage manager on Yizra'el.

While I was on Yizra'el, I was recruited to work for World *Habonim* as a contact person for the Anglo-Saxon movements. An interesting issue I dealt with was a group of about twenty South African *Habonim* chevre (Gerald Brooke, Martin Kessel and others), who wanted to go to a development town rather than a kibbutz and to work in their professions. I didn't know what to do with this as it had never happened before. In the end the idea did not go anywhere but they stayed for the most part in Israel and did all sorts of positive things.

In retrospect how do you see your decision to give up engineering in favor of diesel mechanics?
Meir - I think it was madness actually. It was a crazy ideological decision. I mean Israel needed everything. To think they needed more mechanics than engineers. The *shlichim* may not have actively encouraged this, but they did not discourage it. It was all part of a philosophical fight in the movement about whether *Habonim* should be kibbutz-oriented or part of a more general Zionist movement. I was very involved in all of that.

What was it about kibbutz that attracted you so strongly?
Meir - It was part of who I saw as my people, my nation. I thought that being a member of a kibbutz I would help create a more normal and equal society. Even if the numbers were small I saw the kibbutz as very influential in the labor movement in Israel. I also believed that you shouldn't just talk.

Self-realization was a big thing for some of us. I think a lot of *chevre* left the movement because of the pressure we put on them to go on *aliyah* when they finished their studies.

How have you maintained your ability to devote so much energy to making a contribution to the community?
Meir - When I first came to Tzora, although Bet Shemesh was across the road, I really had no connection. It was only later through my two sons and youth football that I got involved there. Before I knew where I was I created a youth league with a hundred kids from *moshavim*, Bet Shemesh and Tzora.

About fifteen years later I started studying in the *Bet Midrash* of the urban kibbutz (Tamuz) in Bet Shemesh. One day a young woman got me involved in an NGO for human rights. I do a lot with helping to get legal aid but also all sorts of things that people need from furniture to problems with national insurance and so on. I work a helluva lot with Ethiopians. Some days I come home totally depressed. The problems are so enormous and you don't know what to do. But sometimes there is a light at the end of the tunnel and you do achieve things. Basically I came to the conclusion that in the final years of my life, I should try and see how I can help people.

As far as kibbutz is concerned, privatization has finished me. It is everyone for himself. I have actually left the kibbutz internally. I can't get involved here. If I try, I will just get a combination of an ulcer and a heart attack.

How do you manage to do so much philanthropic work when you get no financial backing from the kibbutz?
Meir - As a pensioner here my budget is not enough and I run around doing all sorts of things to supplement our income such as monitoring school exams, etc. People have told me that I am mad and that there is no reason not to be paid for the stuff I do at the NGO. On the one hand, I do want to volunteer, but in the end economic problems will force me to try to get paid for my work. I do have a dilemma about that.

Did you make a conscious decision to educate your family about social justice?
Meir - We have never tried to indoctrinate them. They seem to have come to conclusions on their own and are not all my children are the same. But even if they are materialistic, they also volunteer and help others. These ideas filtered down to them more from activities like the football in Bet Shemesh than telling them what to do.

Have you been active politically?
Meir - I have been the secretary of the Labor party on Tzora for the last eight years. I thought I would be active in the party but it has never really happened. I've been a little cog in a big wheel but had no real importance.

Given a second chance what might you have done differently?
Meir - I would still have come to Israel, done things in the field I am doing today but not on kibbutz. If I could manage financially and if my family would agree, I would leave the kibbutz tomorrow.

Janina Kahn-Horwitz

Netanya
02/03/08

Janina Kahn-Horwitz was born in Johannesburg, in 1964. After spending her matric year as an American Field Scholar she returned to South Africa and in 1986 served as general secretary of Habonim-Dror. She made aliyah to Kibbutz Tuval and thereafter continued her studies in the field of education, specializing in additional language literacy acquisition and learning difficulties. She completed her Ph.D. at the University of Haifa. Today Janina is a teacher and researcher at Oranim and Gordon Colleges. She is a feminist who is deeply committed to attaining equality for all individuals regardless of faith in conflict-ridden Israel. She lives with her husband Neil and two children in the Galilee.

Let's start with a few historical facts about your life.
Janina – I grew up in Johannesburg and went to King David and I was involved in *Habonim* from about standard eight. I decided at some point to come to Israel, I joined the *garin* and lived in the *Habonim bayit* and studied for my first degree there. In 1986 I came with the *garin* to Kibbutz Tuval.

Can you tell us about the movement at that time you were mazkira klalit?
Janina –The *garin bayit* was like a commune and we shared a *kupah*. We all thought we were going to live on kibbutz but the whole feminist issue was big for me. I was not very happy about the role of women in the kibbutz community as I saw it. One of the reasons we chose to go to Tuval was not to fall into the familiar slot that it seemed a lot of women fell into on more established kibbutzim.

We were very involved in the movement and we were clearly coming to live in Israel, but I'd say we were working in parallel with the left there. It was just before the change and a lot of things were happening then. I was doing my BA and I was sitting in the same class as a lot of left-wing people who were involved in the South African struggle. They saw me as going to fulfill my socialist dreams on kibbutz.

Do you remember why you decided to go in a Zionist direction and not pursue the South African struggle?
Janina – My questions were always: where do my allegiances lie? Where do I belong? What is really my struggle? I felt that as a Jew in South Africa, I had less of a role to play. To this day, I have this issue about being a Jew if you are not religious. I felt that if I decided to stay in South Africa it was an active decision not to be Jewish. I felt I couldn't do both. I personally don't like Diaspora Jewishness - it's unappealing to me. If I wanted to acknowledge my being Jewish I had to live in Israel.

Sometimes I say that we were more comfortable fulfilling the dreams of what was expected of us.

By whom?
Janina – By our parents. In terms of my parents and the structure I was living in, I was this revolutionary – I left home at the age of seventeen and never went back again. My father was a great Zionist, so even though I was not doing it in the way he would have chosen, I was.

I always think of it in terms of Erikson's stages of development. In the stage of dealing with identity versus role confusion, you do the opposite but then as you grow older, you go to this comfort zone of what was expected of you after all.

You seem to put more emphasis on your parents than on your social circle…
Janina – That is my analysis in retrospect. I always describe the way I left South Africa to live on kibbutz as being in the clouds – I was on an ideological high. I just did it. If I think of myself leaving here, what

a tearing event that would be for me. I missed nothing about South Africa. I came here and the *garin* was my family. That was just so naïve.

I came down hard and very quickly. About two years later I was already in Jerusalem studying and doing other things. Only then did I start realizing what I had done.

How would you characterize your life as a young idealist in South Africa?

Janina – Extremely exciting. I felt then that I was going to change the world. I could do anything that I decided I was going to do. That is a fantastic feeling. There was this big socialist pull as well. The people I was studying with were envious of me. I was putting it all together. I was going to live on a kibbutz, my Jewish issue was being solved. I nearly didn't finish my BA because I had so much to do and I thought, "What does it matter anyway? I am going to live on kibbutz for the rest of my life." Thoughts of my family values pushed me to finish.

It was comfortable as well. We shared our money in the *bayit* but we all had our own cars, provided by our parents (laughs). By South African standards it was roughing it - we cleaned the house.

What image did you have of Israel and kibbutz?

Janina – Those are two different things. A lot of people who came with us got up and left the country when kibbutz didn't work out for them. For us that did not happen. I felt good about living in Israel. It's a strong cultural identity. It's kind of funny because today I live in an English-speaking bubble to a certain extent but I still am part of and love the culture.

I expected kibbutz to be an extension of communal living. I expected to be able to develop myself and have my own space. I found myself doing all kinds of boring work and felt I was living on top of people. I didn't want to take on positions of responsibility and I didn't want to be working with plants or soldering wires. It seemed ridiculous. It had nothing to do with what I had originally envisaged.

Maybe that was one of the disadvantages of a small kibbutz that was struggling to get established, compared with what a more established kibbutz might have offered.

On the other hand, there was the whole women's issue. Being on Tuval gave me the opportunity to get pretty involved in organizations like the Haifa Women's Centre, the Haifa Rape Crisis Centre, and in Women in Black. All those things were part of that stage of my life. The women in my *garin* were extremely strong. There were some pretty tough characters.

How do you respond to a young South African Jews who today say, "We do not have the comfort zone that you had; there is a lot to be done in South Africa?"
Janina – I would ask them about their Jewish identity. It looks like a lot of them feel very comfortable being Jewish and anti-Zionist.

They are saying that Israel poses a problematic alternative…
Janina – The issue I grappled with at the time was whether it was my own country. "Is this the place where I feel I ultimately belong?" I keep saying there is a lot to do in Israel but where is our voice? We all squirm with discomfort at what is going on but I try to avoid the whole issue. I try not to read Amira Haas and Gideon Levy because it makes me so uncomfortable. And when I do do something, I feel like a progressive person trying to satisfy her conscience.

How do you explain the fact that people are just squirming and not doing anything?
Janina – There is a limit to how much you can do. It has to do with the stage of life – making a living, bringing up children, getting involved in your career. So within your little framework you try to do what you can. I have a lot of contact with the Arab colleagues and students in the Galil. I had an issue whether to send my children to a Jewish-Arab school in the area. In the end I asked myself whether I was trying to stuff my ideology down their throats. "Who am I doing it for? Is it to satisfy my conscience?" These issues are very complicated. I decided

against sending them for other reasons as well.

The issue of the army is also complicated. I am bothered by the fact that my son, now thirteen, is going to go to the army at some point. Is he going to go into the Occupied Territories and do what these kids are doing now? I don't want him to be involved in things like that. If I had to go to South Africa and speak to kids in the movement about things like that I would not feel comfortable. On the other hand, I would not encourage my kids to leave Israel. What did I come here for in the first place?

I am a pacifist at heart. If my son were to turn around and say to me, "I am not going to serve in the army. I would rather go to jail," he would be expressing the ambivalence I feel about the whole thing. He is not going to say that because he is growing up in Misgav and getting a completely different education. He reads *Yediot* every morning and is completely exposed to the mass culture of Israel. He thinks I am off the wall. Then I say to myself, "That is what you deserve; you came here." Then I think that maybe I should have been demonstrating all these years, to offer a concrete example to my children of what I believed in.

Do you feel a disconnect between what Habonim South Africa stood for and the reality of Israel?
Janina – I think there is a connection. My day-to-day existence here is beautiful. Maybe it has to do with belonging. I think there are amazing things that go on here and amazing people involved in the culture and the society. I have found this niche of different things I am involved in professionally and otherwise.

I work in the field of learning difficulties in English as an additional language. I also teach about theories of language learning to Arabic literacy teachers as well as English teachers. I have very interesting linguistic and cultural interactions with people. Many of my colleagues as well as students are Arabs. Because of the position I am in I have been able to offer people interesting opportunities and work. I don't know Arabic but I plan to study it at some point.

In my own way I feel I am very active even though I don't belong to any organizations as such.

How optimistic do you feel about the future?
Janina – Because I am an optimistic person and quite naïve, I still think it will work out. If I have to think about it seriously, I should probably just get up and go somewhere. But I can't. I hope I never have to regret it. Things don't look great. Many of my friends and family think similarly. In order to survive here you have, to a certain extent, to bury all these issues.

I carry on voting for *Meretz* but it's a disaster. It seems there is no left-wing voice. It does not look as if things are going in a direction we would want to see them going in. I don't know what will be.

Hertzel Katz

Ramat Hasharon
04/08/08

Hertzel hails from Benoni. He joined Betar and eventually became head (natsiv) of South African Betar. While doing his BA LLB at Witwatersrand University, he served as chairman of Students' Zionist Federation. After qualifying, he joined the Johannesburg Bar and was a member of South Africa Zionist Federation executive.

Hertzel made aliyah in 1969, re-qualified as an Israeli advocate and still practices law.

As a major figure behind the establishment and management of institutions for South Africans in Israel, Hertzel's activities have been many and varied. He was twice elected chairman of Telfed. Later he became the first chairman of Board of Governors of Telfed. He established Israel-South African Chamber of Commerce and is still a member of its executive. He helped to establish a branch of the Hebrew Order of David in Israel.

Hertzel's energies were not only directed at South African Zionist matters. He qualified as a Traffic Warden and organized seminars in English for promotion of road safety. He set up an NGO for promotion of lawn bowls in Israel. As chairman of ESRA, he initiated the establishment of the Council of English Speaking Organizations in Israel.

Hertzel is married to Lola. They have three children and five grandchildren.

Can you give us some idea of how you were drawn to Zionism and the Revisionist philosophy?
Hertzel - By chance. I was living in Benoni. My very dear, now departed, friend was Gerald Fredman, who rose to be *Manhig* of *Habonim*. We never really understood afterwards when he became head of *Habonim* and I became head of *Betar*, why it worked out that way. If

Gerald had invited me to *Habonim*, I might have gone.

What were the aspects of Revisionism that attracted you?
Hertzel - In *Betar* there was the ideology written by Jabotinsky in 1923 and there were so many points about it that I really said, "That's for me." A lot of it is encapsulated in the *Betar* anthem that Jabotinsky wrote. There was the idea of social justice - every person is born a prince, silence is golden, but speak up if you have something to say, the concept of *hadar* – being princely in all that you do, respecting other people, manners, humanitarianism, and monism. The other aspect of *Betar* was that Israel needed a strong government. Jabotinsky was called a fascist at times. I am not a fascist. He was called a militarist and I am not that either.

To what extent did the adult leadership of Betar dictate what the youth movement should be doing?
Hertzel - Never. The movement was independent, no one dictated to us. And there was never an issue about it.

You paint a picture of there not being much difference between Betar and Habonim. Is that how you experienced it?
Hertzel - At that time, *Habonim* was socialist and we were regarded as fascist. Their emphasis was on *aliyah* to kibbutz. We had very few settlements of our own. When people did go, we did not direct them to any particular place.

Do you remember any dialogue or debate about ideology with friends like Gerald in Habonim?
Hertzel - I don't think there was ever any serious debate. I know we weren't liked by *Habonim* but there were never really any major clashes. Gerald and I remained good friends and we very seldom argued about 'both sides of the Jordan' or Jabotinsky.

Is your impression that the movement leaders of the day were well informed or not?
Hertzel - Sometimes we used to say that at our seminars we talked

about A.D. Gordon and Berl Katznelson and Jabotinsky. And I used to ask whether at *Habonim* seminars they talked about Jabotinsky and Trumpeldor. I don't think they did. We gave a broader view. The *Habonim* leaders were very critical of the adult leadership for remaining in South Africa but many of them did not get to Israel, whereas eighty-eight percent of the leadership of *Betar* made *aliyah*. We recently made the calculation at a reunion we had.

How did Betar handle the South African dilemma?
Hertzel - We didn't get involved in it. Individuals could do what they wanted to, but as a movement, we didn't associate with any other organization, not with the Liberals or whatever. In fact, Mendel Levine, a prominent Revisionist, became very active in the Nationalist Party and that created controversy and ruffled a few feathers.

Jabotinsky spoke about monism – fix yourself a goal and devote yourself to that goal.

Was your own path as straight forward as that?
Hertzel - At university, I became chairman of the Students' Zionist Federation which we set up.

Later I became a member of the Johannesburg Bar and was asked to stand for the Progressive Party. At the time, the party did not stand for 'one man one vote' but for 'make merit the measure,' which was totally acceptable to me philosophically – a qualified right to vote. Colleagues of mine at the Bar and elsewhere said I was mad to do this. For one thing I would be nailing my colors to the mast where people were being appointed to the bench because of national attitudes. Others said to me, "You, a *Betari*, going to join a so-called left-wing party!" I said, "There is no conflict. This is for social justice and that is what I believe in." So my belief in Zionism led me to support the leading opposition movement in South Africa. I actually stood for the party and I was beaten, but did better than expected.

Was your legal work political in any way?
Hertzel - I had a benevolent attitude towards the black people I was

in touch with. I became friendly with one of the leaders of the PAC, Shadrack - a very impressive, articulate young man.

We were talking one day and he said, "Hertzel, when we are march-ing … down the streets, if you are in front of me, my friend, I am going to kill you. There are no emotions involved here. You are white."

He was arrested and at his first trial I appeared for him *pro ami-co* without realizing how it would be seen by others. Everybody said, "What? This white Jewish guy, appearing for a terrorist, as a friend!" He came to me afterwards to say how much he appreciated it. For me there was no hesitation. He had been arrested and every man is entitled to a fair trial. Thereafter I appeared for many Africans. There was no other political work that I did apart from standing publicly for a particular cause and being available for various trials.

Apart from being in the Progressive Party I was really devoted to the cause of Zionism. That is where I was putting my energies, sitting on various committees, etc. That took all my time - professional work, family, and Zionism.

Was there much debate about ideology within the Zionist Council or did local, practical matters absorb the members?
Hertzel - Ideological debates normally took place at election time, usu-ally in the packed Coronation Hall. The debates were political but that was not the major issue. It was always the philosophy of the Zionist Federation, that Israel is Israel irrespective of who governs the country. Never mind what you may think on a personal level, that is Israel, that is our flag, we support the government of the time. The conflict that existed at ground level dissipated when you were talking about support for Israel, which was an amazing thing to happen.

Behind the scenes the party rivalry stirred the whole system. The movement went downhill when the party system almost collapsed.

Was it always clear that you would come on aliyah?
Hertzel - The question was, what was to come first- my commitment to tackling injustice in South Africa or my commitment to Zionism? I decided on the latter. I was still active in *Betar* and then went on to

represent the Revisionist Party on the executive of the Zionist Federation. I was a delegate to the first World Zionist Congress after the Six Day War. Golda Meir was talking about the effect and the ramifications of the war, and issued a call to the Zionist leadership to come to Israel.

I said to my wife that we have an option: either I have to leave the Zionist organization because I am not going to preach Zionism and *aliyah* and stay in South Africa, or we are going to go on *aliyah*. Six months later, in 1969, we packed up and came with our two kids.

What has happened to your own ideological outlook since you came here?
Hertzel - In a way, substantial changes. Firstly, I abandoned the concept of 'both sides of the Jordan'. I never saw that as a realistic goal anymore. I was terribly disillusioned by the existing *Herut* party in this country. Because of my naïveté. Any idealist, let's talk about an Israeli idealist, is going to be disappointed when he makes *aliyah*. You have ideals about what you are coming to and what you hope to see here and I didn't see it. Certainly in the *Herut* Party, which I thought would be the disciples of Jabotinsky, pursuing his basic goals that were close to my heart. I didn't find it. In particular, *hadar*. I am the kind of guy who likes order and procedure and manners, and from that point of view I am not comfortable in this country.

I hate *Popolitika* (popular TV current affairs program). I still get offended when I listen to the radio and hear five people talking at the same time. So, I didn't find *hadar* and I was upset about it.

I never joined the party here. I was never a member of *Herut*. Uzi Narkiss had come out to South Africa just before I left and told us that he could not offer us better homes or better cars in Israel but he could offer quality of life. I came here and I didn't find the quality of life I expected. I persuaded the British Federation and Telfed to launch a campaign called *Koach Kan* to improve the quality of life. We had a conference with nine hundred people present. We had workshops on manners and ethics, road safety, and other things. We tried to say we have something to contribute.

I was disgusted at the way people were advised to get around the Jewish Agency's limit on mortgages and was later shocked when I came out of a government cabinet meeting and was told by a newsman what had just happened in the meeting. I had thought that the proceedings in the cabinet were confidential. Everybody gets culture shock when he comes here.

Do you feel you have had success in any of these areas?
Hertzel - Good question. I was very involved in road safety in South Africa. When I came over here, I wanted to do something about road safety and I became vice-president of MEMSI (AA equivalent). I said to them that we should get involved in road safety, not just in repairing cars on the roadside.

How do you understand the low political profile of South Africans in Israel?
Hertzel - The only MP we had was Shmuel Katz. I don't think South Africans are built for political life in this country. I was a political person in South Africa and people thought I would go into politics but I knew I would not have a chance. Firstly, you don't have the language which you require; secondly, it is a different ball game; thirdly, as I learnt from Begin's right-hand-man, people are not appointed on merit but because they have been loyal members of the movement. So you had to go through that stage and then be rewarded.

Often people have said, "Let's do something." But I have found it very hard to galvanize the South African movement. I suggested going out with placards at various times but I knew I would never get more than ten people to go out and march. I think it is a South African characteristic. People are diffident, scared and apathetic, unaware of the reality of their life. I think it is true for the Anglo-Saxons generally. The Russians have got a big constituency. However, South Africans have made a contribution to this country, a massive contribution. I was instrumental in bringing out the book, *Seventy Years of Achievement* with Philip Gilon. Then there is *Machal* and we had the Academic Achievement Awards.

What would you protest about today if you were going to go out on the streets with placards?
Hertzel - I would certainly protest violence and what is happening in schools. I am upset about what is being taught in schools, the standard is pitiful. I don't think that children in this country are taught any values, e.g. respect for elders, respect for property. Only now that I walk with a stick do people stop for me. Kids now make way for me. There is a feeling of humanity for a disabled person, without knowing why.

What else would I protest for? There was an NGO that was started called the Pleasantness/Decency (Nechmadut) NGO (shows us special little cards with "Nice of You" or "You Made My Day" written on them). They came to see me and I told them my idea of giving out a card for not smoking, etc. This card is what they brought out. I gave a card to a guy who came to fix my computer and his boss phoned me to say he also wanted one. I said, "You gotta earn it."

What are the more overt political issues that concern you?
Hertzel - I am very upset about what happens in the area of so-called justice. I have problems with the courts interfering in things that are not their responsibility. Trial by the press is not acceptable. The harm done is irreversible.

I have never been involved in Arab-Israeli relations. I believe in rights of individuals, human rights. I have been quoted as saying that if I could have peace I would make Jerusalem an open city. Then I define what I mean by peace and until then I wouldn't do it. The peace between Israel and the Arabs needs to be like the kind of peace that exists between Holland and Belgium or America and Canada, where people can go freely across the borders without fear. That is peace and I hope and I pray for peace but not the false peace that has been offered to us at Oslo and elsewhere.

In other words there are not many concessions you would not be prepared to make for a real peace.
Hertzel - Absolutely. That is what should be done. I think that 'both sides of the Jordan' has fallen by the wayside and Begin played a major role in doing that. He didn't wait for the people to lead him. He was a leader and he led the people on the path he thought Israel should be following. Peace with Sadat.

How optimistic do you feel about us reaching something like you thought you were coming to in 1969?
Hertzel - I like to be an optimist. I pray for miracles. On Shabbat, *lehaim* is the standard but I say, "Let's drink to miracles."

What would the nature of that miracle be?
Hertzel - It's the height of naïveté. I don't go to *shul* but I pray every night. When I pray, I pray for mankind. When God is listening to me, I say, "Please let there be no more tragedies." That is what I do pray for.

When you look back on the choices you have made, to what extent do you feel fulfilled and satisfied?
Hertzel - I have never really examined that. My children are all here and I think they are making some decent contribution to the country. I created a lot of things in Telfed which are helping South Africans. I do what I can in voluntary organizations to promote the idea of being of help to our society. I have helped set up trust funds for people in need. I had a very minor role in setting up Bet Protea (senior citizen facility for ex- South Africans) but I get some satisfaction from that.

In a sense, I have done some of the things I wanted to do. I have not succeeded in road safety beyond very minor successes. I have been promoting sport. I helped set up the Ramat Hasharon Bowling Club and sat on the National Bowls Association executive. I am still fairly active. I write letters of praise and complaint. I like to think out of the box. In politics I have been a total failure. On issues closer to the community I have some satisfaction. I have kept a kind of monism. Most of my contribution has been within our community.

Jerrold Kessel

Jerusalem
24/06/08

Born in 1945, Jerrold Kessel left South Africa for Israel after graduating from high school. Despite being appointed captain of the Israeli national cricket team, he never stopped hoping for a call-up from Lord's or Sky Sports.

Jerrold started working as a journalist at Israel Radio and subsequently worked for various foreign publications and the Jerusalem Post before joining CNN. The only CNN reporter with traces of Charles Fortune in his delivery style, he has worked a love and an encyclopedic knowledge of sport into his career as a political journalist. Jerrold is also a regular contributor to Ha'aretz, with his On the Couch sports column.

Named an "honorary citizen" of Sakhnin for his involvement with the town and its football team, Jerrold has recently published a book on Arab Israelis, Goals for Galilee, with fellow reporter/producer Pierre Klochendler.

Jerrold and Lorraine Levin Kessel have one son and four grandchildren.

What made you come to Israel straight after finishing school?
Jerrold – Obvious. The army. I didn't want to go into the South African army. But, obviously also reverberating in the back of my mind there was that telling challenge that Wolfie Mankowitz used to throw out to us in *Habonim* – "Surely you want to be part of history, part of changing the whole history of the Jewish people, all you have to do to be part of that process is to go and live in Israel."

What or who would you consider were the main influences on your world outlook?
Jerrold – John Arlott. He shaped a love of cricket and a love of sport, empathy for cricketers, for players, and the importance of cricket,

through his approach.

Another person who shaped my outlook was Joey (Johanna Ra-marumoo), my nanny. I loved her very much. I am trying to write this radio play called Joey and Mandela, around her influence. She taught me *N'kosi Sikalele* and she taught me what it was to be a black person, to try to be a human being no matter what the circumstances.

My small claim to fame is that even though I was sports mad, I never supported South Africa on the sports-field. I remember making nine shillings and three pence on Jimmy Carruthers, the Australian boxer who beat the South African and world champion Vic Towell. I bet all the time against South Africa. Unfortunately, I lost fairly often, in rugby particularly.

At the time of the 1994 South African elections, the first post-apart-heid elections, I was pretty cut off from South Africa, but on the day of the election, when I had no intention of getting involved, I heard over the car radio a report from the BBC in Soweto telling how women had been standing in line and singing all night, waiting to vote. It was very moving. I called Pog (my wife, Lorraine) and told her that you could vote at the Tel Aviv fairgrounds. Anybody who could show he/she was South African could vote. We waited five hours in line to vote. It was a most wonderful experience. I said I have to vote for Joey – she had died by then. She would have voted for the ANC.

Then there was *Habonim*, of course. At school, an English teacher introduced me to the beauty of English and the literary giants. My exposure to the world at the Hebrew University, the opening up of the world through exposure to great humanist scholars like Isaiah Berlin was wonderful. I was definitely influenced more by literature than by political writing.

Who else? Philip Gillon, the journalist (incidentally one of the founders of South African *Habonim* in the early 1930's) who I met a couple of years after coming to Israel. He once coined a phrase, "The only valid kind of Zionism that remains is Sunshine Zionism." The fact that this is a country where the sun shines three hundred and fifty days of the year and you can play tennis outdoors. "What better reason for living in a country?" he said. His approach was iconoclastic yet, he believed in the endemic goodness of people. It was a very nice role model to have had.

He did have an agenda in his sports writing...
Jerrold – Of course. In his heart he was a great Zionist, but he believed we had made a muck-up of it. He spoke as a humanitarian seeing the collapse of Israel's humanity. People are innately decent and the problem arose when they strayed. When being attacked for being a 'bleeding heart', he'd say, "Bleeding heart and proud of it."

Is decency a theme that runs through your world view?
Jerrold – It sounds terribly pompous but an aspiration to being decent, yes. Overall, as my friend Steve Aschheim says, we suffer more from sins of omission than from sins of commission. All the things I ought to have done, and didn't.

What comes to mind?
Jerrold – Being politically active, socially active. Subscribing to ideas, to values is not really enough. You look around and you see that most of us are guilty of that.

I left South Africa without doing anything. The only reason I came to Israel, I say somewhat facetiously though it's probably got some truth in it, is that it was the only way I could get my cricket cap for my country. Although I still dream of being called up for England.

And in Israel, were you not tempted to get involved in political activity?
Jerrold – By the time I could have been politically effective, I was already a journalist and that gave me an out. I never hid my views although I never espoused them as a journalist. I was already working as a journalist in 1967. I started at Israel Radio then I worked for various foreign publications, served in the army, the *Jerusalem Post*, then CNN.

During the first week I was at university, in 1962, there was a little demonstration, a few dozen people on the lawn at Givat Ram

(Jerusalem University campus), against the Vietnam War. And there was a counter-demonstration that was so angry and so vicious, the tone of which was not for or against the war in Vietnam, but "Why are you concerning yourself with Vietnam when here we are concerned with a little girl in Beit She'an who said she goes to school hungry?" This was a shock to me because we had grown up on Israel's appeal being based on a universalist conception.

At the time of the 1969 elections, we lived in Motza and ours were two out of a total of four votes in our area (of two thousand in the whole country) for a small party called NES. That tells the whole story. NES had this fantastic list – great minds such as Talmon, Arieli, Yatziv, Peled. A peace party through and through. That, you could say, was my politics.

This was just two years after the war. I couldn't quite believe the immediacy of the transformation in the country. I could understand the relief, but was amazed by the euphoria built on the glorification of victory.

Before you came for this chat, I was thinking about the switch that the country made: whether it was intrinsic to Zionism, or whether it came about because of the Arab refusal to recognize Israel. Was Zionism something inimical to itself as a humanist ideology and it didn't matter what the Arabs did? I don't know.

When I was a young journalist, Meir Kahane was a nonentity. Years ago, before he was elected to the Knesset, we heard one of the brothers who ran our neighborhood vegetable store say, "Kahane's is the only way." We decided we were not going to buy there anymore. Sin of complicity. If we stood by that today we would have to go a long way to get our vegetables. The change from Kahane being a nonentity to being mainstream says it all.

Did the demands of your profession clash with your views or not?
Jerrold –The opposite, it helped me enormously to feel morally self-righteous because we were being 'moral' just by reporting what was happening. Somebody once asked me if I was ever under pressure at

CNN to take a stand of one sort or another. Before I later came to realize the wisdom of a certain truism, I suppose I was. It's the reaction to pressure that's important. According to the truism, if you ever even countenance the notion that someone is trying to influence you or to pressure you, you are finished.

I remember a very proud moment when I was working at the *Jerusalem Post*. The *Ha'aretz* columnist Yoel Marcus wrote something about a banner headline I had used when I was the news editor of the *Post*. It was about a four-month old Palestinian baby who had been shot, not killed, by an Israeli soldier - obviously a stray bullet. Israeli soldiers don't go around shooting kids. A few days later Marcus wrote an article noting that the item about the baby was hardly mentioned in any of the other papers. He said, "If we have reached the stage where we take no notice of such events, when we are oblivious to the fact that this is what happens in the battle against the (first) *intifada*, we are finished. We are going to lose."

At that time, the *Post* was followed religiously by foreign correspondents. There was enormous pressure on us to present Israel in a favorable light, but then we withstood the pressure. We just reported the facts, thanks largely to Joel Greenberg who covered events in the West Bank and Gaza. As you know, I left when Conrad Black's group took over the *Post*. Today the paper reflects the Anglo-Israeli community.

Did working for CNN give you a different perspective from the one you had as an Israeli reporter?
Jerrold – It suited me to get beyond a narrow Israeli perspective and to try to understand situations from different points of view. I thought I was better at reporting situations, analyzing them, than getting an opinion across. It was important too. The cause was to let the world know what was happening. Of course, being in CNN at the time of peace-making and then during the *intifada* was amazing – I had a real platform, a world forum.

Are you saying you did not say to yourself, "I can be an influence and I want to be?"

Jerrold – At that stage in my career, I couldn't. At the height of the *intifada*, when CNN was being accused by both sides of fomenting the troubles I was at the center of reporting. I was told that viewers could not tell what my views were or whether I was Israeli or Jewish. I took that as a compliment. Lots of Jews hated me. Arabs too.

How do you see the role of the Israeli media since 1967?

Jerrold – When the great gods of history come to write what went wrong in the formative years post-1967, the popular press and the electronic media will have a lot to answer for. They shaped public attitudes, just like the song *Jerusalem of Gold* did.

A story of politics, the media and sins of omission: While I was at *Kol Yisrael*, we got a directive about six months after the 1967 war not to use the term 'West Bank' any more and to use 'Judea and Samaria' – not occupied territories or administered territories. I was wild, though others took it lying down. My boss felt we should accept the term 'administered territories'. That is the way it went.

Some of the western press and many people in the west are critical of what is going on in Israel. But in Israel the mood is one of self-justification...

Jerrold – Self-justification, yes, but still very depressed. There's the story of a famous clown called Grock who lived in Europe between the wars. One day a man goes to his doctor. He says, "I am finished. I can't get out of this terrible depression." The doctor refers him to the world's most famous psychiatrist. He goes to him and repeats his story, "I can't get out of this depression. Whatever I do there seems to be no hope." The psychiatrist says, "I am very sorry. I don't see how I can help you. Only one thing I can recommend – go and see Grock. Perhaps he can help you." The answer comes back, "I am Grock."

I say, Israel today, for all the bravado, which is basically self-justification, is Grock. It feels very insecure with itself and down in a profound way, relieved by momentary joy. It's down because we don't know who we are.

Maybe it was a pipe dream to believe that once you had the Jews coming into this country and displacing people who were here you could ever just being focused on being Jews. It is certainly impossible when we have the burden of the Palestinians on our backs.

With the benefit of hindsight, can you point to anything you would do differently?
Jerrold – James Cameron (a great British journalist) had this fine thought. He said that one of the perils of growing old is that you have a tendency to focus narrower and narrower, on yourself and everything around yourself. Your whole mind-set becomes narrower. Now, narrow mind-sets lead to narrow views. He said you have to work at it every day.

As they grow older, very few people become more expansive in their outlook on life or more fair-minded in their judgments. So, for me the question is: am I still being open-minded enough?

Do you have any regrets?
Jerrold - Was I absolutely right in my absolute insistence on the unemotional, uninvolved reporter? I do regret one specific incident which had to do with reporting for CNN during the intifada. They wanted to see innocent victims crying. I said, "There are no innocent victims here, other than a donkey in Gaza. Nobody is innocent." Anyway, one morning there was a bomb on a bus full of school kids, in Kiryat Menahem.

With the bus burning in the background my assistant brought this little lady for an interview. She saw what happened because she lived in the building opposite. We were reporting live. It turned out to be probably the best interview I ever did in my life, due more to her than to me. She was amazing - she was so human. She didn't go on about 'Arab bastards'. She pleaded for all this to stop – "For the sake of everybody, us, and the Arabs. It's simply too painful for us all," she said. Then she rested her head on my arm and started weeping.

What do you do? Any normal human being puts his arm around her, says something comforting. Not me, the great proponent of not getting involved. I did nothing. Nothing. I felt so rotten. She was appealing to me to give her comfort and it would not have compromised me in the slightest. I should have.

Where does all we have talked about leave us in terms of the challenge we talked about at the outset - 'changing the course of Jewish history'?

Jerrold - Rabbi Arthur Hertzberg, the forward thinking American Rabbi, once told me in an interview back in the early 1970's: "History will come to judge us – liberal-minded, regular American Jews – for letting Israel down, for letting the Jewish people down; we are going to be held culpable for the direction in which Israel is headed - ultra-nationalist, intolerant in religious matters. If only one million more regular American Jews had immigrated in the last two decades and especially now after the Six Day War, Israel would look, and politically would be, a totally different place." He never came himself, but by gum has he not been right? So maybe what Wolfie Mankowitz said about changing the course of Jewish History just by being here is looking awfully like it's going to prove to be an unfulfilled promise.

David Kretzmer

Jerusalem
06/02/08

David Kretzmer (LLB, LLM, (Hebrew University); Dr. Jur (York University, Canada)) made aliyah to Israel in 1963. He is an Emeritus Professor of Law at the Hebrew University and Professor of Law at the Academic Centre for Law and Business in Ramat Gan. David has been a visiting professor at leading institutions abroad, including Columbia University, the University of Southern California, Tufts University and New York University.

From 1995-2002 he was a member of the UN Human Rights Committee. Main fields: constitutional law, human rights, and international humanitarian law. Books include The Legal Status of the Arabs in Israel (1990) and The Occupation of Justice: The Supreme Court of Israel and the Occupied Territories (2002). He was a founding member of the Association for Civil Rights in Israel and served as chair of its board. From 2007-2009 he served as joint chair of the board of B'Tselem, The Israeli Information Centre for Human Rights in the Occupied Territories.

You left South Africa soon after finishing school...
David – I had to serve in the South African army first, but as soon as I got my passport, I left. And I did not go back for forty years.

What was your motivation for leaving at that stage?
David – I did not think I could do much positive to change the situation in South Africa. I was in a great dilemma, having served in the army. Possibly I did not have the courage to refuse but I was always worried that something would happen and I would have to be part of the enforcement measures of the army. In my wildest dreams I did not think that there would be a peaceful end to apartheid in South Africa.

I thought the country was moving towards tremendous violence that would be fundamentally racial and I would be on the wrong side. I did not want to be part of it.

I had grown up in *Habonim* and I had always intended to come to Israel. I had, and still have, a very strong Jewish identity. I wanted to be a lawyer in Israel and the best place to study law was obviously Israel itself. So I came to Israel and began studying law here.

It seems you knew very early on what you wanted to do. Did your religious belief affect your decision?
David - I was observant then and I still am. I am *shomer shabat* and *shomer kashrut*. Two of my three children are observant. I always was, and I still am, a very political person. I was very conscious of the political situation and I did not want to live in apartheid South Africa. When I left, I said I would not be coming back here while the apartheid regime was standing, unless I had to.

What was your ideological background?
David – It came from *Habonim*. There is no getting away from it. When you think what was done in that movement, it is quite amazing. It came from home as well. I had two older sisters, one of whom was very political and my parents were on the more liberal side. We had some radical friends. It was a combination. King David (School) included. There was a small group of radical teachers there at the time, who could not have found employment anywhere else. There was a more liberal ethos in the Jewish community we moved in, though it may have been a bit hypocritical, because people's lives were dependent on the continuation of the situation. But there was a rejection of apartheid, not necessarily in the most radical terms.

Growing up in South Africa in the early fifties, you grew up with this notion that the Nats were demons. For our parents' generation, this was the pro-Nazi party and in the early fifties people were scared that something would happen, after all their anti-Semitic statements. All these things affect your ideology.

Did you ever toy with the idea of participating in the struggle in South Africa?
David – I did not have a general view on whether the Jews should stay and fight against apartheid or whether they should leave for Israel. I remember debates where some people said the Jews should remain and fight for justice and others said the Jews must go to Israel. I could see the arguments on both sides and I made a personal decision. I did not expect everybody to follow my line. I don't to this day. I certainly don't believe that every Jew should or could come to Israel.

What was the Zionist narrative that you picked up?
David – The Zionist narrative that we all picked up was a narrative that was totally oblivious to the real history of this part of the world. That is generally the establishment narrative to this day - we had this wonderful enterprise and the Palestinians were a wild lot and for some irrational reason, they just hated the Jews and did not want them here, so they used violence. Then the Arab states would not recognize us. The Palestinians began terrorist attacks, and so on. It is not a very sophisticated or convincing narrative and certainly does not reflect the historical reality.

Was there another narrative at that time?
David – There was another narrative on the margins. Today there is a lot more debate and willingness to discuss painful issues, to see the problematical aspects of the Zionist enterprise. In the same way that I was a Zionist in the sixties and still am a Zionist, I am convinced that had I been born at the end of the nineteenth century, I would have been part of the Zionist struggle. I would not have appreciated the perspective of the Arabs in Palestine any better than most of the others who were committed to the struggle. The constraints of the Jewish people and the desperateness of the situation clearly contributed to the fact that they were oblivious to the effects of what they were doing on the indigenous population. But this is what happened and it affects thinking to this day.

Do you feel you were conned?
David – We were indoctrinated, but I don't think it was intentional. The people who were indoctrinating us were as blind as we were. They were giving us what they thought was the truth and it was functional. They did not intentionally hide anything from us. We were adult enough to find out things for ourselves.

Do you have any explanation for the disproportionate amount of Jews who have been involved in struggles for social justice?
David - I don't have anything new to add to what is generally known. It probably has a lot to do with minorities who have suffered. If you look at the activists in the human rights movements in Israel today, there is a disproportionate number of homosexuals. You can ask why? It is a similar phenomenon. People who are used to being discriminated against or victimized are more sensitive to the issues.

If you take the Association for Human Rights in Israel, a number of senior people are homosexuals. In *B'tzelem*, of which I am the co-chairperson, we have two lesbian women on the board. Perhaps it grows out of the same kind of thing. I am sure that Jewish ethics had a contribution, but I don't know what Jewish ethics are. Our Jewish ethics are very different from the Jewish ethics of the 'hill people' in the West Bank.

I am an academic lawyer. Like other academics, I write books and articles. I have been very critical of the courts here and think they could have done more to protect human rights. Nevertheless, when I compare our supreme court to other supreme courts in conflicted societies, our court is doing pretty well. That could possibly be ascribed to some notion of Jewish ethics. I feel that some of the notions of social justice here, which are disappearing very fast, were grounded in Jewish ethics and the social democratic ideal. It is very difficult to separate them.

Did you choose to work in Northern Ireland because it is also a conflicted society?
David – I did. I have worked on states of emergency and on transitional justice. I made my choice of profession very early on. I thought of two

possible professions: when I was young I wanted to be a fireman, but when I grew out of that I knew that I wanted to be a lawyer. My choice was very much affected by the South African situation. We saw these lawyers out there defending people in political trials. I soon decided that practicing law was not for me, so I am an academic lawyer.

Where does your work today touch on the issues that really affect you here?
David – My work for a number of years has revolved around important aspects of the situation here – all the kinds of issues that concern me. I wrote a book called *The Occupation of Justice*, which looks at the jurisprudence of the Supreme Court relating to the occupied territories from 1967–2000. I wrote another book on the legal status of the Arabs in Israel. I deal now with human rights in armed conflict situations. International human rights is one of my fields. I was on the Human Rights Committee of the UN for eight years. In the course of our work in Geneva and New York, we examined reports on the human rights situation in dozens of countries from all parts of the world. When the Committee dealt with Israel's report, I did not take part in the proceedings as Committee rules preclude members from dealing with their own countries.

As an Israeli, how do you engage with international colleagues involved in human rights issues?
David – My closest colleague on the committee was a man from Germany, the same age as I am. He knows the Bible very well and when dealing with countries I often used to say to him, "This is the Job syndrome." When everything is good, he is fine and he keeps all the *mitzvot* and praises God every day. Question is what happens when things go bad. That is fundamentally what happens when you look at the world. Countries are very holy when things are fine but as soon as they start going bad their record changes. You have to see it in that perspective, which people in the human rights community don't always see.

I was involved in human rights from very early on, as a lawyer in the late sixties and early seventies. I got politically involved a short time after coming to the country. I was involved in the 1969 elections with a list called the Peace List. The sort of things we said then are now accepted by nearly everybody. I realized quickly that party politics were not for me and started concentrating on the human rights field. In 1972 I was one of the founding members of the leading human rights organization in Israel, the Association for Civil Rights in Israel. At various times, I served as Chairperson of the Association's board. I was also one of the founding members of *B'tzelem* and of *Hamoked*, the Centre for the Protection of the Individual. Then my wife got ill and I withdrew from public activity for a number of years.

How do you understand the low profile of South Africans in political and human rights activity in Israel?
David – I think that that is a worrying phenomenon. When I originally got involved in politics, I tried to draw in some of the people I knew from *Habonim*, which I could at the beginning. They were thinking along the same lines as I did. But many of them remained solidly within the framework of the Jewish/Zionist establishment perspective. I didn't.

I do not know if the lack on involvement of former South Africans in politics is a matter of ideology or of the nature of Israeli politics. There were some South Africans in the human rights field, the late Leon Shelef, my late sister, Ruth Cohen, and her husband, Stan.

Do you think that for many of us there is a disconnection between Israel the ideal and Israel the reality?
David – I am not sure I see it that way. There is a disconnection in every society. Most people want to get on with their lives as long as they don't feel personally threatened. When they hear about awful things happening in their own society, most people say "tut-tut", but they don't do anything about it. Even more so in a society which is threatened, in which bombs do go off and you have wars, where you are subjected to a constant form of brainwashing. The press here has a lot to answer for.

What does it take to get people moving?
David – I don't know. I am not a social psychologist. When people feel threatened, it is extremely difficult to mobilize them to political action.

To be quite honest I am pessimistic. Nobody knows how we are going to get out of this mess.

Are there days when you ask yourself whether you want to live here anymore?
David – No. I have never felt like leaving. This is my home. This is the country I identify with. As a Jew, I don't particularly like living abroad. Being observant, I feel out of place. I have lived in Israel my whole adult life. I am committed to this country and have no intention of leaving.

You say you are pessimistic, but what about your children and your grandchildren?
David – I think that they will have to change the world. Our generation is not capable of it. My generation is the generation of Olmert and Barak and the rest of the cast of failed political leaders. Perhaps eventually young people on both sides who were not brought up with the same hang-ups as our generation will be able to approach matters from a different perspective.

I don't believe the Jewish State can continue to exist as it is. I very much favor a two-state solution but I don't think it is achievable, implementable, or viable. If we don't get to a two-state solution fairly soon, at some stage the Palestinians and the international community are going to wake up to reality. They will drop the demand for a Palestinian state and replace it with the demand for one person, one vote. That is a demand that can't be resisted. We will then be in a South Africa-type situation.

I must admit that the experience in other ethnically-divided societies is not very encouraging, to put it mildly. And we have not had the last word on South Africa. We know they had a smooth transition from the apartheid regime to majority rule, but we don't know what is going to happen there over the next twenty years. I am not sure they are going to have a stable liberal democracy.

A lot of what has happened here is the result of arrogance, and the prevalent idea, so apparent in the second *intifada*, that you use massive force, and if that doesn't work you use more force. It is a society based on aggression – the use of force to solve all problems.

Legalistically speaking, what concerns you most?
David – Human rights issues concern me most. I am also worried by the hypocrisy in the way we have handled issues on the West Bank and in Gaza. The whole regime in the territories since 1967 has been based on hypocrisy, meaning you do one thing and say you are doing something else. You go to court and lie and the court gives the nod. The Highway 443 case is a perfect example. When land needed for the road was expropriated from Palestinians, the authorities justified this action in court by arguing that the highway was being built for the benefit of the Palestinian population. Did anybody at the time really think they were building this massive road for the Palestinians? Now Palestinians are not allowed to travel on the highway, which was ostensibly built for them.

But you still have respect for the Israeli legal system…
David – I do have a lot of respect. Compared to what happened in other threatened societies, in which the judiciary virtually capitulated, our courts have not done so badly. In Israel itself the rule of law is fairly well-protected. The territories are another matter – in some ways they are like the Wild West.

So how do you keep your spirits up?
David – You go on with your everyday life – children, grandchildren, your friends, your work.

The leaders of South African Habonim today are questioning whether aliyah is a worthy goal. What would you say to them?
David – I cannot give an answer. I have never been one who thinks you should promote *aliyah*. I don't think it is the duty of all Jews to come

and live here. In fact, I think it would be crazy. The paradox of Zionism is that it was supposed to provide a haven for the Jewish people but it is the most threatened Jewish community in the world.

I see myself as a Zionist in the sense that I do believe in the Jewish State, in which Jews have control over their own destiny. I feel easier as a Jew living here than I would anywhere else. Morally, even if I did not live here, the same situation would exist. Those of us from *Habonim* who came to this Israel with ideological commitment can't wash our hands of what we did. We were part of building this country, even if only in a minor way, and we can't suddenly say, "Well, it didn't work out, so bye bye, we are leaving."

I am worried about elites leaving. This is my big fear. One of the disasters of the Palestinians was that the first people to leave were the elites. I hear academic friends saying there is no reason to stay and I say it would be wrong for the elites to leave. You have a responsibility to the people who can't leave. I must add that I am not pretending that staying here is some kind of sacrifice. That would be wrong because I don't have any desire to live anywhere else.

Has the dream shared by ideologically-minded *olim* been lost?
David – Maybe. On Independence Day in the early eighties I invited a whole bunch of former *Habonim* people to my house to discuss and look back on our dream. We had a feeling even then that, "It is not what we imagined." I think we were naïve in some of our perceptions, though some people still hang on to their naïveté. Over the years, I have had very little contact with former South Africans. It would be very interesting to have another group discussion of that kind.

I am sorry to have been so pessimistic. But just look at the choice of possible prime ministers we have. I think the society is in a fundamental crisis and I don't see that it has the potential leadership to galvanize it and pull it out of the crisis.

We could go on oppressing the Palestinians, but I don't think it can continue very long. I don't think our society can face it and neither can the Palestinians. And I don't think the world will accept it.

The one ray of light is that the unexpected can happen. It happened in the last twenty years and it can happen again. Don't ask me what it is.

Ron Lapid

Ra'anana
10/06/08

Ron Lapid (Raymond Lipschitz) was born in Johannesburg in 1943. He matriculated at King David High and earned a psychology degree at Witwatersrand University. Ron and his wife Riwa were very active in Habonim. Riwa served as Mazkira Klalit in 1965. They made aliyah to Kibbutz Tzora the following year. After working as a shepherd, manager of the children's farm and youth leader, Ron was elected food manager of the kibbutz. He introduced significant changes in the organization of the dining room and kitchens.

Soon after leaving Tzora in 1972, Ron co-founded Burger Ranch in Tel Aviv. He personally ran the first restaurant for six years. Over 29 years he and his partners developed the quick service restaurant into an 80-unit chain, which became Israel's leading restaurant company. He served as Managing Director until 1998, and then as Chairman till 2001. After exiting the business, Ron spent a year working in London.

He is a CMT Accredited Master Mentor/Coach, assisting and training small to medium sized enterprises and new consultants – so far in 17 different countries.

Ron is an active volunteer in various social spheres.

Ron and Riwa have four children and nine grandchildren, all living in Israel.

When do you recall first making decisions that were based on what you believed to be right or wrong?
Ron - I remember being exposed to a whole lot of discussions about South Africa at *Habonim* seminar. This was the first time. I had heard of different things going on, but had never put them together in any way that involved ethical or moral judgments.

What was it that affected you at that seminar?
Ron - Racial equality, the value of a human being irrespective of color and what was going on in the country. At home, a kind of curtain was thrown over anything of this nature. There was never any discussion about who our servants were, what they were feeling, or whether they had feelings at all. And despite all of this it was our maid Lena who brought me up to a large extent.

That seminar was a very clear dividing line between "non –thinking" me and "thinking me." It was from that time that I found myself highly stimulated with a need to understand who I was, what I believed in and how I should live my life.

Where did this line of thinking take you?
Ron - Once I got to sixteen the question became, "Do I stay and fight or do I leave and fight for my Jewish awareness which was getting stronger and stronger?" If I try to think of a point at which I said to myself, "I am not staying in South Africa" it was probably the May 31st, 1961 (Republic Day). I happened to be in London where I attended a demonstration in Trafalgar Square. My thinking was, "This is not my battle, this is not for me. I'm Jewish, I'm going to Israel."

You say the Jewish element was very much at the root of your Zionist decisions…
Ron - When I started thinking about the South African situation, things like fairness, equality and justice became very important to me. Then the question became where do I try and apply these ideas? It was obvious to me that I should be a *kibbutznik* as well.

In fact I often used to say that I came to kibbutz more than I came on *aliyah*. I had never considered not being a *kibbutznik*. Kibbutz was where I could try to implement the ideas and ideals that were so important to me.

You were part of the senior leadership when persuasion and pressure were used to create a sense of urgency regarding aliyah. People gave

up university and others left immediately after school. Do you feel this was justified?

Ron - I was aware of it and I didn't feel comfortable with it. There was a lot of emotion used in describing Israel and its challenges. I preferred to look at things more analytically. In fact I did not go with the first group of the *garin* but finished my BA degree. There was a certain amount of ill-feeling against me. I would probably have stayed and finished a second degree if the pressure you describe had not existed. For one year I withstood it and stayed and then I left too, but with a certain degree of unease about not studying further.

What do you think it was that enabled the *shlichim* and the leadership to convince so many people of the urgency of *aliyah*? Was it a classic case of peer and group pressure or were the historical circumstances the main contributing factor?

Ron – Well, 1960 was Sharpeville and Zionist activity was intense at the beginning of the sixties. A lot of people came on *aliyah* during that period, not only to kibbutz. There was a sense that things were going to change rapidly in South Africa. It was easy to paint a pretty black picture, in both senses of the word, and to exploit that. And simultaneously Israel was perceived very emotionally.

The shlichim were passionate Zionists and pushing hard but they were not analyzing South African politics. How was the South African situation exploited?

Ron - I can remember Wolfie Mankowitz giving a brilliant paper that was later printed in one of the movement publications. It included a highly lucid description of how he saw things developing. There was definitely a fear element in his analysis. At some point before it was distributed, it was decided, maybe because of pressure from the Board or the Federation, to destroy it and not to give it out. I remember taking a copy home and keeping it in our room at the movement *bayit*. I don't recall if it was an actual search or a warning, but the Special Branch was interested in one of the *chaverim* who also stayed at the *bayit*. At that point, I decided to destroy anything that might cause me trouble were my room to be searched. Wolfie's paper was amongst the stuff I destroyed. This atmosphere of fear definitely made *aliyah* an exciting and challenging alternative.

Would you have defined yourself as a socialist at that time?
Ron - In so far as I saw myself as a *kibbutznik* perhaps, but I was never part of any political socialist organization. The fact that joining and leaving a kibbutz was voluntary was vital for me. I never saw myself as a missionary who would like to persuade others.

How did the reality meet your expectations once you got to kibbutz?
Ron - When we arrived, we were very much caught up in the highly-charged issue of where our *garin* (Etgar) had settled. Personal, political and ideological issues became terribly interwoven in what developed into something that made us uncomfortable. We were not settling down on Tzora and we moved to Kfar Hanassi for a year.

We were kibbutz members for six years and even today I look back very fondly at kibbutz and the kibbutz movement. I think the kibbutz movement created the most just society I have ever come across. With all the limitations, the achievements were very significant. This was a society with no poor people, nobody was starving. I became even more aware of the egalitarian achievements once we moved off the kibbutz. I felt very good being part of it.

At the same time, there were little irritants that cumulatively were the cause of what ultimately led to a decision to leave - irritants as small as eating in the communal dining room. Sitting to fill a table rather than choosing who you wanted to eat with, remainders of soup being splashed into the *kolboinik*, were examples of things that really bothered me. They bothered me enough in fact to push me into becoming *ekonom* and trying to change things, trying to give people more choice. And I did manage to change quite a lot when I was in the job.

Another irritant which may seem minor but really got to me at the time, was that I really wanted to go on with my studies. In the six years I was a member, I was never offered that. I did not want to go and ask a committee.

To me it was totally acceptable that one should give according to one's ability and get according to one's needs, and I still think that way. But I slowly began to realize that there were a lot of people around me who thought like me but there were also quite a number who were just takers. That irked me.

The final observation was of people who I held in very high regard who had become disillusioned and bitter. When I saw this bitterness, I was determined that this was not going to happen to me.

With all the positive feelings and beliefs that I had and still have about kibbutz, I came to the conclusion after six years that it just wasn't for me. Leaving was not an ideological decision.

What took you into the fast-food business?
Ron - I saw a 'want ad' for a new American-style burger restaurant opening in Tel Aviv and applied. I saw this as being temporary, but it turned out to be the first step to becoming one of the managers and owners of Burger Ranch. Luck and circumstances played a role in putting me somewhere that I loved almost from the word go. There was scope here for organization, team building, marketing, attracting clientele, planning, accounting; everything was there in this business and I just loved it.

Can you tell us something about trying to retain what was important to you in the Israeli business world?
Ron - I found it very comfortable. I could express myself and influence things that others never thought of. You ask yourself why someone would work for a minimum wage and work hard, smile, and be happy. Part of why these questions interested me was that I still basically had the *madrich* mentality. We built training programs that were designed to make the worker feel worthwhile. I saw kids who started as fifteen year olds, becoming soldiers, working well in other places or even their own businesses. As part of our corporate culture, for many years we gave a number of study bursaries to kids who had been spending time as volunteers for at least a year. We did lots of things like this which made me feel most at ease morally and ethically with what I was doing.

Riwa (wife) - Ron was never a regular kind of boss. When a young manager was getting married or needed a loan, he would go with him to the bank and use his pull to get the maximum for this kid. When somebody was doing well, he got the praise he deserved, when somebody was not doing well he was told but he would get another chance. From the person who delivered the rolls to the manager, everybody was dealt with as somebody.

Ron - I do feel that I did not have to make many compromises on what was important to me. I have found expression for my abilities in many ways that helped me maintain my integrity. As I suggested earlier, I believe very strongly in leaders. In politics as well, I think leaders are more powerful, both positively and negatively, than we tend to think.

How do you feel about where Israel is today ?

Ron- Greatly troubled. I see the positive things but they are less obvious. I had a very clear vision of peace coming to the country. That vision has been clouded over the last ten years or so. Although I still believe … I don't see any future for Israel without peace. I still maintain that belief, and believe we should continue to express it in what we do.

As far as corruption is concerned, I think we are as bad as any other country in the world. The standard of leadership is very troubling although there are some good guys too. I am not nearly as simplistic in my outlook as I was forty years ago - thinking about Israel and kibbutz in utopian terms. I don't see it like that any more. My underlying belief in people is still there. A lot of people do what you expect them to. The higher your expectations the higher the results tend to be.

Have you ever considered a role for yourself outside of the business world?

Ron - There have often been moments when I thought I should and could have done something in politics. But it never worked out and I suppose that I was never at ease with getting into that world. I was also involved in business and it was not easy to combine that with anything else with any seriousness. It could have been rewarding but didn't happen.

I think that the security fear has encouraged a lot of people to put principles aside. Not necessarily with ease, but uncomfortably. I wish we didn't need a Wall but have never gone to demonstrate against it. Maybe that is because I am not the demonstrating kind, but also because I see the short term in which it may be helping the security. I am one of the people who has not done anything, who has gone somewhat in the direction described as a bystander.

How do you handle that? Do you do other things? Do you compensate?
Ron – Well I feel that so much of my life is meaningful, that I am doing things that I am comfortable with. I now know that life is so complicated, that I can't do everything that I would like to do. There are certain things on which I compromise. I try not to do this on major issues. I feel quite at ease with myself.

Given the chance, is there anything major that you might have done differently?
Ron - A lot of our lives is fortuitous. There is less planning than we once believed. I think I could well have ended up doing something else, probably with satisfaction, but I don't have regrets. I don't look back in anger. I look forward. My general attitude to virtually everything, and this is both a function of my personality and life experiences, is that I try not to spend time, effort and emotions on things that I can't influence. I try to learn from my mistakes and to develop myself further. I think about how to be a positive member of my family, and of Israel, and of the world. I don't look back with regret.

Zeev (Wolfie) Mankowitz

Jerusalem
16/07/08

Zeev participated in the Machon Lemadrichei Chutz La-aretz in 1959, returned to serve in the movement and settled in Jerusalem in 1963.

In 1973 he, became director first of the Institute for Youth Leaders from Abroad and then the Jerusalem Fellows, a program to develop educational leaders for Jewish communities. He subsequently served for six years as director of the Melton Centre for Jewish Education at the Hebrew University, Jerusalem.

Zeev has been Visiting Professor at Old Dominion University, Yale University, and the University of Cape Town, as well as a visiting research fellow at the Oxford Centre for Hebrew and Jewish Studies and a Fellow of the International Institute of Holocaust Research, Yad Vashem. He is also an academic consultant for the New Museum of the Holocaust, Yad Vashem, and has lectured widely in the US, Canada, Mexico, Argentina, South Africa, Australia, Britain, Austria, and Poland.

Zeev served as an academic consultant in the planning of the new museum in Yad Vashem and chaired the Board of Yesodot - the Centre for the Study of Torah and Democracy and that of Ir Amim, a non-profit organization devoted to the well being and viability of all Jerusalem's communities.

Zeev Mankowitz continues to serve as a member of the International Advisory Board of the Melton Centre and has recently been appointed Director of the newly created Diana Zborowski Center for the Study of the Aftermath of the Shoah at Yad Vashem, Jerusalem.

Zeev - My family lived in the Gardens at the meeting point between white and colored Cape Town. My grandfather was the *"gabbe"* of the Constitution Street Shul that was in the area that became colored.

The formative significance of my growing up in Buitenkant street was two-fold: I developed a warm and lasting attachment to our religious traditions and, secondly, I grew up very much aware of all the differences that divided South Africa. My exposure was different to the one that a lot of people go through.

We weren't well off. My dad died when I was 10. My mom was what the family called "ferociously independent." She gave me this feeling that I didn't want to be dependent on anyone in South Africa. I didn't want anyone to do me favors, I didn't want to apologize to anybody, I didn't want to be beholden to anyone; I wanted to be free. To be free meant to live in a country that I saw as my own and according to values that I saw as my own. If there is anything in my Zionism that has deep roots it's this sense of wanting to be independent of minority hang-ups, minority sensibilities and minority concerns which were very much part of who I was as a South African Jew. I was not able to just wave these things aside; they spoke to me with an enduring urgency.

The year I spent on *Machon* in 1959 was a life-changing experience. I had given my mother my word that I would go to university when I got back and I did. But then came the Eichmann trial and Sharpeville. The feeling was that we had to get ready to move as many young people out of South Africa as possible. So I gave up university after a year and a half.

Sharpeville sent a shock wave through South Africa. We saw it as the first tremors of an unstoppable uprising of the black population that would lead to civil war. In this war the Jews who were identified as supporting the black cause would be caught in an impossible situation. Our job was to create what was really a parallel of youth *aliyah* and that is why I went to Johannesburg.

Did your analysis influence Habonim's way of thinking in this regard?
Zeev - In Cape Town yes. I saw a film on the Eichmann trial at the Adelphi in Sea Point. Sharpeville was still pressing hard in the background. I came out of the film and asked myself how so many people in Europe could have had an intimation of what was going to happen and just sat around not taking any action.

Zeev shows us a snippet from what he describes as "a somewhat pretentious paper," given in August 1963.

It gives you a sense of what was going through my mind at the time:

1.   That everyone in this country is being led, without any recourse to protest and non-violent dissent along a path decided by the government that must end in disaster.
2.   That in such a conflict the sides that one takes will almost certainly be predetermined by the color of one's skin.
3.   The people who are not committed to apartheid will be caught up in a fight which is not really theirs.
4.   That within this complex of forces the Jews because of their peculiar minority status, historic relationship with the white population and ethical code will find themselves in an untenable position.

(Minutes of the Habonim Ve'ida, Johannesburg, August 1963)

In Johannesburg we started organizing and working towards getting our version of youth *aliyah* off the ground. We also worked on explaining to the *shlichim* what we were thinking about bearing in mind that their kibbutzim were a critical part of our plan.

As things turned out the violent disaster that you predicted did not take place.

Zeev - It's difficult to know what the future holds. At the time we did all sorts of other things: We wanted to feel confident of our ability to protect our community if the need arose. We spent many hours in a type of basic army training but without arms - how to move around at night, how to keep watch and even how to *pish* quietly. I tell you this not because the training was serious but because our reading was that the situation was threatening and that we had to move quickly. By the time I went on *aliyah* it was clear to me that our predictions were premature. As time went on it became clear that we were not on the edge of a revolution.

Where did your thinking about kibbutz come from?

From our shared commitment to social justice and our experiences on the *Machon*. We had an incredible four months on Kfar Blum. We were a powerful group and we met up with people on the kibbutz who were equally powerful. But for me it also had a lot to do with our work assignment in the fishponds - going out to row in the early morning and the 9 o'clock breakfast - fresh bread scrambled eggs and mint tea made by a co-worker from Morocco. Starting at 4 in the morning, dipping into the refreshing waters of the Jordan, the Hermon looming above us. Just beautiful. This had very little to do with ideology and everything to do with a sense of heady freedom and the feeling that we were doing our bit. What moved us was a sense of values rather than a well articulated approach to socialism. The socialism didn't only come from the kibbutz but it was an inspiring example of how it could work.

My socialism had more to do with the labor movement in Britain and even then it is Isaiah Berlin who more than anyone else has guided my thinking. In truth, I don't remember much discussion about socialism at all.

And yet the debate about *chalutzik aliyah* was fierce...
Zeev – The ideological formulation was about a group orientation, a collective ideal as opposed to a more individualistic, liberal ethos. It also had a lot to do with going to kibbutz and living a life that embodied the key values that we were talking about. This is the way the argument for *chalutzik aliyah* went: "We believe in social justice and equality, we believe in individual freedom and living a life of independence in the Jewish state. Where can you do that best? On the kibbutz." All these ideals pointed to the fact that what was going on in South Africa was absolutely unconscionable and intolerable but given the fact that we are Jewish and feel a sense of solidarity with our community that limits our freedom of expression, the best thing to do was to ask, "Where can I create this world of freedom and social justice?" Our answer was clearly the kibbutz. This was our highest aspiration.

The counter-argument was that *aliyah* was our highest ideal and that each person must be autonomous to decide how and where they wanted to live their lives in Israel.

There was also an academic dimension to the debate: collective commitments did not allow for untrammeled intellectual honesty, argued Mike Kuper. He wanted to know how we related to the 1948-49 war as the War of Liberation when it spelt disaster for the Palestinian Arabs. His sharp mind and powerful arguments left us floundering. Finally, there was also an element of personal rivalry – my best friend in Johannesburg was Steve Aschheim and we argued about everything including these issues. Even though we still occasionally find ourselves at loggerheads our deep friendship remains firm – at heart, this is what the movement was really about, caring profoundly about one another.

So you left South Africa adamant about kibbutz...
Zeev – I had this very deep loving commitment to my mom and so I first went to university as I had promised. After four years studying, I had married my late wife Gene who wasn't interested in kibbutz and it wasn't too difficult to convince me to do an MA. The intellectual world began to consume me. At first we used to go to Yizra'el every two weeks. Then this became every three and then once a month. It was, and remains one of the great failures of my life. If I had gone to kibbutz I would have had a very different life.

My life was public in that it was institutionally bound, I worked at the *Machon* and then it was Jerusalem Fellows, then the Melton Center at the Hebrew University. All those were institutions with a mission but a public life of a different kind. Politics remains the path not taken. The political activist side of me that I got from *Habonim* might have come to the fore had I gone to kibbutz.

Do you have any reservations about the *tochniot* and methods used in Habonim education?
Zeev – The person who led the movement ideologically was Giddy Shimoni. He wrote the *shomrim* handbook and did a seriously impressive job. His way of helping us understand what Israel and the Jewish

community in South Africa were about was important and definitely most influential for me.

Some of the stuff we wrote in movement publications does make me blush when I read it now. Phrases like, "The choking dust of materialism;" things that are just youthful effusiveness. But by and large I see movement education in a positive light -tremendous seriousness and an attempt to give young people a chance to understand and come to terms with the world they lived in by giving them the tools of critical thought.

But there was an ideological atmosphere that had its own rules. When groups went on educational trips to Israel, we tried to be honest. But those setting out for Israel were imbued by a romantic, even heroic sub-text that our "realism" only reinforced and that went something like this: "While everyone else is warm in bed we shall be redeeming the land of Israel, untiring, determined pioneers of the Jewish renaissance."

Another big question was whether to get involved in South Africa. Our approach was, "eyes on, hands off." You couldn't develop critical thought except against the real background of people's lives; equally, given our position that we did not want to embarrass or endanger the community in any way, you could not be engaged in any activities that would lead to closing down the movement. If you wanted to do something like that you had to move over to other settings.

How do we explain the fact that our understanding of Israeli history in Habonim did not in any way foresee a Palestinian problem?
Zeev - There was a side of the movement that wasn't intellectual. I shudder today when I remember the song, (sings) "We are the Arabs we used to live in tents. But since the Jews came we live in apartments. Tumba ta tumba," etc. I blush when I think of that because I didn't put an end to it.

Was it naiveté that made the Palestinians seem irrelevant?
Zeev - When I came on *aliyah* in 1963 the laws about freedom of movement for the Israeli Arabs were moving towards liberalization and the question of the Palestinians was not a persistent headache and many of

the countries and people who mattered to us were perhaps critical of various policies but, nonetheless, basically sympathetic to our cause. The crucial factor, looking back, was the context of the small, pre- '67 Israel. There was a completely different dynamic at work. Jordan was on our doorstep with this gigantic country and a good half of the West Bank. Egypt was in Gaza and Syria on the Golan Heights. We had a teeny bit of rough country. The feeling was that we were basically decent. There was a lot of work to do but we were not doing anything that was vile or violent.

The troubled feelings that we have had since '67 were not in any significant way reflected in what happened prior.

How have you dealt with your change in perspective?
Zeev - As each year has passed I have become more introspective, a little less public…deeply engaged and involved in things that concern me about the world we live in and that go beyond political activity. I think the most important thing that Israel needs today is a new kind of poetry, a new series of stories around which we can begin to organize the idealism which often remains untapped. I've come to the conclusion that the legend of the 36 righteous men and women should not be understood literally but as a symbol of the significant minority of idealistic people that exist in every generation. They are there. I don't know how it happens but that is how I read that tradition.

Now that I have retired this is more and more becoming the challenge that I am thinking about. From that point of view, from about fifteen years ago when I was still pretty religious I went through a period of looking for what I was lacking and couldn't find in the religious framework. I could never find a group of people that fully shared my sensibilities. The Reform were too assimilated, the Orthodox were too orthodox, the Conservatives too American and the kind of easy inconsistencies that we brought from South Africa was something I refuse to surrender.

When talking about South Africa, you referred to the unconscionable situation. How has this translated into your life here?
Zeev - The easiest thing to notice is in our voting pattern. I always

voted Labor. Because I think we need large consensual parties I never voted for lists that were close to my heart but marginal in the election process. When I became religious I became involved in creating Oz Veshalom, the religious parallel of Shalom Achshav.

I have a profound sense of the many things that have gone badly wrong in our country. I imagine that one of the symbolic things I have done was influenced by my late teacher Prof. Rotensterich who never set foot in the occupied territories. With me it has been roughly the same. But to say that this has been at the center of my life would be overstating the case.

For a while I took a leadership role in Ir Amim, an NGO that is working for a Jerusalem of equity, stability, and social justice, with a negotiated political future. I have also headed an NGO called Yesodot which works in religious schools and seminars promoting democratic thought based on Jewish sources.

So our commitments, I suppose, tell who we are. I know that these organizations are doing important work and I am helping it to happen. I wouldn't say it is major but it is something.

But to go back a bit, when I took off my *kipa* after our family tragedy, we remained kosher and observant to a degree. I suddenly realized that there was nothing more important to me than what we had tried to educate towards in *Habonim*. It could not be defined just as youthful enthusiasm. These were serious commitments and now it was time to actively take on the things that we believed in with the hope of making a difference to the country. The only thing that I am sorry about is that if you work in education you will know how long it takes to bring about meaningful change.

People who have taught and studied with you have pointed to your teaching as being imbued with an ideological fervor. Has this been a conscious thing?
Zeev - I'll say that my commitments raise questions but that I never try to give answers. At the end of a course people often asked, "So where do you stand politically?" and that was fine by me. But I got people engaged in thinking about themselves and the world from a

value perspective. What I did was simply what we called *hadracha*. Right until retirement and now beyond, I was as much a *madrich* as a teacher, a combination that remains central to my very being.

How do you see the students today? Are they capable of making the kind of shift that is needed if we are to see significant change in Israel?

Zeev - One interesting thing is that on the whole they are a lot younger than when I started teaching – early or late twenties, less life experience. If we find the inspiring narrative that helps us reorganize our life and create something different ... I accept the analysis that says that since 1967 there's this bone in our throat that we can't swallow and we can't spit out called the *shetachim*. Everything is still stuck around that issue. I'm just not sure that at a time when there are so many threats around us, many of them blood-curdling, if there can be a generosity of spirit that we need in order to move towards a settlement. But I remain pretty certain that with any real chance of peace and concerted international pressure, what looks firm and fast today will begin to unravel.

As South Africans we can affirm that no matter how dark the horizon, the march to the equality of rights cannot be permanently restrained. Alexis de Tocqueville said this magnificently in the 1840's and has yet to be proven wrong.

How do you see the low visibility of South African *olim* in dealing with issues of social justice that were so high on our youth movement agendas?

Zeev - One thing that is important is that South Africans tend to continue talking English in their family and social circles. Most South Africans have a workable but not a rhetorical Hebrew that can stir up passion and enthusiasm. This is not an explanation but it is part of one.

The second part is that we come from a very diverse group of people and found it difficult to recognize that many Jews who came from South Africa identified very strongly with Likud or settler policies. We may have kept this support and identification with Revisionist thinking out of sight but I think it is very important. There is no homogeneous

South African community that has a shared voice on matters of vital concern to our country. When we were young *Bnei Akiva* were very much like us as far as kibbutz goes but all that has gone out the window.

I think the third thing is our civil culture. It didn't prepare us for the abrasiveness of Israeli political practice. It leaves people worried and bruised and disgusted and unable to think they would ever want to be engaged in this kind of thing.

A lot of really important contributions have been made by South Africans but these have been in the context of institutions such as the universities, hospitals, the professions, business, industry as well as a few municipalities. In the end our small numbers count against us in the political arena.

If we look ahead…
Zeev - If we just avert our gaze from the daily helping of horror handed out by the media and focus on those we live and work with we all know what we find – remarkable people living in a special country.

We still have so much to do. Taking the long view we might say that we have just got started. Important developments have their own gestation time. We just don't see that significant shifts take a long, long time to mature. Our lives are overflowing with challenges, pain and a kaleidoscope of fascinating change.

Here in Israel our return to history has brought us an overload of daily stimulation. Much more than we ever bargained for.

Raphael (Ray) Melmed

Moshav Bin Nun
11/03/08

Born in Port Elizabeth in 1938, Raphael Melmed grew up in Bulawayo. After studying Medicine at UCT, he did post-graduate studies at the University of London. He made aliyah 1972 and took up a post as a physician in the Department of Medicine, Hadassah Hospital, Jerusalem, where he worked until his retirement in 2005, and was also Associate-Professor of Medicine at the Hebrew University - Hadassah Medical School. He was formerly, Israel Weckler Professor of Medical Education and Head of the Unit of Behavioral Medicine in Internal Medicine.

All three of Raphael's children, Yair, Michaela (died 2003) and Gidon were born in Israel. He has three grandchildren.

Tell us a bit about your early years.

Ray – I came from a very Zionist background. My late father and his family in Port Elizabeth and Queenstown were all gung-ho Zionists. My parents were both born in South Africa and they died in Israel. My father became a Zionist Revisionist at a critical phase of his life.

How did that happen?

Ray – That was quite an interesting event. He was an unusual guy. He was first of all a Zionist. My late grandfather, Meir Melmed, died in Queenstown in 1916 at the age of forty-two, when my father, the eldest of six children was nine years old. They were extremely poor. I still have the obituary from the *Zionist Record*. When Meir Melmed died, he asked that his coffin be draped in the Zionist flag and that they sing *Hatikva* at the grave. I think it was part of the Lithuanian tradition, which was very strong on the nationalistic side of Jewish existence, the notion of creating a homeland for the Jews.

In 1945 when I was about five or six there was a Zionist election in South Africa and my father said he was going to read each party's manifesto. He read the Revisionist manifesto and said, "My goodness. This is an exact expression of the way I feel about things." He became a Revisionist from that day on. He made himself extremely unpopular because the Revisionists were exceedingly unpopular in those days. My father became the chairman of the Central African Zionist Revisionist organization and vice-president of the Zionist Council in Rhodesia. All my life I knew about his activity. I was a school boy when Begin came to Bulawayo in the early fifties to stay at our home called by my father "Beginvilla" (much to the amusement of the Jewish community).

What do you think it was that attracted him to Revisionism?
Ray – I think it was the nationalist element that was a true representation of what should be. I don't think it was the maximalist stance. That became part of it. They spoke in terms which he could identify more clearly.

How specifically did he educate the family, or was that just something you imbibed?
Ray – I was a member of *Habonim* for a long time. My first Zionist camp was a *Habonim* camp. In those days there was no *Betar* in Rhodesia. Then they came along and said they want to create *Betar*. My brother and his friend Jonathan were the first *Betarim* in Rhodesia. After a while I joined as well.

Can you remember what you were thinking at the time? Why did you make the switch from Habonim?
Ray – It is a very difficult thing to know. I am not sure I can say. It was not popular to be in *Betar*. There were members of the community who accosted us at Zionist functions and literally cursed us. These were people who were strongly Zionist-socialist and they spoke about the militarism of Jabotinsky's philosophy. The intensity of feeling was very substantial.

I think my father presented it in a way that sounded reasonable but he never at any stage said, "You are becoming *Betarim* and forget about anything else." There was no such thing in our home, but clearly an influence there must have been.

I went to Cape Town, I was one of the leaders of *Betar*. There was a camaraderie there that I am sure was shared by all the youth movement activists. You believed in a cause, there was an ideology, and you were young. There was a kind of a purposefulness to life, which was great.

I hated the apartheid system in South Africa but I felt that at the end of the day that had to be sorted out by the blacks. The majority had to deal with it. I felt as a Jew I was peripheral to the big issues, that I could only express my disdain for apartheid in a symbolic way, at the most. I felt I had to look after my own future as a Jew in a historical sense.

Who were the people in Betar who had an influence on you?
Ray – There were figures older than us but I think the real motivation came from reading. We had easy access to the literature and it made very good sense. If you go back and read some of Jabotinsky's writing you will see he spoke about human rights for the Arab minority of Israel, in a way that no other Zionist leader did. He laid it out in a very clear, categorical way. But at the same time he said that after all these years we have our right to national expression.

In a sense, the Zionist-socialist theme seemed to us to be that the Jewish State was a necessary step in creating a Jewish socialist society. There was a spin there which we did not find attractive. The socialism seemed to be the essential element and that to us was less persuasive. We found the Revisionist literature more persuasive than the Zionist-socialist literature.

You can also talk about the way the Revisionists were ostracized. If you read Begin's account of the Altalena, they had a point of view. They were not there to upset the apple cart. They had an argument which we accepted. It became a matter of what you supported.

Can you give us a sense of what the atmosphere was like among Jewish youth at that time? Did you have friends who were not in Betar?

Ray – There was argument more than dialogue. Each person tried to persuade the other as to the veracity of his perspective. There were differences of opinion even among members of the family. My father and his brothers had the most violent Zionist discussions that soured the atmosphere between them for months and years at certain times. They went hammer and tongs at each other. We were a microcosm of what was happening in the general Zionist world. The attack in the S.A. Zionist press against Begin, when he visited Rhodesia, was bitter and ugly and clearly the youth picked that up as well. But at the end of the day we still had our friendships and we still socialized and we went to the same parties and when we were dancing with the girls we were focused on the girls. My Zionism flew out of my mind when I was looking at Janice.

Betar was one of the smaller movements. How did you relate to this?

Ray – It didn't disturb me. I might have absorbed it from my father. He was a very courageous man. He was a leader who had the courage of his convictions. He was not a natural politician in that he presented his genuine beliefs with passion, not what he thought people wanted to hear. I have been a risk-taker all my life but in a calculated way. I came to Israel as a very determined Zionist wanting to make a go of it here, so the career path I chose was an enormous risk in academic medicine.

There are not many examples of doctors who left Israel, did well outside and came back. How did you prove to be the exception?

Ray - I did not lose my residual Zionism. I had every intention of coming back. I figured I was going to make a serious attempt to make it work. And I had a bit of luck. The right job was available when I was ready to take it, i.e. when I had had the appropriate training.

How did the reality of Israel match what you had anticipated?

Ray – I kind of accepted it as it was. By nature I am not a very judgmental person. There were problems and I could see them. I did not walk around feeling that this was paradise but at the same time this was the society I wanted to identify with and these were the problems I would have to grapple with as part of that society. I took it in my stride.

In subsequent years I came to believe very strongly that those people who came to Israel not as Zionists, very often did better than the Zionists, because of this issue. People who came without an ideology were more disposed to accept the reality, in the sense of riding the waves, whereas the ideologues were constantly being challenged by the imperfections they did not want to have to deal with.

Does that mean you do not consider yourself an idealist?
Ray – Zionism was my ideology. That is why my generation of *Betarim* have succeeded brilliantly in Israel, because we were brought up to believe that the Zionist socialists were screwing up the country and when we came to Israel in 1973, that is exactly what we found. There was still a *Mapai* government and we were constantly presented with the shortcomings of the *Mapai* leadership.

What was it about the Mapai style of socialism that you disagreed with, and in what way were they 'screwing up the country'?
Ray – There were many things that we found objectionable and I am not sure it is inherently socialist. First of all, they politicized everything, including sport. To me that was outrageous. To be a member of a particular sports club you had to be a card-carrying member of the party. Promotions in government institutions, particularly the army, had to do a lot with whether you were in the *Haganah* or the *Irgun*. We knew many instances of outstanding people who had been in the *Irgun* who could not get beyond a certain point. There was a ceiling. There was enormous power in the hands of those who had the power and they frequently abused it. A lot of this had begun to thin out by the time I got to Israel but we knew about these things.

We knew, too, that investment was frightened away by the conditions that the *Histadrut* imposed on anybody who wanted to bring capital to Israel. Today we know better.

Then there was this intense animosity which made you feel defiant.

Did that mean that you had great expectations of what would happen when the regime changed?
Ray – My contention was that Israel was a democracy in name only. The day that the opposition became government was the day that democracy would be born. And that happened. Israel became a democracy. There is nothing in the DNA which says right-wing, left-wing. In England I voted for the Labor Party because I felt more comfortable with them.

Once Begin was in power, did things start to move in the way you wanted them to?
Ray – I was very realistic. I didn't think there was a magic wand. Let's face it, the irony of Begin's position is that he spoke to the masses better than the Zionist-socialists did. As a social phenomenon that was fascinating. I am a pragmatist essentially. I have voted for Labor in Israel in subsequent years when I got cheesed off with the nonsense of the *Likud* and *Herut*. I am not one of these diehards, who says, "Never this or never that." Israel has become a much more pragmatic place anyway. The old ideologies have weakened. People don't invest the same intensity as they did, other than in the religious issue, which is emerging as the focus, in a very uncomfortable way for me.

Has the question of Greater Israel been an issue for you?
Ray – I never thought that the Greater Israel was a feasible proposition. It might have been a valid concept at a certain time. It was historical and I saw it in that context.

Are you more or less satisfied with the direction that Israel has taken since you are here?
Ray – Overall, I suppose so. Israel has been an incredible experiment of integrating cultures. I think Israel has done amazingly. Rees-Mogg, a past editor of the *London Times*, wrote a number of articles many years ago saying that were it not for the Arab threat, Israel's economy would still be based on agriculture and textile manufacture. I strongly agree

with that and in many respects I think that the challenges have moved Israel on by decades.

If you look at the Arab world, you can see something similar. As a Diaspora, the Palestinians are top-class people in many fields because they have been challenged through their own hardship.

I think challenge is healthy. I think it brings out the best. Lack of challenge is disastrous for a society, for example in Scandinavia, where people are bored as hell, alcohol becomes a massive problem, etc. I think human beings atrophy when the challenges are removed.

How do you feel about the human rights issues here?
Ray – I get extremely disturbed when I hear about injustice and abuse of authority, regardless of who it is directed at. It is something I don't tolerate. I was conditioned by the South African situation. From an early age, I had an awareness that the African man working in our house was an adult and I was a child. I did not sit on my backside and ask for things to be brought to me. I got that from my parents. I never heard prejudicial statements in my home directed towards people in a less fortunate position. Never ever. I carry that into my life here.

Are there aspects of Israel that trouble you?
Ray – There are two areas that are of major concern to me. The one is the Jew-Arab, and the other is the religious-non-religious. It does matter to me that Israel treats the minority citizens appropriately. I am extremely worried about people who are driven to dictate political reality in the belief that this is what God has decreed. That worries the living daylights out of me because that virtually has no limit and no answer, other than what could be a disastrous confrontation.

Are you troubled by the implications of the continued occupation?
Ray – The effect of the occupation is troubling. I think it is a reality we are forced into and I don't think we have worked hard enough to provide a clear answer to what that can do in undermining the value system of our society. I am not convinced it is healthy to say we'll give up the occupation and that will rid us of that negative influence, because

you cannot walk away from the reality of the innate and sustained hostility of the Arabs towards Israel. So you walk away from the occupation and you expose yourself to what is happening in Gaza, which will be the story in the West Bank. So, we are carrying an incredible burden but we don't have the answer. It is worrying.

Are you optimistic?
Ray – I am an optimist by nature. I look for solutions to problems and I continue grappling with them until I think I have found them, in relation to my own life. I think that at the end of the day we will prevail.

Do you feel good about the choices you have made in your life?
Ray – You win some, you lose some. Overall I am very grateful and very fortunate that my grandparents left Lithuania. In July 1943 the Nazis came into Polevez, where the Melmeds came from, and in three days the community was gone. When I read that, it was like being hit on the head with a hammer. That would have been us, us. I was five years old in 1943.

Tzvi (Pantz) Pantanowitz

Zichron Ya'akov
23/01/08

Tzvi Pantanowitz's voice was well-known to listeners to Kol Israel in Eng-lish, where he worked as a reporter, editor and news presenter. His last five years at Kol Israel were spent in the Hebrew news department as "assignments editor."

Born in Klerksdorp in 1935, Tzvi made aliyah to Kibbutz Yizra'el in 1960 after qualifying as a pharmacist.

He lived with his wife Dots in Jerusalem for many years, where they raised three children. They now live in Zichron Ya'akov and have nine grandchildren.

Tell us a about your family and others who might have influenced you.
Pantz – I was born in Klerksdorp in 1935 to a family of immigrants from Lithuania. When I look back now, I see that my family was pro-foundly involved with survival. If they could get over the hump of sur-vival and keep this family together, that would have been enough for them, considering what they went through in Europe. Survival was my father's total *raison d'etre* throughout his life. My mother was a *mensch*. If anybody was an example to me it was her saying, "You must never hurt anybody that you don't have to hurt." I trace the values that have guided my life to her.

What was the Jewish content of your lives at that time?
Pantz - I was utterly turned upside down by the Holocaust. Not that I was so conscious of it. But I remember in 1943 I saw my mother stand-ing in the lounge and crying. She had just heard that the whole fam-ily had been wiped out in Europe. I can remember that as a seminal

moment for me. And then the State was declared in 1948, and all these feelings about being involved in Judaism and all the prayers about 'next year in Jerusalem', I thought we would all rise up, the Jewish people in the Diaspora, hold each other's hands, and march across the border to Palestine.

Habonim gave me an ideological framework for carrying out what I was thinking about. The two things came together and gave me another resonance so I could move on. But it came first from an emotional standpoint and the ideology just gave me a wider understanding of what I had to do.

What significance did the South African context have?
Pantz – I was politically aware in the sense that I read newspapers avidly when I was a child. So I knew what was going on, more or less. But if I look back on the way I behaved I think I was totally unaware of the political and the social ramifications of what I was doing as a person. For instance, as you know, in our house there was a room for the servant in the garden. I used to go in there quite often. The toilet had no seat and she had a candle for light. I never said a word about that, not to myself and not to my parents. I think it is a total failure of my sensitivity to what was happening around me.

I went to a dual-medium school and although I suffered in a small way from anti-Semitic remarks, in the end I fitted quite well into the system. To this day, I have a perverse sympathy for the *Boers*, because in a sense they were in a similar situation to what we were – a small people, not sure how to behave. Except that our reaction to that situation was to be correct and moral and theirs was survival and they didn't care how they treated their blacks. So, I look back in disgust at the way I behaved as a South African Jew in the South African situation.

At the time you were a student, did you not have thoughts about what could or should be done in South Africa?
Pantz – I did go to demonstrations and I remember a meeting with a Labor Party leader in a private home in 1953. He said to us, "You guys have to decide where you want to be. If you want to be involved in

South Africa it has to be a total commitment and you know the danger of being jailed. You can't pussy-foot about it, i.e. say you believe in it and not do anything about it. Or, you have to get up and leave and build up your own country." I said, "I am going to Israel. I won't be able to do anything about this situation and maybe I am too frightened of going to jail, as well." That was my decision.

When the chips are down, I think I am prepared to endanger myself. For instance, now I think the Palestinians are very much in the situation the blacks were in in South Africa, except that there I ignored it and here I don't. I have got involved with Arabs in Israel.

How did you get involved with Habonim?
Pantz – In 1945-46, post Holocaust, *Habonim* started in Klerksdorp and we were taught standard scouting things and songs, Yiddish songs like *arum der fire*. Yiddish was terribly important to me.

I went to a seminar in Meyerton when I was twelve, in 1947. The cream of *Habonim* leadership of the time was there and they had just come back from the *Machon* and they were so enthusiastic about Israel. Everything that happened at that two-week seminar just flowed into my body. I embraced it all and became part of it.

What was it that fired you up?
Pantz – Until then my life was concerned with cricket and *kennetjie* (stump) and suddenly there was substance as to what life was about. It was no longer a matter of whether you were good at school or not. There was something you could believe in. There was your nation, your identification, your culture, your music, the dancing. All these things just jelled together - the intellectual part and the emotional part. The only thing I hated was scout-craft. I was with all these wonderful people – Eli, Isaac, Meir, Muzz - and a wonderful *madricha*, Debbie. I would have followed her into the fire. There were those who challenged us with "If you are not committed to go to Israel you have no moral right to remain in the senior group, *Shomrim…*" Sometimes a dissonance emerged. The gods that inspired us stumbled, and in my eyes betrayed what they had preached.

You had to become involved with the future of the Jewish people. You couldn't just sit and talk about it. We were given a God-given chance to make a home for the Jewish people. It was now. You were history. It was a potent time historically. The emotion was the influence for me, more than the intellectual.

Where did the kibbutz idea fit in?
Pantz – When I came to Johannesburg, I lived in the *bayit* and became totally involved in *Habonim*. I had no interest in my pharmacy studies. Everything became the movement that year.

I suppose I am an extremist. Once I believe in something, I go with it. Joe Lucatz had a strong influence on me in the socialist direction. It seemed that was what I really cared about and believed in – equality, each according to his needs... all those slogans seemed to fit into what I really thought. I suppose it had a healing effect for me also. What I was doing professionally was totally in contrast to what I believed in, so I had this dissonance in my life. This just made me feel whole again.

I met Dot (wife) when I was at the *bayit*. She wanted to go back to Israel just as strongly as I wanted to.

How did the reality of kibbutz Yizra'el match what you expected?
Pantz – I loved Yizra'el. I know this is going to sound like a lie. When I came to Israel, I felt I had come home, in a real sense, not only as a physical place – emotional, cultural, and in terms of security. It was considered a border settlement. Everything came together. I was very happy. The moment our child was born things changed for Dot. And ultimately we decided to leave.

In retrospect I don't think we made a bad decision but I love Yizra'el to this day and I still see it as my home. It is a terrible thing to say but I would love to be buried there. I have got good friends there. I identify with them. I know the kibbutz is not the same as it was when we were there and that terrible things have happened. Only the rich kibbutzim have kept their way of life. It's ironical.

I was happy in that *tzrif*. I thought that is the way you are going to have to live – a bed, a book and a simple cupboard. You didn't need anything else. Everything was provided for and you were all sharing together and the *hagim* were wonderful. I was mad about that place.

Where did you get your intellectual inspiration?
Pantz – From people like Shaz (Leon Shelef). He could articulate how Jewish values should inform the way you live your life. Your *halacha*. I don't live like a socialist today but I still feel that my sympathies lie that way. In a sense, I have denied my original beliefs. We live in a nice home with a fairly decent standard of living. There are various symbolic references to my beliefs, like the car. It's an old car - I have never bought a new car. But it is an affectation. My heart is still with the people on Yizra'el and I admire them for staying.

How do you view ideologies today?
Pantz – Today I am scared of ideology. We know that communism failed and liberal socialism is possibly the best framework for advancing society. I am trying to think what we gave our children. We think that we did not pass on to our children the intense ideological involvement we felt, but I see they got something by osmosis. They are not left-wing but in their day-to-day behavior they behave like *menschen*. I think it comes from *Habonim* ideology, which I think was based on Jewish *menschlichkeit*, not something that Marx wrote. I don't think we have to regret anything we have done. The ideological mantras made us extreme. Although I still think that kibbutz was the most amazing social idea of the twentieth century. There isn't anything like it. It failed because of our human frailties.

I am proud of the moral basis that the movement gave to me to this day. That is the way I should behave in relation to my fellow man, to my family, and to the Arabs around us.

Are we upholding the idea of being *menschen*, of *halacha*, in Israel today?
Pantz – We are not. We have done some terrible things and we are doing terrible things all the time. I am involved in a group called *Si-kui*, which tries to bring Jews and Arabs together inside Israel by first

learning about each other. I am involved in the neighboring village of Jisr al Zarka and I have been down there several times in the last year. I wrote an article in the local paper, the theme of which is that just as in South Africa, you pass the village every day, see it out of the corner of your eye but you don't think about it. The only time it is reflected in the local press is when something goes wrong, whereas there is a whole universe inside there. We have kibbutzim around and Caesarea, one of the richest communities in Israel. How do they live together with the poverty of the Arab village? They don't, of course. But interesting things are happening. In the field of Arab-Jewish relations inside Israel, I am hopeful. There are lots of groups trying to do something about it.

I am doing something because I feel guilty I didn't do anything when I was in South Africa. The situations are similar but at least the Arabs have the vote here. Economically and in other ways they are discriminated against. The majority of Jews don't want to have an Arab living next to them. I would be proud to be the neighbor of families I know there.

We have gone picking olives in the territories a few times. We don't do enough. We have been supporting a family from Darfur and we try to do the right thing. That also comes from *Habonim*.

Does it trouble you that Habonim graduates are not involved?
Pantz – It does but the country has changed and so have we. I don't think Israel is always right. We should have been a light unto the nations and to ourselves. And we are not. People explain it away by saying, "Our problems are so big and we cannot handle this as well." That is an excuse, of course. We can handle survival and other things at the same time.

Is it not ironical that here we are bemoaning the shattered dream, whereas in South Africa they cannot believe the miracle?
Pantz – That is an accident of history. It could have gone the other way. There could have been a bloodbath there. We must not be too harsh on ourselves. There is something that was instilled in us which governs the way we conduct our lives and infuses most people from *Habonim* that I

know, even if they are not politically active. We have to make a distinction between day-dreaming your ethics and living your ethics. I think that just living in a fair way to your fellow man is also something. Not being active is a matter of courage of your convictions. People get tired.

I also go once a week to read Hebrew newspapers to a group of older women. I love it.

You can still go to South African Jews and say there is a challenge here. It is harder to be here than in South Africa. We need a moral leader. Ben Gurion had his limits but he did give you a sense of vision. Surely our generation will throw up somebody.

How do you look at the key choices you made in the past?
Pantz – I must admit I have few regrets. It may sound arrogant but I am glad I came on *aliyah*. This is the country I want to live in. I am proud of the fact that all my children want to live here.

Somehow this fear of survival and of the other has overwhelmed us, governing all that we do. I see lots of secular groups looking to their Jewishness and Judaism to find a moral basis to what they are doing. We did not come this far with nothing. We carry baggage, from our Jewish past, what the Holocaust did to us, the education in *Habonim*.

I am glad I went to kibbutz. I see that as the pinnacle of my life here I retreated from the ideals I had. I am not sorry about the ideology I believed in, even though it may have sounded simplistic. The only regret I have is that I have not done enough to make sure there is no poverty in this country. And that maybe I have not done enough to bring peace about. But I am trying to do it with *Sikui* - a very small chance.

Benjamin Pogrund

Jerusalem
28/02/08

Born in Cape Town, Benjamin Pogrund holds four degrees from the universities of Cape Town and Witwatersrand. He was employed by the Rand Daily Mail for 26 years, specializing in reporting black politics and existence. He was jailed for refusing to divulge an informant's identity, prosecuted for his reports exposing abusive prison conditions, and for possession of "banned" newspapers, and denied a passport for five years. He was deputy editor when the newspaper was closed in 1985. He emigrated to Britain and was chief foreign sub-editor of The Independent. After a year in Boston as editor of The World Paper, Benjamin moved to Israel in 1997 to found Yakar's Center for Social Concern, to foster dialogue, where he was Director until 2010. He has written three books, on Robert Sobukwe, Nelson Mandela, and the Press under Apartheid, and is co-editor of Shared Histories: A Palestinian-Israeli Dialogue. He is married to Anne Sassoon.

Can you tell us about people who might have influenced your thinking during your early years...
Benjamin – When I was a young teenager, I was very conscious of the political situation in South Africa and very much against what was going on in the white community. I am at a loss to explain this. It might have been through access to books because we had a lot of books in the house.

There were no influences that I can remember.

I matriculated when I was sixteen and by then I was already well formed in my view of being totally against apartheid. In *Habonim*, when I was thirteen to fourteen, I ran a group in Woodstock/Salt River and can remember bringing in coloreds from the neighborhood to have meetings with the kids. In May 1948, on the night of the elections, when the Afrikaner Nationalists won, I stood outside *The Cape Times* to see the results on a big screen – I was already politically conscious. I was fifteen. When I went to university, where there were black and colored students, it was just a natural scene for me to get into student politics.

There was a major break between me and the extreme left, which happened inside NUSAS. For various reasons I stood up against the communists in the organization and they went for me. Whoa! It was my first taste of a most vicious personal assault. It coincided at that time with my reading of Arthur Koestler's *Darkness at Noon* and also *The God that Failed*. Those two books had an enormous effect on my thinking.

What were the issues in dispute?
Benjamin – I was the national director of research in NUSAS. There was a conference and Harold Wolpe, a student at Wits, submitted a paper which I had to pass. I said it was not research, it was just Marxist polemics. I put the problem before the executive and they said they would back me. I agonized over the matter and decided not to accept it. David Cooper, a friend of mine who had, unknown to me, become a member of the Communist Party, came to see me and told me that he had been ordered by the party to run against me. I threw him out and never again spoke to him. I won the election and it was a turning point in NUSAS. From then on the Liberals dominated student politics. I was horrified that somebody could put an ideology ahead of personal friendship. It changed my outlook totally. I became vehemently anti-communist. I viewed them as inimical to South Africa as the apartheid people. I hated them and they hated me,

Life is very strange. Years later I fell in love with a woman who was a member of the underground Communist Party. The comrades used to come round to see her and they found me there, so they stopped coming.

By that time I had made a break with *Habonim*. I had intended going on *aliyah* to kibbutz Tzora and even went to *hachshara*. But my mother said, "No. First a career, then you can do what you like." And in those days one listened to one's mother. So I went to UCT and got caught up in student politics.

Of the people in *Habonim*, Len (Loony) Atkins had a profound influence on me. Also Muzz Hill. I grew up in *Habonim* on the Trumpeldor credo: "It is good to die for one's country." It took me a long time to shake off those ideas. When I came to live in Israel in 1997, I had to re-examine myself and I am not through with it either. It is worrying. Things happen here which are not very good. I write a lot and speak in defense of Israel and it is difficult because there are tricky issues.

Take us back to university days and the move to the Rand Daily Mail.
Benjamin – I got more and more involved with student politics and decided that if I was not going to go on *aliyah*, I wasn't going to preach to others that they should go. So I left *Habonim* for that reason.

As a student in Cape Town I got involved with the Liberal Party. I was a part of a group within the party, which at the time believed in what they called the 'qualified franchise', whereas we believed in a non-racial South Africa. Athol Fugard was also in our circle.

I decided to go to Johannesburg because I knew that was where things were happening. After a few months I got to know a number of black writers. I used to run meetings in Sophiatown and one night the ANC Youth League came to break up the meeting – we were intruding in a black area. I was on the stage when I saw a huge guy on the floor below me with a bottle raised above his head. I ran down, tapped him on the shoulder and said to him, "Can't we talk about this?" And he put the bottle down. We became good friends, Steve Segale.

I got a job at the *Rand Daily Mail* without a background in journalism. I was given an interview and got the job. Laurence Gandar had transformed the newspaper from the rag it had been. That was the luck of life, timing.

Laurie was writing under the name of Owen Vine and he wrote a series of amazing articles – critiques of apartheid – which created a buzz around South Africa.

The newspapers at the time were white-owned, white-run, white-staffed. There was not a single black in sight, except as cleaners and workers. The papers were aimed at white readers, the advertising was aimed at whites. Blacks didn't feature, even in news reports, except in criminal trials, in times of rioting… "last night the police shot five natives dead because they were throwing stones", and things like that. Occasionally you got a paragraph about a black leader saying something. I remember seeing a headline once: "Elsie Hall, the pianist, plays for natives". I thought this was wrong.

Through my visits to the townships I had got to know Mandela and Tambo, and I developed a close friendship with Sobukwe, who was lecturing at the university. In those days you could not meet at a café, so he used to come to our flat and I went to his home in Soweto although it was illegal. I used to sneak in. I started writing, under a pseudonym, for *Contact*, a Liberal magazine run by Patrick Duncan.

I would get word of imminent raids by the police from the crime reporter and I drew up a list of who I thought would be raided, some of whom were friends of mine. But I never tipped any of them off. I couldn't. I agonized over it. I believed in the code of ethics for journalists and I went to prison for it, for refusing to identify an informant. Secondly, I could have done it once and then I would have been finished. Eventually the *Mail* changed and we were no longer writing police stories and became more and more critical of the police and the torture was starting and the deaths and we were writing about this.

I started working full-time on black politics and gradually black lives. This was something that had never been done before. By this time I had resigned from the Liberal Party. What I wrote as a reporter and what I wrote under my own name were two different things. As a reporter I was dispassionate. I became African Affairs reporter and started covering the surrounding countries.

This was the late fifties and the ANC was in turmoil. They had tried a defiance campaign and all sorts of things against the government that were described as: action>reaction>counter-action. The government would do something, the ANC would respond, and then the government would clamp down on them. Scores of people were being raided and arrested, the Treason Trial was running, there was a lot of agitation, marches, people were being shot, and in parliament the apartheid laws were being rammed through. The press was slowly waking up, following the lead of the RDM (*Rand Daily Mail*).

Black education became one of my passions, and poverty wages. I did the first big series on malnutrition. I went through the country writing about starvation and was denounced in parliament as a liar for it.

Did you want to stay in South Africa when the paper was closed down?
Benjamin – The *Rand Daily Mail* was closed down in 1985. If I'd had a job I would have stayed but I was filled with despair about the country. My friends were in jail, murdered, and the country was in a terrible state. My son was thirteen. I could see five years down the line he would be eligible for military service and if you refused to serve you could go to jail for six years. I did not want to do that to him. I was just sickened by the place and we left. I was lucky to be able to get into Britain.

What are your views on the notion of 'the man and his time' with regard to de Klerk's role in the transition to majority rule?
Benjamin – I liked de Klerk because he had a sense of humor and I think that is wonderful in a politician. He was a conservative but we got on well. He was elected as a conservative. I did not anticipate what happened. I thought these guys were *bitter einders*, that they would fight to the bitter end, like they did during the Anglo-Boer War. I saw lots of horrible things happening and de Klerk was part of that. But something happened in him.

Sampie Terreblanche, professor of economics at Stellenbosch, says that the big turn came in August 1985 when the American banks refused to roll over the loans to South Africa. The rand dropped in value by fifty percent overnight. That was the beginning of the end. The then governor of the Reserve Bank told the cabinet it was finished, that apartheid was over. They could hold the situation but the townships were becoming ungovernable. The economy was screwed.

From then on it was a rearguard action. My reading is that de Klerk thought he had to give way but he thought he could control the situation, that they were going to ride the tiger. They were not yielding. They believed they were going to go on holding power and give a semblance of power to blacks. This is an important point here. Human events cannot be controlled, whatever the leaders want. Once you inject an element of change, as happened in South Africa, it can go anywhere. Also, the Nats got outplayed by the ANC, by the lawyers.

How do you feel about the current situation in South Africa?
Benjamin - Skweyiya, the Minister of Public Works made a statement in which he said it was an impossible task to turn South Africa round. The problems are so immense they cannot be solved in the foreseeable future. A lot of this is the heritage of apartheid.

I used to make the point in my editorial writing: the longer apartheid goes on, the more difficult the transition will be. Mandela gave the place a grace period of reconciliation but he did not get to grips with the problems. Mbeki was meant to save the situation but he failed on AIDS and on health.

People say crime was not as bad under apartheid. That is rubbish. The townships were murder places. The police didn't give a damn. People forget that. It has become equalized. But the crime is terrifying.

All these problems are there and I don't think they can overcome them easily.

After all this, how did you land up in Israel?
Benjamin – Over the years, I was somewhat disconnected from Israel, though not really. I came to Israel several times as a guest of the government.

Then our eldest boy came on *aliyah* and we started having this contact with Israel. We had close friends here. Compared to South Africa, journalism in London was boring. Then I stumbled across Yakar and got to know Rabbi Mickey Rosen. Somehow I got involved in organizing discussion meetings. I went to America, Mickey came on *aliyah* and kept saying to me I should come and do the same thing in Israel that we were doing in London but on a bigger scale.

We went to South Africa and nearly stayed. We were very happy there. Then we came here to start this dialogue center. I have kept it small. I do projects with Palestinians and I run meetings.

How do you balance your thoughts about Israel today with what you write in articles for the Guardian, for instance?
Benjamin – When I first came, I used to say it was like apartheid, etc. I only began to focus in detail shortly before the Durban Conference in 2001. I had never been associated with government but after I was sent material that was coming out of Tehran, I was outraged by the lies about Israel and I agreed to join the official Israeli delegation. My stance was that in public I would not criticize the government but in private I would say what I liked.

I don't go along with the idea that Israel is perfect. No society in the world is perfect. I say we are doing horrible things but then try to explain it and discuss it within the context and also look to the future.

What disturbs you about Israel?
Benjamin – At this stage I am concerned, firstly, about the settlements. I think we are digging our graves. I believe in the Jewish State. I am an old-fashioned Zionist. I believe in the state for survival, a haven. I visited Auschwitz and that reinforced my view totally. On one of my trips to Israel I was taken by the Ministry to Yad Vashem on the first morning. After that, everything I saw was in terms of survival.

What we are doing now is going to destroy the Jewish State. Two years ago, in an article, I was derisive about people who support the one-state solution. Now I don't feel the same way and I have heard a friend saying we have passed the point of no return. I hope to God she is wrong. Those settlements are going to make two states impossible. And the occupation also brutalizes the Palestinians and it brutalizes us.

When I talk abroad, I always talk about my own personal experience. Some years ago I was in hospital. My surgeon was a Jew, my anesthetist was an Arab, the nurses were a mixture. Half the patients were Jewish, half were Arab. I watched the interplay between people and it was wonderful to see. I have seen the same thing when my daughters gave birth. I tell people in South Africa – same facilities, same treatment. Are you telling me that is apartheid?

The establishment religion worries me enormously. I think it is intolerant. You can count on one hand the number of rabbis who talk up for behaving decently as Jews.

I often refer to the lessons that can be drawn from South Africa. One of the most important ones is making contact. In the worst days of apartheid people maintained contact. There were enough people who knew each other and trusted each other. So my mantra in my work is: make contact, create trust. You have got to have it to make peace. And that is why I work with Palestinians. The place is worse than South Africa in some ways because of the passions and the hatred. Here you have the religious element which you did not have in South Africa. In South Africa the churches played a big role in ending apartheid. Here religion leads to division.

Another lesson is non-violence. In 1961, when the ANC took a decision to engage in violence they took a decision not to kill white civilians. That was crucial, because apart from a few isolated instances, whites did not fear being driven into the sea. I keep telling Palestinians, "You have driven most Israelis to the right, with suicide bombing."

Is there anything that you can see on the horizon that could change things dramatically here?
Benjamin – Not boycotts. Boycotts are not a principle but a tactic and you apply them according to the situation. They don't always work. It was part of the factor in South Africa but not as great as many say. It won't work here.

What will work?
Benjamin – I think American pressure.

Do you think there is going to be American pressure?
Benjamin – I think Bush has betrayed all of us. The Americans have let the settlements go on. I just hope that the next American administration really pushes. That is the only way we are going to do things. It might be too late because we might simply tell the American to go and get lost.

What do hear from the Palestinian side?
Benjamin – It depends who you talk to. Someone I work with says *Fatah* are totally corrupt and *Hamas* are a bunch of thugs. We have this problem with *Hamas*: we don't want to talk to them and they don't want to talk to us. They want to talk at the moment because we are killing them. We are talking to them behind the scenes, possibly through a third party. We'll have to talk. No country in the world can tolerate those rockets. What are we going to do?

What I like is the Saudi Peace Initiative. I am sorry we are not going along with it. The Gulf states are changing. They are investing and building. They want stability. We should be exploiting this.

You are not a young man anymore. How do you keep going?
Benjamin – There is so much to write. South Africans were treated like pariahs and that is happening to us. People are seeing images on television and reading things, most of which are accurate, but extremists are picking up grains of truth and using them against Israel. You can't just stand by and let it happen. You have got to fight it. How, is another matter.

Gideon Shimoni

Jerusalem
21/07/08

Gideon Shimoni was born in Johannesburg in 1937. He was active in the Habonim youth movement, serving as its Secretary-General in 1959-1960. He graduated with a BA (hons) in History from Witwatersrand University. In 1961 he married Toni Block and they settled in Israel, where he completed postgraduate studies, MA and PhD. degrees at the Hebrew University of Jerusalem. He was concurrently a lecturer at the Institute for Youth Leaders from Abroad in Jerusalem. In 1966 he served as an educational Shaliach for Jewish students at South African Universities. From 1971 he was on the faculty of the Hebrew University as a lecturer in Jewish History and Contemporary Jewry, and also held the Argov Chair in Israel-Diaspora Relations, until his retirement as a full professor in 2005. Over the years, he directed several international conferences of Jewish intellectuals and community leaders convened under the auspices of Presidents of the State of Israel, and lectured at universities and publicly in many countries. His academic publications include a major study -- The Zionist Ideology, and also Jews and Zionism: The South African Experience and Community and Conscience: The Jews in Apartheid South Africa.

How did Hebrew come to be spoken in your South African household?
Giddy - My parents happened to be one of a few dozen couples known to me who, after coming to Palestine as *chalutzim*, mostly from Lithuanian towns, ended up in South Africa, thinking that it was a temporary stay. This was my parents' social environment, and I grew up as part of its second generation. These families used to get together on Friday nights and much of what they did was conducted in Hebrew. One interesting thing about them is that almost all did come back to Israel, in

most cases after their children had done so.

Most of the children in these families grew up in homes that were permeated with an implicit Zionist atmosphere. I don't remember any time in my life when it wasn't crystal-clear to me that when I grow up, I would "go on *aliyah*", as South African Jews customarily phrased it. It was axiomatic. My first language was Yiddish and I spoke Yiddish with my brother and cousins until the age of about six. I had some difficulty with English when I first came to grade one.

My parents never really invested in having a future in South Africa, but ended up staying about thirty-eight years and both my older brother, Emanuel and I were born there. They flourished when they eventually came back to Israel in 1968 and lived nearby to our home in Jerusalem.

When did you join Habonim?
Giddy - I was about eleven. But the first camp I went to was a *Bikkur Holim* camp. Our family had never been on a holiday, except for a few days to Parys, on the Vaal. We were really not well off and lived in rather poor circumstance. In those days in Doornfontein our toilet was not even inside the house, it was in the back yard.

I got involved in *Habonim* through a friend who told me that the uniform was much better than the *Bnei Zion* uniform and I agreed to go. There was a very fine unit of *shtilim* – *Mashtela* Trumpeldor - that met at the Jewish Government School.

Coming from my home background, I didn't need *Habonim* to turn me into a Zionist. Very quickly I found myself almost being in the position of a *madrich* within my peer group. We did not have a *madrich* who was good enough to lead us so we arranged that we would function without a *madrich*. I conducted most of the *sichot*. We won every *hitcharut* competition. At the age of fifteen, I decided I was not going to camp and went to work at *hachshara* in Brits instead.

Were there other movements active at this time?
Giddy - All the movements were strong in the Doornfontein area. *Hashomer Hadati* (later *Bnei Akiva*) was strong, and the debate

between the movements influenced us. For example, for a time we decided there was not enough Judaism in *Habonim* and we started going to the Wolmarans Street Synagogue as a group. At one point, I was asked to participate in a 'living newspaper' of the Zionist Federation where I spoke about my plan to live in Israel and it was just a matter of choosing what kibbutz to live on.

Was the kibbutz ideal central to Habonim at that time?
Giddy – Absolutely. No question about it. All the *madrichim* that we looked up to were already on *hachshara*, including my brother, Emanuel, who was not in *Habonim* but in the Zionist Socialist movement and one of the founders of *Dror*.

How many of these people landed up on kibbutzim?
Giddy - A fair percentage. Some of them ended up in other places all over the world.

Where did South Africa figure in all of this?
Giddy - My exposure to thinking about what was going on in South Africa started under the influence of Gerald Fredman, a wonderful *madrich*. He was very socially concerned, charismatic, and intellectual. Our seminar programs included quite a lot of discussions about what was happening in South Africa.

The other influence on me was the *chalutz* leadership core of the movement. This led to studying socialist texts. My first reading of the *Communist Manifesto* was within the framework of the movement and it made a tremendous impact on me. It was clear to us that the members of the *chalutz* group – those who were "on *hachshara*", as the phrase went, were the spearhead of the movement. When I was a kid, they had already accomplished the transformation of the movement from a Jewish scout movement to a Zionist *chalutz*-oriented youth movement.

Was there serious debate in Habonim about getting involved in the South African struggle?
Giddy - That happened later when we were already *madrichim*. In

that period there were members who became very critical of the move-ment. One of the critical points was the soul-searching dilemma of conscience in 1960, when we were asked to participate in the national anniversary celebrations in Bloemfontein. I was *mazkir* of the move-ment at the time. We consulted with the Zionist Federation and they said, "You can't refuse." *Habonim* had special status and was recog-nized as a movement representing Jews in South Africa, parallel to the *Voortrekker* movement and the Boy Scouts. We reluctantly went ahead and did it. Some people threatened to leave the movement as a result.

Our view on internal Zionist politics was where we differed from *Hashomer Hatzair*, not on *chalutziut*. They were connected to Kibbutz Artzi and *Mapam* and were extremely dogmatic. We argued that *Ha-bonim* was not party-political. *Habonim* was *halutzik* but not socialist. The term that we used was *klaliyut* (generality). We turned it into an ideological position. We said, "As a youth movement we determine our path ourselves, we do not take dictates from senior parties." Therefore there was no sense of declaring ourselves a socialist movement. There were people with socialist views and there was a general appreciation of the Marxist interpretation of history, but we were not affiliated to any political group. We stuck very strictly to that.

Did you never consider South Africa as the place for your struggle?
Giddy - In my generation, say from 1956 till 1961, the arguments were mainly about how far the movement should go in participating in things that were government-sponsored. People who believed that they wanted to fight for the cause in South Africa had already left the movement. Very few of my circle pushed off and went to fight against apartheid. One or two of my friends, mainly from *Hashomer Hatzair*, did that.

Do you think that this period was a watershed in the sense that people were making choices between broader humanitarian values, expressed as wanting to fight the South African cause, and narrower Zionist values?
Giddy - The stage at which these dilemmas became activated was once people were at university. At university, people were exposed much

more intensely to ideas and activities of involvement in the resistance in South Africa. Then it would be reflected in discussions inside the movement, over concrete things such as: do we join the bus boycott march of the people of Soweto and Alexandria? And how actively do you get involved in the actions of the anti-apartheid student movement? Some said one should do something, even something small, while one was still in South Africa. Others said it was "all or nothing", and in the end it would be at the expense of *aliyah*. The balance of opinion was definitely against serious involvement locally. The Zionist cause and the personal planning of one's *aliyah* had priority.

We talked a lot about what was going to happen in the future. There was a sense that within who knows how many years the Jews of South Africa will start being persecuted and the crunch will come. Then it will become necessary to bring all the Jews to Israel. Everything had to be on the basis that we were preparing for that time. There was the sense that this is what is going to happen – a classic historical repetition of what happens to Jews in the *golah*. This speculation went on into the early sixties.

There wasn't an actual split in the movement between those who said the movement should devote itself to the anti-apartheid struggle in South Africa and those opposing such active involvement. There was a certain amount of personal conflict, a few got pulled into the student movement and they generally left the movement. Between 1956–1961 most of us were deeply involved exclusively in the movement, although extremely unhappy about living in apartheid South African society.

When I was *mazkir* of *Habonim*, I was open-minded about the issue of the movement not dictating kibbutz *aliyah* as its only goal. Although I personally was in favor of kibbutz as the goal, I was very much against making it an imperative.

Do you think that the focus on Zionism precluded a more universal set of values?

Giddy – No, it didn't. As a Jewish youth movement, our primary orientation was humanistic in a universal sense. It involved a goodly measure of socialist belief about the world. But it was the Zionist-Socialist conception that this could only be realized by first normalizing the situation of the Jews through Zionism. It was not viable while you were in the Diaspora. Our conception was that through *aliyah* and one's life in Israel, one is participating ultimately in the most universal of causes.

In retrospect, as a scholar whose field is largely the history of Zionism, I see this conception as part and parcel of labor Zionist ideology as it had already been prevalent in Eastern Europe. The difference was that in Eastern Europe Jews themselves were the persecuted group, whereas in South Africa our special dilemma arose from the fact that we were part of the privileged group.

My interest in ideologies led me to write something on this subject as a university student. Its theme was 'Jewish Universalism and Particularism'. What I articulated was that particularistic Jewish values and universalistic human values were incompatible in the condition of Diaspora that we were experiencing in South Africa. Our allegiance to Jewishness and the Jewish community clashed with universalistic allegiance and you had to choose between the two, which meant that, in terms of your values, you were living as a split person. The community was saying: "Do what you think you ought to do against the system in South Africa, but not as a Jew." This was tantamount to an abdication of Jewish values. You were told not to practice the very values that should have been coming from your Jewishness. This dichotomy made it impossible to be a man and a Jew at one and the same time. This was what *galut* meant in the South African situation. I argued, in retrospect rather naively, that this dichotomy could only be resolved through *aliyah*, because living in a Jewish autonomous environment meant that everything one does is at one and the same time Jewish and human.

Did you consider going to kibbutz?

Giddy - Yes. I personally had no doubt about going to kibbutz. What affected me in not going with a *garin* was that Toni had come back from the *Machon* absolutely convinced that kibbutz was not for her. So between us it was a serious issue. The second thing that affected me was my brother. After *hachshara*, he had come on *aliyah* and was a member of kibbutz Tzora and his wife was very unhappy. I did not want to come to kibbutz knowing in advance that the chances were that I would find myself leaving because Toni would not be happy. A lot of people felt that the kibbutz could be used as a way of easing one's integration into Israel but I felt that this went against my own sense of integrity.

Bearing in mind the relatively low number of ex-South Africans who have remained on kibbutz, do you think *chalutzik aliyah* was an appropriate ideology for South African youth?
Giddy - Yes I do. Absolutely. I think that the kibbutz did embody and focus the pre-eminent ideals of the movement. It was the way in which the movement was part and parcel of Zionism, of the labor movement in Zionism. The fact of the matter is that those members who did not think that kibbutz life was for them simply didn't go to kibbutz.

By contrast, the South American youth movements undermined themselves by their exclusive emphasis on kibbutz. In South African *Habonim* there were people who made it clear that it was never their intention to go to kibbutz. When I decided not to be part of the *garin*, Toni and I went ahead with our *aliyah* and were not ostracized for not coming with the *garin*. We did feel a bit *lo naim* because in our own minds, in principle, the most important thing was still the kibbutz.

If you could say that a lot of people were prevented from coming to Israel because of the emphasis on kibbutz, as happened in some *chalutzik* youth movements, then you might say this was a very bad thing.

And yet there are those who claim that their kibbutz experience had an adverse effect on their lives...
Giddy - I think it is very individual. I do not think that people's lives were harmed by a period on kibbutz. It might apply to some people, but not to others. For many people, it was a major part of their life, a formative experience in their personal lives, and they managed well in whatever they did afterwards. No regrets.

You could apply the same assessment to *aliyah* in general, especially given the disappointment with what has happened in Israel over the years. Some would say that the movement's influence, leading to *aliyah* spoilt their own personal welfare. Others will say it was a positive part of their lives.

Nevertheless, was there not a certain mismatch between the reality of kibbutz and the movement education about kibbutz?
Giddy - That is only because of what has happened in later years. The kibbutz ceased being for Israeli society what it was, say, up to the sixties. Anita Shapiro has written very beautifully about this phenomenon. The society changed, but people went on speaking anachronistically as if the former values still hold, until their dream was shattered. And that is what happened to the kibbutz as a movement and that is why the kibbutz lost its real power of attraction.

Would you agree that despite our desire to live a full Jewish life in Israel and our sincere commitment to Jewish culture, Habonim did not provide an in-depth Jewish education?
Giddy - This is a very difficult aspect to ponder because I can only answer it from a personal point of view. From my personal perspective, living in Israel the way I do is a natural and satisfactory fulfillment of the Jewishness that I had before coming. Living as a self-fulfilled secular Jew is much more possible for me in Israel than it would be if I lived in the Diaspora, especially the South African part of the Diaspora. If anything, this sense has been strengthened by my reaction to all sorts of things that have to do with the moral record of the politics of those who are strictly religious.

I am very skeptical about so-called inherent Jewish values. The values are imposed onto the Jewish tradition. What we have difficulty explaining is exactly where they come from and how. In other words, Judaism is in a sense value-neutral in crucial matters of society and politics. Those who come to it with liberal conceptions and values read these into Judaism. Those who come with opposite conceptions and values can equally read theirs into Judaism and find in its tradition all the proof-texts they need. The idea that unequivocal social values inhere in Judaism is a myth. Actually, this is an argument that has been going on within the Zionist movement since Ahad Ha'am published a famous article, in which he argued that what is unique about Judaism is its value emphasis on *Tzedek*.

Interestingly, in my book *Community and Conscience: The Jews in Apartheid Society* this is what I conclude in my attempt to explain how it is that some Jews held that Jewish values made it imperative to actively oppose apartheid, whereas others did not interpret Jewish values in that way at all. Indeed, I found a negative correlation between the degree of Jewish religiosity and the degree of liberal opposition to the apartheid system. The ones who were liberal read it into their Judaism. They were a minority.

Following on from that – today virtually all aliyah from the west is comprised of religious people. There is hardly any *aliyah* based on secular values. What does this mean for Israel?
Giddy - This is a process that we are not going to be able to change. This type of *aliyah* from the west is contributing to religious-nationalist fervor in the country and I expect it is going to get worse. You feel it particularly in Jerusalem, which is moving more and more in that direction. It has affected my own family. My son is moving out of Jerusalem particularly because he doubts the prospects for non-orthodox education of his children. He believes that the options for him and his children in Jerusalem are going to close. Here in Beit Hakerem we are an island. We should declare ourselves an independent secular republic (Laughs). The *aliyah* that is coming is feeding into this trend.

Those of us who have a secular cultural approach to our Jewishness will become increasingly what sociologists refer to as a cognitive minority, which has its advantages, because cognitive minorities become creative and they have a cause. We also have to hope that there will be a degree of gradual sobering-up from the national-religious fervor. We are living in an historical cycle of religious revival and it will play itself out eventually but, I think, beyond our lifespan. The interesting thing is that the period of our upbringing and youth was when the historical swing was still the other way.

In your book *Community and Conscience*, the phrase you used to describe the dominant mode of the political behavior of the South Africa Jewish community is 'bystander quietism.' Are you not surprised that the phrase sounds like an appropriate description of Habonim graduates in Israel who are content to limit their expression of idealism to voting for leftist parties?

Giddy - I think it results from our background as big fish in a small pond that then become small fish in a big pond. The environment into which we entered was so much more ramified and more established than we were able to cope with as immigrants. We turned inwardly to ourselves. Another factor is that there was a considerable material strain to actually make ends meet, which occupied the formative years of our lives in Israel. In those early years many people were involved with bringing up their children and throughout the world that is a phase when people turn inwardly to themselves and are less involved in societal matters, except perhaps in South Africa where people had a support system that allowed them time for those activities. A lot of the people who were very active in South Africa had servants to look after their children.

The people who are a greater surprise in this regard are those who went to kibbutz. One would have expected that they would have produced many more active people in political life.

Do you think that at the same time there has been an erosion of values?

Giddy - I think social values have lapsed somewhat, which may indeed indicate that they were not very deep in the first place. People conformed to the preached norms when they were in the movement, but they tend to become conservative as they get older. It is a great disappointment to find how many *olim* from South Africa, including graduates of the movement, have views that I would consider abominable on issues concerning conflict or peace with the Palestinians and the future of *Yehuda and Shomron*, for instance. You can't assume that people who came on *aliyah* through *Habonim* are all 'progressive' in their political orientation. I conclude that these are people who are reverting to type and their liberalism wasn't very deep in the first place.

But the more general question of why people from the movement didn't become heavily involved politically or have not been more critical of the mainstream is interesting. A lot of them might be disappointed about the way Israel has changed, but this disappointment does not express itself by going out onto the streets to demonstrate. The few people who have gone out on a limb seem to have done so as part and parcel of their professional lives, for instance as academics.

You have argued very strongly against the use of the word apartheid in the Israeli-Palestinian context. But what are the lessons we can learn from recent South African history?
Giddy - The main thing that I have been at pains to do is to show that there is no empirical foundation for comparing the apartheid system to what we do vis-à-vis the Israeli Palestinians. At the same time, to show that there is a segment of Israeli society, mainly the national-religious segment, which has a conception of what Israel should become through holding on to occupation of the entire West bank, that is very much comparable to the conception once held by the *verligte* elite of apartheid's proponents.

In terms of conflict resolution is there something we can learn from South Africa?
Giddy - What we can learn from South Africa is: a. What we are doing is not moral, and b. It won't work. In South Africa, the *verligtes* eventually realized that it was not working, it couldn't be sustained. When the Soviet Union collapsed, the communist bogey fell aside, which allowed the Afrikaner elite to say, "Now is the time to negotiate a solution." Most Afrikaners believed that de Klerk would succeed in negotiating the kind of solution that would preserve white's group interests. He succeeded partially, in the first phase. Now they are at a crossroads and even committed people are concerned.

I was told that when de Klerk was here on a visit a few years ago he said, "For God's sake, you have the possibility of partition. We never had it. You have got to take it." That was his message. That's a very telling lesson. I think most of Israeli society accepts it.

Looking at your journey from Doornfontein to Jerusalem, how would you describe your life in terms of the way it has turned out in relation to the things that were important to you?
Giddy - Completely good and satisfactory personally, but I'm extremely worried about our collective future in Israel and deeply upset at the imminence of a nightmarish situation. That we would willy-nilly be doing the kind of things that so appalled us in the years we lived in South Africa. I would never have thought in 1961, when we came to live in Israel, that the time would come when that nightmare would loom so large.

From a collective perspective it is both worrying and hard to be optimistic. As an historian looking back, every major change that has taken place in this arena came after a war: the 1948 war, the Six Day war, the Yom Kippur war, and the *intifadas*. Each time, complacency settles in and the only thing that will shake it is something very terrible, like war.

I try to make a distinction between these things and one's personal life. The achievements of Israeli society are fantastic in so many respects but this nightmare of what we are going to become if we go on suppressing the Palestinians… It is not entirely our fault. We see what they are doing after we have left Gaza to them, and that they will do the same thing from *Yehuda and Shomron*. And we know that the *Hamas* is likely to take over there too.

I don't relish discussing these things with my son and daughter, both born here. They seem to live their lives without thinking too much about the political situation. The last thing I would want is to encourage them to be disillusioned. Fortunately, they don't let these things disturb their lives. The question of where values come from is fascinating. I am fond of the statement that values cannot be taught, they can only be caught.

Itz Stein

Herzlia
21/08/07

Originally from Benoni, Itz Stein was a member of Habonim and later became mazkir of the movement in Cape Town. He made aliyah in 1956 and studied history at the Hebrew University.

Itz was a professional Zionist in the full sense of the word. He was the Director of the Telfed office for five years and spent two years as an Aliyah Shaliach in Cape Town. He was a member of the Executive Council of Telfed, an active member of various committees. In his later years he was elected as a member of the Board of Governors of Telfed.

Itz played a role in the activities of a number of kibbutzim where South Africans had settled. He assisted with the establishment and running of Hostels for olim in Givatayim, Efrat and Kochav Yair. He was seriously wounded while serving in the army but never allowed his suffering to affect his positive disposition. After retiring, he developed an abiding interest in plants and biology. Itz was married to Shirley. They had four children and nine grandchildren.

Itz was ill at the time of this interview and passed away on 28th of April 2009.

Were there contemporaries and friends of yours whose decision to stay in South Africa had to do with the struggle for black freedom?
Itz - There were a few. One prominent one was Albert Kushlik. He was very involved in what he called "The Freedom Movement", when he went to varsity. On one occasion I nearly became involved by association. My whole background was a Zionist and Jewish one. At home, we spoke Yiddish. I was the *mazkir* of *Habonim* in Cape Town when I had a phone call from Barry Fabian. He asked me to meet a black man who was on the run and looking for a way to skip the country. I met him, but

his friends from the Communist Party put him up for the night. The next morning I took him to the harbor and he sailed off from there. For the life of me, to this day I can't remember his name. This was 1954 and would have been considered very revolutionary and dangerous by the movement.

It is not as though we ignored what was going on around us. We used to discuss it a lot but we decided that our place was here. We were not optimistic about the future in South Africa. We saw our role in Israel as part of the endeavor to be a light unto the nations. This was a very strong belief.

Did your experience working for Telfed lead you to any conclusions about South African *olim*? Are there generalizations to be made?
Itz - *Aliyah* in the 1950's was very strongly ideological, and influenced very little by South African issues. After Sharpeville there was a large group who wanted to get out of South Africa. When I was at Telfed after 1966, a lot of the *olim* were very difficult. They had huge demands and unrealistic expectations. There was very little Zionist background or motivation there. That hasn't changed all that much over the years. Apart from religious *olim*, *aliyah* for many has not been an ideological decision. It is the last choice for those who can just cannot make it to Australia or Canada.

South Africans are a positive element in that they look to do things. They have made a significant contribution to changing the face of Ra'anana. But this is not coming from an ideological position. South Africans are go-getters. They get things done.

Would it be true to say that South Africans who did come from this ideological background have slotted into an Israeli mentality and not really been prepared to go against the current?
Itz - I think that is true to a large extent and it is difficult to explain why. We are deeply influenced by Israeli society. Israeli society is anti- to a large extent. Anti-Arab, anti-this, anti- that. There is a racist element here and a lot of South Africans have brought that with them as well.

Was it realistic to expect that dynamic youth movement and com-munity leaders who rejected the lack of social justice in South Africa would become involved in this issue here as well?

Itz - A new immigrant's need to find his feet in this country, work, and master the language etc. has often proved overwhelming. Some people decided not to stay. Others get involved in their own narrow circle. The travails of absorption often determine which way a person goes. Some never learn Hebrew.

There is also the *lo naim* factor. In South Africa you were expected to behave correctly, to be accepted. Americans for example are more confrontational.

Do you think education in Habonim was naïve about Israel?

Itz - So many years ago… I'm talking about the early 1950's. We saw this as an ideal country. We idealized everything. Expectations were great but so was the downfall sometimes.

Meir Winokur

Ein Karem
20/08/07

Born in 1943 in Cape Town, Meir Winokur made aliyah in 1961. After army service he studied for a BA in Psychology and English and MA in Clinical Psychology at the Hebrew University of Jerusalem. In between he studied painting and drawing at the Art Students League in New York City and later did a Psy.D degree (Doctor of Psychology) in Clinical Psychology at Rutgers University, New Jersey. On returning to Israel, Meir undertook psychoanalytic training, and is currently a Training and Supervising Analyst and teaches at the Israel Psychoanalytic Society and Institute. For many years the Coordinator of Training at the Students Counseling Service of the Hebrew University, in Jerusalem, he is currently in private practice in Jerusalem and Tel Aviv. Meir is married with two children and lives in Jerusalem.

What role did your family play in influencing the important decisions in your life?
Meir – Both my parents were very prominent in the Cape Town Jewish community. My sister, who is seven years older than me, was in *Habonim* from early on and was on the *Machon* in 1952. I could not have had a more Zionist background and it was clear to me at the age of twelve or thirteen, that when I finished high school, I was going to go on *aliyah*.

At school round about that time, standard six, we had to give lectures in English and in Afrikaans and I had a standard lecture on the Sinai campaign. I would proudly explain the whole story in both languages.

I was very involved in *Habonim* until the age of about fourteen when a few of us kind of broke away from the movement mainstream.

We were influenced by things at the time: late fifties, beat generation, and books like *On the Road* by Jack Kerouac. We were seen by the rest of the movement as ivory tower intellectuals and we were very pleased with ourselves.

When I eventually left Cape Town at the beginning of 1961, I saw it more like an adventure. But it could not have been by chance that the adventure started by volunteering for *Machal*, the Israeli army. I had to do some weight-lifting in order to improve my posture. And it could not have been by chance that I have stayed here.

If somebody had asked me at the time why I was doing what I was doing I would have recognized it as being some kind of a Zionist thing. I would have added an angle about it being some kind of adventure, something about apartheid. I used to work for the Liberal Party in the last few years of high school.

My sister was very involved in the SRC and was very anti-apartheid, and we were too. We were perhaps the only unit in *Habonim* to bring black people to come to talk to us about what the black experience was like in South Africa. We had a small band with a colored man who was a jazz pianist. We were very much engaged in that and the adventurous spirit of the beat generation, at the same time as the Zionist agenda.

Can you tell us a bit more about what set the tone at that time, people, books, etc....
Meir – We were four friends. In the last two years of school we used to get drunk together, girlfriends together, go to retreats in a place called Kronendaal. It was a big adventure and we lost interest in the old Zionist stuff. Nevertheless, I was quite still quite prominent in *Habonim*. I was arts editor of the *Habonim* newspaper and *rosh kevutzah miztayen* at a national seminar and I was proud of it.

We also had our own private, rebellious things: anti-apartheid, anti-anything establishment, including the *Habonim* establishment. We thought we were seen as a bad influence and we were proud of it. I was probably influenced by the fact that my father died when I was fourteen, which perhaps contributed to my rebelliousness.

How did this young intellectual rebel land up in the Israeli army?
Meir – I would say now that the main reason I chose that avenue was to prove myself and my manliness. The army was attractive also because I thought I was going to stay on in Israel and it meant only half-time service and it had other benefits if I was going to remain in Israel. I also imagined that I would go back to South Africa on a visit and show all the girls I was this great returning hero from the Israeli army. And there was also some Zionist spirit there.

Did the madrichim not try to draw your group into the movement?
Meir – Our *madrich* was the supreme 'bad influence', part of the story of doing our own thing. I remember the gym teacher at school, a big guy, who, in front of the whole school said to Rafi (one of the gang of four) who was talking when we were supposed to be singing hymns, "Altman, I hear you are a beatnik over the weekends." It wasn't so extreme. We got a little drunk on Saturday nights. I read books like Aldous Huxley's *The Doors of Perception* with interest but we did not take drugs. And we continued to participate in *Habonim* activities, as I remember it.

Was the anti-apartheid struggle ever an alternative for you?
Meir – Yes. If I had been asked then, I would have said that it would not have been right to live in South Africa without acting against the government but I was aware of what the dangers were. It was a difficult decision but I decided that my direction was Israel, which was a deeper part of my identity.

What was your image of the Israeli army before you enlisted?
Meir – A lot of it was imaginary. On the one hand, I imagined becoming a soldier-hero; on the other I thought the army gave you short pants, a *kova tembel* and you went around with a shaft of wheat in the corner of your mouth and an Uzi over the shoulder. I had a naïve, mixed up view of Israel, army and kibbutz. I hoped to find a home. I don't think I ever thought about killing Arabs but there was something about borders and developing the image of a fighting person.

We have noticed that siblings from our background have often taken different paths. Has that been an issue for you?
Meir – By the time I went to Israel, my sister (see interview with Shula Marks) was already living in London. Because I did not feel that I was doing it out of Zionist ideology, I did not disapprove of her landing up in London, and what is more, she was thinking at that point of coming to Israel. So there was no conflict at that level. I did have a conflict with her in 1967 during the Six Day War. She had become quite left-wing in London and she had an even-handed view of the tragic situation in the Middle East, as an historian. I was in *milium*, opposite *Givat Hatahmoshet* (battle site in Jerusalem). I saw horrifying things going on around me. She was horrified at this catastrophe in the Middle East and I was very identified with Israel. At that point, it irritated me that she could be so internationalist from the privacy of her well-carpeted apartment in London. And that goes on to this day, to some extent, albeit not in the same tone. I have also shifted. I see the Israeli- Arab conflict as a more two-sided thing.

Are you saying that your views have moved closer to hers?
Meir – Generally, yes. But not when the bombs are going off. I cannot think about the (Palestinian) refugees when that is happening. I do think that Israel has made some terrible mistakes. I do see it as a two-sided situation, which I didn't when I first came here. Even at the time of the 1967 war it did not get close to the point of a cut-off in the relationship and tensions tended to subside when we were not in the shadow of an immediate conflagration.

Where do you stand on human rights and social justice issues in Israel?
Meir – I am a member of the Labor party but only because I forgot to cancel my membership after I joined to support Sali Reshef years ago. I was identified with Peace Now and that is where I would put myself politically. I was never a very active member. I do have concerns but I am not politically-oriented. I do go to demonstrations. I was there the night Rabin was murdered. Our kids were with us and we came back

here distraught. My sentiments are there and they have not become any more or any less extreme. They have become more differentiated and I am clearer about why I think what I think. It is somewhere between active engagement and disinterest. I am certainly not totally disinterested.

At times, I do think that things seem to be so noxious here, across the board - the quality of political life, the dishonesty of politicians. At certain moments, I find it very bothering, and it includes Israeli military actions when they seem unjustified. This does not mean that I automatically side with the Arab side or that I condemn things across the board. I do think that the occupation is central and I have been opposed to it from 1967. I voted for the *Reshimat Hashalom* at that time. Sometimes I feel it is so depressing and so obnoxious.

I sometimes think that the price we pay for having a Jewish State is not worth it. We don't have what we were brought up on in *Habonim* – light unto the nations, equality. People are out to screw one another. It is difficult to find an honest person to give you the right advice at more or less the right price, say to fix the air conditioning.

I am engaged in my work and I do not have the energy or the interest to be politically involved and I am really turned off about many elements of life in Israel today although I have a satisfying life here and don't entertain the possibility of leaving. I do sometimes wonder why not, considering the nuclear threat to this country.

To what extent have you tried to pass your ideas onto your children?
Meir – That's quite heavy. I have not adopted the kind of position that would allow me to educate someone in my footsteps. I would like to think of myself as a decent human being and hope that my children have taken something of that. My son did not want to go into the army and I was quite conflicted about it because I came here as a volunteer. But from where I was at that point, I could, somewhat ambivalently, put myself behind his clear-cut intention to get out of the army. My daughter, on the other hand, became a shooting instructor in the army. And neither of them is politically involved though their views are

similar to ours. My son did fight for a black musician not to be deported from Israel. He is a soldier in the army of music!

I have no sense of wanting to educate them to be anything other than decent human beings.

Elsewhere

Sidney Bloch
Sam Fanaroff
Michael Hayden
Manfred Kagan
Ronni Kahn
Richard Kuper
Shula Marks
Vivian Rakoff
Michael Schneider

Sidney Bloch

Tel Aviv
09/09/08

Sydney lives in Melbourne. The interview took place while he
was on a visit to Israel.

*A medical graduate of the University of Cape Town, Sidney trained in
psychiatry and was awarded a PhD. at the University of Melbourne. He is a
Fellow of the Royal College of Psychiatrists and of the Royal Australian and
New Zealand College of Psychiatrists.*

*Current appointments are: Emeritus Professor of Psychiatry, Adjunct Emeri-
tus Professor in the Centre for Health and Society, and Senior Fellow, School of
Philosophy, Anthropology, and Social Inquiry at the University of Melbourne;
and Honorary Senior Psychiatrist at St Vincent's Hospital, Melbourne.*

*Sidney has had Visiting Professorships in the Chinese University of Hong
Kong, the University of Hong Kong, the Hebrew University of Jerusalem, and
Columbia University.*

*He has published 13 books, several of which have been translated into nu-
merous languages. Russia's Political Hospitals (1977) won the Manfred Gutt-
macher Award of the American Psychiatric Association in 1978 for the best
book published in forensic psychiatry, and An Anthology of Psychiatric Ethics
(2006) won a commendation award from the British Medical Association in
2007. He has published over 200 articles and chapters, chiefly in the areas of
psychotherapy, psycho-oncology, and psychiatric ethics.*

*Sidney, together with his son, produced a film exploring aspects of his
South African roots. The film was screened on Australian TV in 2010.*

**Was Habonim more of an influence in shaping your ideas than the
home?**
Sidney – Once I declared to my parents that I didn't see my future in
South Africa there was never any opposition to that viewpoint. Later

on, they encouraged me to make my way to Israel. They were Zionists themselves. They belonged to the Zionist Socialist Party and would meet regularly as part of that group.

Ultimately the movement became my spiritual home - morally, socially and politically. In retrospect, morally was the most important. It gave me a place to be a person that was respectful of the human rights that one would have wanted in the broader society. Looking back, I don't know that we did all we should have done. I think you would have to say that we were much more geared towards preparing ourselves for another life in Israel than doing something about our current lives and fulfilling some of our moral aspirations.

I remember a couple of things that caused me heartache. There was one annual camp in East London where we would throw out so much food. It was terrible, morally unacceptable. We used to put the food in gigantic oil drums and I can remember on at least one occasion when the local black folk would come by and forage. Why we didn't just say, "Here's bread and other food for you," beats me to this very day. It is mind-boggling to think back to it. It was shameful. There was a certain degree of moral blindness.

I did have my solitary activist initiative in 1956, when I was fifteen. They introduced the bus apartheid system in Cape Town on that day. I hopped on the bus outside the post office and immediately noticed the new signs: In front of X whites only, etc. I sat in the wrong side of the bus in terms of the new law, which did not find favor with the conductor, who said, "I didn't make these laws but I have got to carry them out."

The conductor then stopped the bus opposite the Caledon Street police station and said, "Either you move or I take you into the police station." After a few minutes of reflection, I moved. For me it was a watershed. Later, when talking to Albie Sachs about this, he said, "Your 'mistake' was doing it on your own. If you had done it with others you would have carried on the protest."

You are talking about your sense of morality that was already well-formed...
Sidney – It would be good to know that it was. I did not agonize about protesting in the bus. I hadn't read about the American south and I am not sure if I knew then about Rosa Park's bold protest action in Alabama. It just seemed a good thing to do on the day.

At no stage in *Habonim* did we say, "We will not go to a segregated seaside resort for a picnic." I remember going to Seaforth, and enjoying a wonderful picnic. There was no sense of: "Hang on, this is a whites-only beach." I was a prototypical moral bystander. I was not a perpetrator. I wasn't acting in a way that promoted racism.

Do you think you could have done more?
Sidney – Definitely, yes. There have been many moments of regret. About inaction. Not about leaving South Africa, but about not fulfilling my moral responsibility. One thing that was alleviating (in South Africa) was my work in SHAWCO. I did my bit there for three years, working in the clinics in the shanty towns, one evening a week. There was nothing dangerous or profound about it. Most students did it but I am pleased I was one of them.

More significant than this voluntary job was my decision to combine my *wanderlust* with making a contribution and finding a morally sane place to do it, namely the rural mission hospital. I went to work in Lesotho, the Transkei, Zululand and Swaziland. I chose different places and different church denominations. They were multi-racial and the government was not watching over our shoulder. They were all terrific experiences which I'll never forget.

What was your aim in making a documentary film in South Africa?
Sidney – It is designed to serve as an educational resource for kids in Australia. The key goal is it to show the students a human story and let them know that you pay the price for moral bystanding. The idea is to use this resource to promote social inclusiveness in the school and in society generally.

Where is South Africa in your scheme of things today?
Sidney – The film has brought South Africa back into my mind in a major way. The other thing was the fortieth anniversary of our graduation class which occurred not long ago. I corresponded with some former class mates to say that we really should do something about apologizing to the twelve students of color in our class of about one hundred and ten. They were not allowed a whole range of things: going into the white only wards, attending post-mortems of white bodies, dissecting white corpses, etc. Discrimination was never raised in our six years of medical school, which is terrible.

Together with a few fellow students who had been thinking along these lines, we organized this event. Alas, only twelve people came, including only two colleagues of color. We had our conversation and we all said what we felt.

When I asked one colleague, a colored, who is now a professor, why he had not come, he said, "There is no point. Nothing has changed. You guys are still as racist as you ever were." A spokesman for the colored group said he thought meeting together was a good thing but that it was all too late. "You had your chance and you missed it," he lamented. An Afrikaner colleague then angrily declared, "It is all very well talking about the minority of non-white students but what about the minority of Afrikaans-speakers. There were only six of us and you treated us like shit." And he went on to say that he had done more by staying on in South Africa than those of us who had labeled him a racist and then run off. Intense stuff.

This sounds like South Africa in a nutshell... a real drama.
Sidney – Yes. When you consider these incidents, they remind me that we have unfinished business. In our family there has been a sense that justice must prevail. However, in another sense we are still moral bystanders.

You seemed to be on a Zionist path yourself. How were you diverted?
Sidney – Six of us went to the same hospital in Israel and did our internships. I got diverted by a romantic development and a year later

found myself in Australia.

Over the course of time, the spirit of those days of Zionism waned. I have always had a great sense of affiliation to the country. When we had to choose a place for a sabbatical ten years ago, we had no hesitation in choosing Jerusalem.

I always see this as a second home. I have always thought that when I retire, which is imminent, I would spend more time here and that is on the cards.

I have to say that my Zionism in the pure, ideological sense has waned considerably. To some extent that is linked to the moral issues here, which I would find just about impossible to deal with, because I think the occupation of the West Bank is morally indefensible.

One thing I have learned and it has taken me a long time to do so, is that it is not for me to do anything about issues that affect Israel because I am not going to bear the brunt of any convictions or arguments that I offer.

It seems that generally speaking movement graduates living outside of Israel are more critical of the country than those who live here. Do you feel that people here have lapsed into bystander apathy?
Sidney – I do not equate apathy with bystander. I think it is enough of a judgment to say, "You are a moral bystander." Being a bystander is a form of behavior: you see things you are fully aware of, you are not in denial, but you stand by. I don't believe it is through apathy because apathy means non-interest.

I think the moral bystander position as I have come to understand it through the film is possibly as difficult as is that of the victim or the perpetrator. You don't suffer directly like a victim and the perpetrator has his own conscience to deal with in the end. But the bystander is in an anomalous position. To put a judgment onto it by saying it is apathy is too simplistic. I don't know enough what the moral bystander looks like. All I know is that it is the most a common position to take, about loads of things, and we are all involved.

By and large, it is mostly: I have this life to lead. I have got these children to educate. I am not a hero and I can't take on the world. I am not ignorant of the issues around me but what am I to do as a singleton?

Many of us were committed to a cause when we were younger. With time that commitment has faded. Do you think it is simply a function of age or are there other factors?
Sidney – We were very different human beings because of our provenance. Our origins are exceptional – growing up in South Africa is one. *Habonim* was an incredibly cohesive and wonderful instrument for us to exercise our beliefs. I think that is quite unusual, if not abnormal. Obviously it was helped by the South African environment. In democratic Canada, the fervor we felt would not have been so great. Inevitably, if it was so intense then it has got a longer waning possibility.

Also, as I have seen it in myself and my *chaverim*, everybody got caught up with our lives, some coping with early illness, premature death, struggling to get careers going, and so on. Other people had opportunities elsewhere, which it would have been foolish not to take advantage of. To live with that original fervor does not seem feasible. Personally I have not lost that fervor, nor have a lot of other *chaverim*, but it is not manifested in the same way as formerly.

What is driving you? What is the passion behind it all?
Sidney – Half my professional career has been in the field of ethics. The other half is more clinical - psychotherapy.

The pursuit of ethics as an interest commenced by way of a stumble. By chance, in 1971, I came across the political misuse of psychiatry in the Soviet Union. From that point on, I became absolutely committed to the idea of learning as much about this as possible, with the goal of bringing it to the attention of the world. That was a big, ideologically driven aim - no medical person should be so perverted from their moral path as to lock up people who do not warrant the designation of 'patient'.

In 1977 together with a colleague I published a book called *Psychiatric Terror*. Then a follow-up book, and articles. Finally, in 1985, after a decade and a half, the battle was won. There was acknowledgement that "mistakes had been made" and the perpetrators were removed from office. We regarded this as a huge moral victory.

I have done much writing on ethics. I guess that one of my identities is as the psychiatrist with expertise in psychiatric ethics. I have also been involved in creating a code of ethics for psychiatrists in Australia and New Zealand. The ethics activities are something I am immensely joyful about because you want to do something worthwhile in your career.

If you could revisit the choices you made in the past would you do things differently?
Sidney – As Erik Erikson talks about in his last stage of the life-cycle: integration vs. despair – I look back at this point when I am close to retirement and say, "I have made a reasonable contribution; ethics, the Russian abuse, helping hundreds of patients, good teaching, conducting useful research, raising a family, and so on. They seem to hang together."

Sam Fanaroff

Pevensey, Sussex, England.
17/12/08

Raised in Johannesburg, Sam was a staunch member of Hashomer Hat-zair from an early age. In 1948 he made aliyah to kibbutz Beit Keshet and remained there for a year and a half.

In England, he discovered his ability to make jewelry. Working initially in copper, he developed his skills and later became a founder member of the Sussex Guild of Craftsmen, when it was set up in 1969. Sam was one of the driving forces behind the Guild, and an active member for about thirty years. He soon gained a reputation as a teacher of jewelry-making and is recognized as a leading metal-smith.

Today Sam's interests are in physics and the sub-atomic particle, and astronomy.

Sam, can we start with a bit about your background...
Sam – I joined *Hashomer Hatzair* when I was nine years old. I was dragged by my bigger sister to the first meeting house although I was far more interested in playing football than solving the Jewish problem. This was in Jo'burg in 1938 or thereabouts. I stayed in *Hashomer Hatzair* for sixteen years, until I went on *aliyah*.

My age-group was in conflict with the movement because they wanted us to stay on in South Africa and take over the running of the movement. But as we had already done four or five years of *hachshara* we were in this mad rush to get to Israel. So we broke from the movement and threatened to go on *aliyah* on our own accord.

In the end we became part of *Aliyah Bet* and went to Israel dressed as tourists.

What was it that caught your imagination in Hashomer Hatzair?
Sam – *Ezrat ha'am*. Doornfontein was virtually a *shtetl*. Many families had lost relatives in Europe. After the war we were very moved by the newsreels of people coming out of Belsen.

Part of the ideology of *Hashomer Hatzair* was to transform the Jew along the lines proposed by A.D.Gordon and Borochov.

When I was on *hachshara*, I was very proud to plough the land. I ploughed with sixteen oxen in them days. So I was very proud of this transformation. Strangely enough, the farm near Potchefstroom was called Klein Jerusalem. The Afrikaans neighbor, who had a lot of sympathy for the *Irgun* in Palestine, would say to me, "*Wel jood, hoeveel rooinekke het jy vandag geskiet?*" (Well Jew boy, how many rednecks did you shoot today?)

Were you not drawn to the South African struggle?
Sam – You had a choice. In the movement, some people did break away and identified with the African struggle. I was not prepared to do that. I saw my duties as being with 'my nation, my people'. It had real meaning about it at that time. Nowadays we can be cynical about it. There was also some anti-Semitism in South Africa, with the Ossewabrandwag. And my present nose is the result of a clash with them.

That must have affected you…
Sam – We took it in our stride in them days. I hit him with half a brick but he broke my nose and I didn't dare go home because my mother would have gone *meshuga*.

So you were in the front line against the Ossewabrandwag…
Sam – We all went to the town hall to protect the left-wing speakers, where the Ossewabrandwag and the Nazis were trying to knock them off their perch. It was not part of official *Hashomer Hatzair* policy. We did it as revolutionaries, as socialists.

We recognized that there was an African problem. We did not treat Africans like most people. But I don't want to give you the impression that we were involved in the African struggle. Those who were involved, left the movement. There were at least half a dozen who became Trotskyites, one of whom was Baruch Hirson.

Did you read a lot in those days?
Sam – You had to. It was part of the *Hashomer Hatzair* curriculum. You read A.D. Gordon, Freud, and Reich. Reich was the great revolution in the South African movement, not the Fourth International. His influence was profound. If you mature as a young person you are going to confront your sexuality and it was introduced in the movement at the right time. There were consequences: mothers were frightened for their daughters. They had good reason to be. It should be said that the Reichian influence did not in any way disturb the thrust towards *chalutziut* and kibbutz.

How did the kibbutz reality match what you were expecting?
Sam – I did not find much conflict in that area. I stayed for about a year-and-a-half on kibbutz Beit Keshet, where we were badly needed for security duties. In retrospect I was a bloody fool for not staying on longer. That is part of my guilt.

There was one area of conflict with the kibbutz. When the Arabs vacated some land nearby, another kibbutz tried to take possession of it and Beit Keshet thought they should have it. We were recruited to confront the other kibbutz. And somebody said, "Bring a revolver." I thought to myself, "You are confronting *yids*." So I said, "I won't go if you take revolvers. They are not Arabs." I didn't go. They didn't like that and they called me a coward.

There was another incident where I felt that things were not right. There was an inquiry into a shooting incident and they blamed me for causing undue alarm. I felt it was very unfair because my courage was in question. After that I felt I was like a square peg in a around hole. The original people on the kibbutz were all *Palmachniks*, all bloody heroes. I think that gently edged me out. I went to live in Tel Aviv. I worked on boats and I was a hotel-keeper.

Did you feel the kibbutz was cramping your artistic bent?
Sam – I didn't even attempt anything like that. I thought it was totally out of keeping. We had to plough the land, build the houses, and guard at night. It is only when I came to England that I started.

Is your impression that the *shlichim* painted a utopian picture of what life was like on kibbutz?
Sam - They did, no question. Nobody ever questioned whether your make-up can meet the demands of the kibbutz. I can only put my leaving down to the fact that I was immature. I did not have the good sense to work it out. I also wanted to see the world.

I left Israel not because I was ideologically against it but because I could not stand the religious aspect. I recall a conversation with two survivors from Buchenwald that had a profound effect on me. What bothered me most was that on Shabbat they would still sing the prayer (in Hebrew): "The Lord will answer when we call." And where was God when they were shoveling them into the furnaces? I could not accept that they kept saying this.

I was schooled in an ideology of spiritual renewal, creating a different human being. As far as I know this ideology has gone down the drain on kibbutzim.

What were the implications of choosing Zionism?
Sam – Choosing the Zionist path was a conscious decision, not a chance event. When we went on *hachshara*, we gave up apprenticeships and some stopped university studies in the middle. You really had to step out of your tramlines and fight against the pressures of family and friends. It was made even harder because we could not tell our friends and relatives that we were leaving. You just disappeared one morning. I think my mother cottoned on when I started packing.

Are you happy with your decision to live in England?
Sam - I had to adapt to English society and I married a Baptist and occasionally I go to church. I am just as critical of the Christianity as I am of the Jewish religion, perhaps even more so. We all had to adjust

and it was a bit of a problem adjusting to English sensibilities. We have survived here but in retrospect I quite often have a conscience. I should have stayed for longer. I went back to Israel with the intention of settling in Ein Hod, in 1962.

What is left of your belief system?
Sam – I don't think there is a lot left. The basic thing about being an honest man still governs my life. I won't go and kill myself to make an extra few quid because I don't feel that is imperative any more.

I think I would be classed as a liberal. Some of my friends have hung on to their ideology of fifty years ago but it doesn't make sense to me any more. In those days we wanted to destroy capitalism but we have all done pretty well out of it. For me sufficient is enough. I don't aim for anything else. Most of my friends are quite well off although we all once subscribed to the idea that we wanted to destroy capitalism. A hypocrite I am not prepared to be.

My current interests are in physics and the sub-atomic particle, which is a world I had never come across, and astronomy.

Where do you stand in relation to Israel today?
Sam – Part of the family is there. My sister goes there regularly. I have an interest, I read whatever I can. I would be very happy if there was peace. From what I gather, the Israel I knew has long disappeared. I would have expected there to be people in Israel, particularly from the kibbutzim, who are looking for a wider, spiritual meaning. If you take the religious component out of Jewish life, what are you left with? And I can't come to terms with the religious aspect. To me the God has failed, though he is still demanding sacrifices.

Michael Hayden

Vancouver
20/03/08

Born in Cape Town, Michael Hayden played a distinctive, rebellious role in Habonim before graduating in medicine from the UCT. He completed a post-doctoral fellowship in clinical genetics and was an instructor at Harvard before joining the UBC Faculty of Medicine.

Michael is the Director of the Center for Molecular Medicine and Therapeutics, UBC, and is a world-renowned geneticist. He has made outstanding contributions in the areas of genetics, Huntington's and other neurodegenerative diseases, lipid disorders, and type 2 diabetes. He is the recipient of numerous awards including CIHR, Canada's Health Researcher of the Year for 2008, and was one of the five finalists of the Globe and Mail's Nation Builder competition in 2008. In June 2009, he was awarded an Honorary Doctor of Science by the University of Alberta. In September 2009, he was awarded the Order of British Columbia.

Michael is currently spearheading a fundraising campaign to build a centre for at-risk youth in Cape Town.

Was your upbringing typically South African Jewish?
Michael - I grew up very differently to any of my friends in South Africa. I grew up poor. My parents were divorced when I was eight. I lived with my mother, who was this kind of rebel. She never had a car and never had a servant. She had a Vespa scooter on which I rode on the back. We had blacks and gays and music in our house all the time. My mother would take me to Langa, Guguletu, Woodstock etc. for poetry readings. This was the 1960's.

My mother was impossible. She spent most of her time telling me to do less school work and have more fun. Homework became my illegal activity. It was a pretty wild time, very cross-racial. She had a black lover of course, for twenty years, an artist who had spent time in jail as an ANC prisoner.

I used to talk to my mother about joining the ANC. It was a discussion we had but it was much more serious for me to pursue a life of science. I knew I had the talent but there was no way I could do that in South Africa.

How serious was your involvement in Habonim?
Michael - I was the only one of all my friends who didn't join the *garin* although I was very involved in *Habonim*. I was a Zionist but I never really saw myself living in Israel.

I was always pretty committed to South Africa. I regretted that as a young person *Habonim* distracted me in some ways from that. In *Habonim* I was pretty active but always doing things a little differently. A lot of Karl Rogers, psychotherapy, imagine you're a rose bush kind of things. I would run these *chugim* at camp – the feely, feely era. And it wasn't just all about love and sex, though that was an important part of it. It was really a different way of viewing things and relating to people.

While still at high school, a small group of us felt *Habonim* was too narrow. We formed our own movement called *Achdut*. We joined up with some people from *Bnei Akiva* who we thought *Habonim* was alienating. And there were also some really good-looking girls in *Bnei Akiva*. We stood for semi-religious *aliya*, which could mean anything. While *Habonim* camp was going on, we actually ran an alternative camp on the slopes of the beach at Onrus. I can still sing you our anthem. It goes like this:
(Sings)
Semi religious aliyah
Our light is the Torah
By the ideals of Achdut
We'll leave the golah...
It goes on and on for about six verses.

At the end of every evening, we'd stand together and sing this song convinced we'd be able to break the barriers of this reactionary *Habonim*, which was too focused to encompass people who saw things differently. They were making divisions. We were making the compromises. It was the ultimate political move. It was a somewhat flagrant act of defiance.

Did your defiance express itself at medical school as well?
Michael - I was leader of the medical students in Cape Town. In the medical student council we tried all sorts of things. We said, for example, that if the black students couldn't come on the white wards, the white students would not go on the black wards. I was never imprisoned, but was known to the police and had been detained. I realized they knew everything about me – every colored girlfriend I had been with, every grade I had got throughout medical school. For me at that point it was a matter of whether to join the ANC and get involved in the violent struggle or to pursue some work in science, in a field where I felt I could make a contribution.

What project are you undertaking in South Africa?
Michael - Our medical class had a reunion in Cape Town 2005. That class included about forty non-whites. Sixty percent of the class had left South Africa. In the first slide of our final year class shown at the reunion, there was not one black. The guy showing the slides said, "I bet none of you even noticed that we were not in the photo."

It came to me before the reunion that this was an opportunity to mobilize the class to do whatever we could for a community in Cape Town. We decided to do something in Masipumalela, a town where the AIDS rate was tremendous. We had the knowledge, we had the means, and we were going to do something to make our little contribution to this mammoth problem.

My mother was not wealthy but she had a small home in Camps Bay. We decided not to take any of the proceeds of the sale of the house out of the country but to start something in the area of Cape Town.

These funds helped to get the class project off the ground. We retook the class photo, this time with all of us, of course. We were starting again.

What has happened since then is very interesting. Here in Vancouver when we asked for small amounts of money I got some very angry letters. The worst have been the Jewish doctors living here, in Florida, in Australia and all over the place. I had a letter for example asking if I was crazy and saying that furthermore the writer wanted nothing to do with anything of which Bishop Tutu is the patron because apparently Tutu is pro-Palestinian. There is anger of that kind, as well as, "Why not take care of your own community first?"

I am not asking these people to feel any responsibility. I am just saying, "Have some compassion, hey, you were born there."

Have you tried to raise money in South Africa?
Michael - We have many friends who are still there and many of them are extremely wealthy. I have turned to them for help with the project. And they say, "You know we don't have to feel guilty any more, blacks and whites are equal now." Now this is coming from the most intelligent, wonderfully sensitive people. You look at them and your jaw drops. Why isn't there some way to accept some diminishing of your own wealth in the interests of others?

How do you feel about Israel?
Michael - I do think a lot of what happens in Israel is very ugly and troubling, but I know it is not the whole story. I strongly support Israel and its right to exist but in some ways it's like being back in South Africa. You hate what the government does. You feel it doesn't represent your viewpoint, you feel helpless and hopeless and yet that doesn't diminish your love or your support for the country. You still somehow believe that there is a possibility to do things better and put together a coalition of the right people. Perhaps that is as naïve as I was in South Africa in those days.

My ability to have some role in participating in Israel feels less and less likely. But let me say this. If there was something meaningful that

I could do in Israel today, just like I am doing something in South Africa... I'd love to find a framework to do something in Israel that was akin to crossing boundaries, is meaningful, and has integrity.

Manfred Kagan

Kibbutz Tzora
10/08/07

Manfred lives in Toronto. The interview took place while he
was on a visit to Israel.

*Born in 1948, Mannie Kagan suspended his University studies to volunteer
for six months in Israel in 1967 after the Six Day War. After completing his
degree in Electrical Engineering in South Africa he lived in an urban kibbutz
in Carmiel, Israel in the early 1970's. He subsequently returned to South Africa
and completed an MBA degree at the University of Cape Town.*

*Mannie has worked in high-tech. and computer-science related industries
in various capacities throughout his career, in Israel, South Africa and Canada, where he currently works as an IT Consultant for a large information
systems company. He lives in Toronto, together with his wife Aura, children,
grandchildren, and large extended family, and retains a life-long passion for
reading history and science.*

What was it that set you on the path to Zionism and *aliyah*?
Manfred - I grew up with a mother who was hard of hearing and as a
result I could never really communicate very clearly with her. My father was a very hard working guy who I hardly saw. In a sense, I think I
grew up intellectually starved. My intellectual awakening began when
I joined *Habonim*.

Our *madrichim* at that time (I was about fourteen) were very influential. We looked up to them, in my case intellectually as well as
everything else. To this day, I remember a lot of the stuff we did. It was
like pouring water on baked earth. I just drank it in.

When did you first come to Israel?

Manfred - I came to Israel as a volunteer in 1967. In my peer group there was a split between those going in the direction of kibbutz and my group who were interested in a new enterprise of a communal framework in Carmiel. I think I could have gone either way. When I came as a volunteer, I was actually supposed to go with the kibbutz guys who went to Kfar Hanassi. Something got screwed up with my passport and I ended up going a week later to Amir. My life might have taken a very different direction in other circumstances. I would most likely have been part of that group who later went to Yizra'el.

After being on Kibbutz Amir for a couple of months we were given the opportunity of going to the *Machon le madrichei chutz la'aretz*. A number of amazing lecturers opened up a whole educational world for me. This was the first I had ever heard about the new field of Holocaust Studies and it became a topic that has been with me ever since.

When I got back to South Africa, I joined the Zionist Federation library and devoured it from beginning to end. That too had an influence on my thinking.

Would you say that the picture you had of Israel was realistic?

Manfred - I don't think I am particularly idealistic. I have a fairly cynical streak. I never even toyed with the idea of staying in South Africa. Going to Israel was a given. What I would end up doing in Israel, kibbutz or something else was not clear. I was not dead set on living in a communal setup forever. My thinking was more or less this: "I'll give it a try, see what it is about and if it doesn't work out, then I won't stay there." I don't think I had a particularly rose-colored perspective.

Are you saying that your decision to set up an urban kibbutz was not an ideological one?

Manfred - I wouldn't say that I was out to change the world. In many of my life decisions I took a practical approach. I could have done arts or education but I said, "I can read at night or on weekends. I can do a technical profession so that I can earn a living." And that's exactly what's happened in my life.

How did you relate to the situation in South Africa?
Manfred - I was violently against what was going on there. But you can be strongly opposed to something without thinking you are going to fix it. One way to cope with a situation like this is going somewhere else.

I don't want to give the impression that I was somebody without all the impulses young people have to change the world. We all wanted to change the world and believed we could.

In retrospect do you think you or your peers were manipulated in some way by movement education?
Manfred - Oh absolutely. I think everybody was. It's a question of degree. Luckily my wife Aura and I weren't damaged because we had careers. In fact that whole Carmiel experience was totally positive for us. We were there for about a year but it didn't work out. We in fact took the decision not to encourage our second *garin* to join us.

As things worked out we ended up going back to South Africa for a period of time.

What 'damage' are you referring to?
Manfred - I think some of our peers were encouraged to go to Israel without a profession or training. There was also a lack of preparedness due to the kind of thinking that said, "I can do an arts degree or not even study because I am going to kibbutz." They didn't think that they might have to earn a living. So there were guys who ended up leaving kibbutz in their forties with no specific training or profession and landing in trouble. It sounds funny but I even heard comments like, "We should have a class action against our ..."

Had the Zionist idea worn off by the time you were ready to leave South Africa for the second time?
Manfred - It had worn off and in fact we saw a lot through the eyes of our friends who were living in Israel. In some cases they advised us to think very carefully about coming back.

I saw the extremely aggressive business climate in Israel as an obstacle. In fact in South Africa I found some of my own behavior had taken on some of this rudeness. I wouldn't say all enthusiasm for Israel had dissipated. As a young adult you just move into a different phase with a different perspective. We had not become cynical. It was just a slightly different slant on how we saw things.

What role does being Jewish play in your life today?
Manfred - Tremendous. Being Jewish is a fundamental underpinning of my identity. I love reading history so I have a cultural historical identity. When I look at myself in the mirror, I see a Jew.

Can you elaborate a little about how you see the strength of a Jewish identity that is not based on religious belief?
Manfred - You could argue that one of the ways of escaping from being Jewish is to live in Israel. In Israel you are like a fish swimming in water that happens to be Jewish, but you don't have to know that or explicitly express that in any way. In the Diaspora you have to take decisions about your Jewish identity. One thing I have come to understand is how powerful the Jewish community is in Toronto. You can almost live immersed in a Jewish environment.

What is the Jewish content of this community when religion is not the core factor?
Manfred - Jewish identity for me consists of a lefty outlook when it comes to political agendas, concern for the welfare of the world, ecology, endangered species, and so on. Jewish identity for me is living as part of a community of Jews with a similar background. Together with that goes a certain consciousness of Jewish history, the dangers regarding the future of the Jews and a concern and a love for Israel. This is in contrast to the segment of the Jewish community that is incredibly conservative. We have moved to a left-wing synagogue community recently. So you find yourself in a very compatible group of people with who you could form a social network. And that is a personal picture of how I find I can express my Jewishness.

What is your sense of how your kids see the world? Is there any of that young zeal to change the world in some way?
Manfred - I think that young people today are very, very different to the way we were. There has been a move to the right. There is not really any viable socialist or communist country any more. They reflect the shift in the thinking of the entire world. They are much more practical than we were and they have to be.

It is very rare today to meet kids that are like we were, kids who would have these kinds of discussions.

What would the young Manfred Kagan be involved in today?
Manfred - I think I would be a rabid environmentalist if I were younger...

Ronni Kahn

Poland
30/07/2007

Ronni lives in Sydney and was interviewed while attending a
family wedding in Poland.

*Ronni Kahn was born and schooled in South Africa. She went to university
in Israel where she received a BA in Fine Arts . She lived on a kibbutz for 12
years, moving to Haifa before emigrating to Australia in 1988 with her family.*

*Stunned by the amount of food wasted by the hospitality industry, Ron-
ni founded OzHarvest in November 2004. OzHarvest now delivers around
125,000 meals each month to 195 charities in Sydney, Wollongong, and Can-
berra with its fleet of six vans. Since its inception, over 4.5 million meals have
been delivered to those in need.*

*She has been in the event industry for 20 years, most recently running her
own company, Ronni Kahn Event Designs.*

*Ronni was been awarded the Australian of the Year Local Hero in the Aus-
tralian of the Year Awards 2010.*

**Was there anything ideological about your decision to leave Israel
for Australia?**
Ronni - It was never really a question of principle if that is what you
mean by ideological. We had left kibbutz Yizra'el with nothing, and
were living in Haifa. We understood that to ever attain some kind of
economic security in Israel was going to be bloody difficult. That was
a major reason.

The loss of Neill Freed and Dudi Silbowitz in the Yom Kippur war
was a traumatic event for most of us on Yizra'el. Neill was my brother-
in-law. A second motivation was definitely my wanting my teenage sons
to have the choice of whether to be in the Israeli army or not.

I want to add something about my kibbutz experience. One of the reasons we left was that I felt that if I was not prepared to fully participate, sit on committees, and be involved as a contributing member I shouldn't live there. In some ways it could have been easy and comfortable but kibbutz is a communal society. The quality of that society is a function of how fully its members participate. I wasn't going to be doing enough if I stayed there.

So ideological - no. It had more to do with emotional and practical issues. And life in Australia was to a great extent a continuation of the search for security and stability.

What lay behind your decision to set up OzHarvest?

Ronni - Selma Browde caused the epiphany but the change started prior to that. I had been in Australia for sixteen years and worked my butt off. I had got divorced in that time and in terms of my own business had reached a point of financial security. The overriding factor was realizing how blessed I was with a roof over my head and two healthy children. I wanted to do something that was more meaningful. I had also been in a relationship where I was showered with material goods and wealth and funnily enough that made me aware that that wasn't enough either.

At that time, with this sense that I needed to do more becoming a minor crisis in my life, I visited South Africa. This was the first time I had been there since Mandela came to power and my picture was of the old South Africa. I was blown away by the vitality and the vibrancy of the change. I felt that those friends and family who had stayed by conscious choice had actually made a difference. I felt how meaningful their lives had become by living through this change.

Selma took me with her to Soweto where she had to check up on AIDS clinics that she had set up. She told me about that program and I felt, "Wow!" I knew she was fantastic, but now here she was in her seventies and still totally committed to making a change. While we were driving around and talking about the changes she said, "You know, during my time in politics we were responsible for bringing electricity to Soweto." And I thought, "What difference have I made to anyone's life other than my own? I get up and go to work, happy and motivated, but what difference have I really made beyond that?"

When I think about it more, I have always regarded Selma, who was our next-door neighbor in Johannesburg, as some kind of a mentor. She was always a role model. Until that visit, I think it had been subliminal. It was only then, however, that I consciously asked myself, "What am I going to do that will make a difference?"

That visit to Soweto galvanized my decision to return to Australia, the country which had allowed me to build personal economic freedom, and to give something back. I didn't feel that I should stay in South Africa and make a change, or go back to Israel. At the same time, I quickly became aware that what I am doing can impact on both those countries by my showing and sharing the model with them. I hope I can be a catalyst for something good coming from it elsewhere too. I am totally committed to the expansion of the program. Almost anywhere that people eat there is food left over and unfortunately there are levels of hunger of and levels of poverty that we need to deal with.

Was this determination to make a difference as sudden as it sounds or can you identify other signs of it at earlier times?
Ronni - You know, even in Haifa I volunteered to work with families from battered homes. I didn't have many skills but had been doing aerobics for ages so this is what I did with some of the women as often as I could. They seemed to love it. In Australia I registered with Jewish Care. They would phone and arrange with me to take people to the doctor, or to do chores for them, etc.

I don't have any real answers about any legacy my parents left outside of the family. There was my father's accident which nearly killed him and left him badly crippled. Do you know how many people helped my mother? I was six. I couldn't have known. About ten years ago I met a woman in Sydney. She told me that after the accident she gave my mother a Kenwood mixer to help her with all the baking she was doing. You know how many random acts of kindness there must have been in that period? We can't afford to ignore even a smile or a thank you. They are so important.

How has working on OzHarvest affected your life?
Ronni - My whole life changed. No satisfaction I ever imagined or no fulfillment I ever dreamed about could have been as good as the reality of doing what I have done. Phoning people to thank them for a fifty dollar donation can be more satisfying than closing a business transaction for a huge sum of money.

I'll tell you something else. When I look at many of the people we feed, I sometimes think, "What's the difference between them and me? Why are they on that side of the fence while I am here? I could just as easily be on that side." Honestly, I often don't know what puts people where they are. Sometimes you see homeless people who look no different to you and me. Not everybody who is helpless is a hopeless old alcoholic. Circumstances are sometimes beyond people's control whoever or whatever they are.

I am so blessed to know that what I do can be important to some of these people.

Richard Kuper

London
28/05/08

Richard Kuper was born in Johannesburg in 1941 and now lives in London. He has degrees from Witwatersrand University and Cambridge and an MA from the London School of Economics. He has been, variously and overlappingly: polytechnic/university lecturer in social philosophy, sociology and European politics, rank-and-file trade-unionist, political activist on many fronts, publisher at Pluto Press, researcher and organic farmer. For much of the past nine years he was Chair of Jews for Justice for Palestinians. His abiding interest is in the development of an eco-socialist politics of transformation that takes the best from both the red and the green traditions, fusing it with a radical, deliberative-democratic approach to political organization and decision-making.

Where does your ideological bent come from?
Richard – It's odd because it doesn't start immediately from home. Home was uncomfortable in South Africa, like a lot of other families, particularly Jewish families. My parents were not Zionists in the slightest. There was no thought of going to Israel. And no real politics. There was more a kind of politics of fear, particularly with my mother. I was never brought up with the feeling that South Africa was where we were going to be living for the rest of our lives, but Israel didn't figure.

After my *barmitzvah* I got involved in a Zionist group called *Young Israel*. It became a major social world for me. It billed itself as a Zionist group in which all ideologies were welcome. In fact, people who had ideologies were in *Habonim* or *Bnei Akiva* or *Betar*. It was basically a friendship group, but for me it was a revelation and I got absorbed in it and it became my social world.

We had a close family friend called Joy Harris, who was involved in the Black Sash during the fifties. They would talk about things, so this was always somewhere in the background – South Africa. But it was just an uneasy perception.

I think what really changed me was reading Trevor Huddleston's book *Naught for your Comfort*, which just shook me to the foundations. He was working with these people who were being treated unfairly. It was a very gut-level reaction, no deep politics to it. I just got involved in liberal politics, which were just about people being treated equally.

When I went to university in 1957–1960, it was the time when they were trying to close Wits to black students and I got involved in the campaign to keep the university open. My parents asked me if I want to leave South Africa because they were freaked out by my participation in a demonstration for which I and a few others were briefly arrested. I had no ideology whatsoever. I didn't believe in any political party. I found out afterwards that many of my friends were Marxists and aligned with the Communist Party. I was in a classic sense un-political. But already very committed and insofar as I thought of going anywhere, I would have gone to Israel.

At the end of my second year at university, I went on *Machon Hachoref* and I loved it. But I also felt uneasy, seeing these Arabs. It just echoed something. I remember having arguments about how the Arabs were being treated and people said, "You are a fine one to talk, coming from South Africa." I thought: "I don't like it in South Africa and I don't like it here." At the same time, it was all remarkably uncritical.

I do not remember being ideological in South Africa, except feeling that the system was totally wrong.

Yet somehow you moved from this point to becoming very ideological...
Richard – In everything I have done since then ideology has been a way of making sense of what I have seen around me. And when a particular ideology or organizational form hasn't made sense, I have left that form but still kept the deep underlying commitment. That is what

has influenced everything I have done.

You left for the U.K. soon after graduating ...
Richard – I just couldn't wait to leave. I went to Cambridge, where I got involved in the Socialist Club and there was also a Labor Club.

What took you there?
Richard – I don't know what took me there. I already had this commitment to the radical egalitarian movement. I couldn't abide Marxism, although I knew almost nothing about it, because of Russia. At Cambridge I studied Marxism, and England was so stifling that labor politics seemed to offer an alternative. There was a mood for change in the country. What I was experiencing was shared by lots of people who had grown up here. So socialism became important and Marxism eventually, when I discovered you could be a Marxist without supporting the Soviet Union.

It was a tremendous emotional breakthrough when I came across a group called the International Socialists (IS). At the time, their formulation was that Russia and Eastern Europe were a form of state capitalism. I would not put it like that now, but at the time it was the most liberating thing I had encountered. I joined in 1964 and stayed there until 1976.

Was Jewishness still a factor for you?
Richard – Not consciously. Not at all. Jewishness had just disappeared. I had identified with the Jews in South Africa who got involved with politics there and Jewishness seemed to me to be my kind of radical egalitarianism, transposed into what you did in particular situations. Jewish meant being active about it. That is all it meant. I unconsciously drifted away from Israel until 1967, when I supported Israel at a gut level. At a political level, I said a plague on both your houses. I was then shattered to discover that the organization I was now part of supported the Arabs in this war. There were huge debates and discussions. I realized that the occupation needed to be unwound as quickly as possible but I didn't rethink Israel. It was too uncomfortable to do that.

My greatest disillusion, very early on, was third world politics. Finding IS and finding that the key to it all lay with us, here, I got involved with British politics at a grass-roots level. I was quite active in the Labor Club and in the Socialist Society at Cambridge. When Labor failed to deliver, I drifted out of it slowly.

I was also at LSE and I was involved in the students' union. We took Vietnam politics into the students' union.

I started writing for the IS newspaper, *Labor Worker,* as it was then called. And I just got more and more absorbed into that kind of politics. Then, in 1967 we had a sit-in at LSE, which I was prominently involved in. The sit-in was essentially about student rights and the right to protest. We succeeded in lifting a number of student suspensions.

There is a whole world of political development associated with a sit-in; we stayed in the building for ten days. It was the first occupation in Britain. It became a benchmark for future activities. Then, the next year, in 1968, with that experience behind us, it became more politicized. We were saying it is not just about democratic rights, it's about the world system, it's about capitalism. These people are part of capitalism. They are training a cadre for the new capitalist world.

Was it not unusual for a South African to get so involved in things here?
Richard – It was, but that was partly to do with the political world I moved into, which said that the key to change was not in South Africa and not in black Africa. Here and America was the heart of it all. This was the place to change it and this was where you act. I always intended to go back to South Africa when I first came and I knew enough not to get involved in the anti-apartheid movement. It was riddled with spies and you just knew that anyone who was involved was known to the South African secret service. There was nothing immediate to go back to and no feeling that a white could do anything there.

In addition, the anti-apartheid movement was fairly Stalinist and dominated by the Communist Party and I was in an organization that was fanatically anti-Stalinist. My politics were then done not as a South

African or as a Jew, but as a universalist, an internationalist. That is what I related to.

It seems that you fitted perfectly into this environment...
Richard – Yes, it gave me an identity. It was a solution to all my personal problems, of who I was and what I was doing. I did not have a clear feeling about myself before. I remember thinking: I need this organization - it makes me whole. It gives me a way of being in the world.

It did not last for long, it has to be said. Already by the early seventies it was changing, it was becoming entangled in organizational arguments. I was at the heart of it and I used to write editorials for the newspaper. Perhaps there is always a sectarian impulse in organizations like this.

Anyway, by 1976 I was fed up with the way things were going and I decided to leave.

How were you integrated into the working class movement and what did you achieve?
Richard – We built a strong rank-and-file pressure group within the technical teachers' union and had a significant effect on debate within it. We also had this huge achievement in the student movement in 1967 and 1968. After that we recruited a lot of people at LSE to IS.

People from IS were often among the leadership of student movements up and down the country. By 1969–1970 it had disintegrated, along with the Vietnam protest but we had also been very important in the Vietnam Solidarity movement.

Was IS effective outside the student world?
Richard – Yes it was. That was part of its great appeal. It had shop stewards from all over the country. We had this group of workers we could go and speak to and who valued us. There was a tremendous feeling of mutual support. We spent out time in the student movement saying the struggle isn't in the universities, it's outside. And we took students out. There was a building workers' strike at the Barbican in 1967 and we took students down there to support the strike and be on the picket line.

And were you there?

Richard – Absolutely. There was a great feeling and in a sense we were ahead of the game in the Marxist movement because a lot of the other Marxist were third-worldish and we were the ones saying that the industrial working class was the focus.

Did you expect things to happen?

Richard - Oh yes. We thought they were going to happen in four, five, six years. But we thought things were changing, that we were vindicated. People had written off the industrial working class and now everyone agreed it was a major agent for change. There was a great feeling of being in the forefront. It was incredibly exciting times. Then there was the invasion of Czechoslovakia and we led the protest against the invasion.

Was there a lot of intellectual ferment?

Richard – Yes, there was a lot of intellectual ferment. Already at Cambridge in the early sixties, the young Marx had been discovered and we were all reading that. A more humanistic Marxism was emerging. This provided an underpinning for the view that forces for change were in the developed countries. We were part of a process of de-subordination in England at the time. It was a widespread phenomenon. The whole old system of authority was crumbling.

Stories abound of you selling newspapers (The Socialist Worker) in Camden Town in the early seventies. Was that part of the ethic?

Richard – That as well. Lenin believed in the 'paper' and we believed in it too. But in reality what it achieved was limited. Once or twice in the five years I sold the paper, I actually had a conversation with one of the people who bought it, let alone recruited anybody. They all agreed with you, but the real problem for them was the UFO's that were coming at us. People's ideas really are a weird mixture of insight and prejudice. I wouldn't write it off as a fruitless activity, though getting up at six o'clock to go to the factory and have four of you sell one paper was not much of an achievement.

I was involved in writing leaflets for the bus garage in Chalk Farm.

Were you acting as the voice of the proletariat?
Richard – We believed we were, or the vanguard of the proletariat. After 1976 you had a Labor politics that we never knew how to deal with. We just regarded it as a sell-out. Politics slipped from our grasp and never really recovered.

Did you not feel you wanted to be an academic?
Richard – No I didn't. I wanted to be a revolutionary of some kind. Being a teacher was quite a good base for it. I enjoyed students and having arguments with them.

What was the thinking behind your starting Pluto Press in 1969?
Richard – The thinking behind it then was that it would propagate IS ideas or bring ideas into IS. The first publication we did was small. Books, in their thousands, were sold into factories. On the basis of this we commissioned other books. We translated one on Gramsci, one on Rosa Luxemburg and Alfred Rosmer's account of early days of the Revolution, *Lenin's Moscow*. We had some real influence on broader politics through the publishing.

How did you then get involved with Middle Eastern matters?
Richard - We are now into the nineties and being Jewish does not figure. I disliked what was going on in Israel. I totally supported the first *intifada* and I supported Oslo. Whatever the terms of the agreement, the paralysis of decades had gone. It offered opportunities. I somehow assumed that the problem would be solved.

The personal resonance came in the second *intifada*, partly because of the Not in Our Name appeal from South Africa, but mostly because my partner went to side with Women in Black (in Israel) and the ISM (International Solidarity Movement). We set up a group, agreed on a statement, which we sent out for signature. People signed and then said, "What else are we going to do?" We slowly became an organization called Jews for Justice for the Palestinians, and Palestine became the centre of our politics.

What is happening in Palestine is inconceivably horrible. It may not be as bad as genocides that are happening elsewhere but the fact that it is happening under western eyes and with western support, justified in terms of our values, makes it worse than almost any of these other atrocities. It is a perversion of what we stand for.

Why are you involved? Is it your identification with one of the parties, or is it your wish for justice?
Richard - I don't know. At one level, it is something very deep to do with who I am and the world I was brought up in, hearing that this is being done in my name. I wanted to dissociate myself from Israel's conduct but also to say there is another Jewish tradition – a very positive statement, not just a personal cleansing. I had been Jewish in my politics without knowing it for the past forty years. My Jewishness was expressed in my internationalism and egalitarianism and this to me is what Jewishness is about.

In effect, my view is that anti-Semitism in the Diaspora is fed by what is going on Israel's occupation policies.

How has the community responded to Jews for Justice for the Palestinians activities?
Richard – Originally with great hostility. In 2002 there was an Israel rally in Trafalgar Square and Netanyahu spoke. We had a silent vigil on the steps of St. Martins. There was a lot of hostility to that. We got hot coffee thrown over us. For about two years we were not reported on and not recognized by the Jewish community. We were quite beyond the pale.

Over the years, we have been able to change that. This year, we put a *Pesach* advertisement in the *Jewish Chronicle* with over four hundred signatures. It stated that Israel should talk to *Hamas* and that what is happening in Gaza is unacceptable. The JC published an exchange of letters on the issue.

Our claim to demand justice for the Palestinians became a demand for pluralism in the Jewish community here, the right to speak out and be recognized. For me that is one of the most important things we have done.

How have you taken to the change in South Africa?
Richard – I was phenomenally optimistic about it. No one believed there could be a peaceful transition. In that there is a lesson for Israel. The difference is that in South Africa there were a lot of people working towards integration on a daily basis, whereas in Israel the separation between Israelis and Palestinians has become almost total. From that point of view it is not optimistic but I take tremendous encouragement from the fact that you can have reconciliation. I don't know how stable the thing is in South Africa but I think there is still room for optimism.

Do you feel you want to get involved again in South Africa?
Richard – At a certain level. I have been involved over the last ten years in sending books to resource centers. We set up a group called Friends of Workers' Education in South Africa. Often the best thing you can do is give people material, books – making resources available. I believe books are incredibly valuable. Books never hurt anyone. In Palestine, books matter. Students don't have books. In Palestine, what we found is that people want basic books: nursing, physics, maths. We just sent a load of books to the Palestine IT Association and to Hebron University.

How does this activity both in South Africa and in the Middle East fit in with your revolutionary ideas?
Richard – I think I have become more sanguine about the overall revolution. I don't expect to see it in my life time. I have suspended judgment about whether that outcome will materialize. I still believe that is what we need but it is crucial now to get involved in ecological politics. I am involved in the Red-Green Study Group which meets six times a year to discuss ecological issues and the material base on which production takes place. We have done some small-scale interventions.

Is it difficult to retain your belief in creating a better future?
Richard – I have to say I am tired of some things. I can't say I am optimistic about anything in the short-term. It's the way I grew up in South

Africa. Somebody once said, "No matter how bad things are, they can always get worse." In the sixties, things seemed to be getting better. Suddenly things seemed possible. But most of the time, things don't seem possible to me. You are acting without hope. You do not see how it is going to lead to improvement but nonetheless you hope you are providing something. When the change comes, as in South Africa, you can have all sorts of unexpected upheavals.

So, in a sense, while acting without hope, there is hope. You are acting without any understanding of how what you are doing is contributing to the change you want. But you believe that those kinds of things will contribute, are therefore worth doing and encouraging other people to do.

Shula Marks

London
23/05/08

The daughter of ardent Zionist parents, Shula Marks was born in Cape Town in 1936. She spent a year in Israel on the Machon le Madrichei Chutz L'Aretz in 1953. She emigrated to the UK in 1960 and received her PhD. from the University of London in 1967. Since then, Shula has lectured and written widely on late-nineteenth and twentieth-century South African history. Apart from ten years as Director of the Institute of Commonwealth Studies, she spent her academic life at the School of Oriental and African Studies where she is now an Emeritus Professor and Honorary Fellow. She has honorary degrees from the Universities of Cape Town and KwaZulu-Natal and is Fellow of the British Academy.

Let's start with a bit about your early life, in terms of people, books and circumstances that shaped your thinking early on.
Shula – The starting point should be that I grew up in an intensely Zionist house. My mother was involved in Zionist activity before she got married and my mother and father met through a common Zionist interest. It was hard not to be involved intensely in all of that. Then when I left school I went off to Israel on the *Machon* and actually I decided that I would study in Israel. But I decided to go back to South Africa just before the Suez crisis because my father was terribly ill.

Besides the home influence I was very involved in *Habonim*, where there was also an intense involvement with what was going on in South Africa, and this was as formative of my identity as my home. This was what being Jewish was all about for me – freedom and righteousness and not oppressing others – taken from the teachings of the prophets.

What did you read as a child and what books made an impression on you?
Shula - I was ill for a year and people used to send me history books. Some of them were dreadful and some were excellent, like van Loon's *History of Mankind*. But I read voraciously. Later I read a lot about Jews and prejudice. *Madrichim*, like Muzz Hill were important. There were teachers at university and people I met at university who influenced me.

What was the ambience like in Habonim?
Shula – It was totally exciting. There was a real ferment, between Zionism and non-Zionism and also between socialism and non-socialism. I worked at the *Habonim* office in Burleigh Street and next door to us was the *Guardian* newspaper. I think a lot of my ideas were influenced by the people who worked there. Then at university being on the SRC and working in SHAWCO affected me. Those experiences were all formative for me.

When we left for England for Yitzak (husband) to specialize, it was intended as a stop-off on our way to Israel.

How did you resolve the dilemma you faced in South Africa, of whether to stay and join the struggle or to leave?
Shula – To an extent it was a copout. I felt we did not have a real role in South Africa because this was a national struggle. However, I was much more torn than Yitzak, as I was drawn to the socialist aspect of the struggle as well, but the Zionism was much stronger. There didn't really seem to be a good option.

We came here (to the UK) and Yitzak was offered a job in Israel but he wanted to delay going for six months until he completed his training. This was around 1967. I was working on colonization at SOAS when suddenly I thought, "This is a dividing point in my life". Here I was writing about colonization in Africa and we never asked ourselves about other forms of colonization. It was a very painful moment and my brother (see interview with Meir Winokur) was taken aback.

I was appalled by the arrogance of Israel after the 1967 war. I had left South Africa because I disapproved of what was going on there and this was not that different. The processes were similar, namely, this is ours because we were here three thousand years ago. It was as though this was a sudden revelation to me. From that point I really queried whether this was going to solve the Jewish problem.

We continued to live in England and I spent three months at the Hebrew University and, as always, I loved being in Israel, unlike in England, where I have rarely felt at home. While I enjoyed being in Israel, I struggled with it and we came back to London, and I still struggle with it. It's close to a love-hate relationship.

How does this express itself now?
Shula - I think one has to engage critically, insofar as one has a responsibility. And that is what I told the members of *Habonim* I met recently in South Africa. I have not been tremendously active since I got a job at SOAS, where I have been bound up with South Africa.

Were you involved in the protest movement here?
Shula – I was having kids after we arrived but I was shocked by the levels of racialism and prejudice I found here. I heard people saying things here that I had never heard in South Africa. I suppose it's true that the less you know about people the more prejudiced you are likely to be.

How do you explain the success of negotiations in South Africa compared with the lack of success in negotiations between the Israelis and the Palestinians?
Shula – There were more people listening in South Africa, neither side believing that it had the absolute truth. The two narratives there were not as contradictory and the common objective was always a single South African state, whereas in the Middle East the central idea has been a two-state solution, which is changing a bit now. In South Africa there was a single, unifying religion – Christianity. In the Middle East, religion is an area of conflict. In South Africa there was modernizing

elite, both among the Afrikaner and the black communities.

My impression is that your work is not purely academic, that you are driven by a greater passion that has carried you through your life. Is that correct?
Shula – The issues that I have been interested in have essentially been to do with restoring the sense of agency and a sense of their own history to black people. Another of my other interests was to establish how apartheid happened, what alternatives were there. I don't think that is a million miles from what I believed in generally, what I am passionate about.

Does that go back to your Judaic roots?
Shula – It does, but it also comes from my father, who was known as a very generous man. There is a marvelous story about my father from the time of the Korean War, when I was about sixteen. I had gone to an anti-war demonstration and a friend of my father's saw me there and told him. He never said anything to me but later I heard that when my father heard I was there he said, "Firstly, at her age I would have done the same and, secondly, it is none of my business." That was the kind of household I grew up in.

There certainly was a connection between being Jewish and being radical in South Africa. Something like four percent of whites were involved in anti-apartheid activities, and of those about forty percent were Jewish. That is disproportionate and I think it is something about the immigrant experience, exile experience, and experience of the Holocaust plus the awareness of anti-Semitism and prejudice. Lots of my reading was inspired by what was going on in the country.

What is your feeling about South Africa today?
Shula – I suppose that during the first ten years of ANC rule people were optimistic and now they are pessimistic. They are either right up or right down and there is never a kind of balance. What could you expect when people had such euphoria, such expectation, such fantasies of what could happen in South Africa when there had been such

inequality and broken families? It was a totally unrealistic expectation, and I think that is still the case. It is a bit like Israel, with its utopian fantasies.

What is required for things to improve in South Africa?
Shula – I think serious redistribution of wealth is required, and it should have happened in 1994-1995 when a lot more could have been done, but now I don't see it happening. Something has to happen about crime. AIDS has been a tremendous problem. There were two tragedies the moment the new South Africa was born. Firstly, there was a prevailing sense of market fundamentalism and it was very difficult for South Africa to stand outside of it. Secondly, there was a reluctance to discuss the culture of sexual relations, particularly the possible implications of having unprotected sex.

What are you working on at the moment?
Shula - I am currently working with a couple of colleagues on a book on the struggle for health in South Africa in an international context. It takes as its starting point the establishment of the health centre at Pholela in KwaZulu Natal, by Sidney and Emily Kark, who later settled in Jerusalem. Pholela was important because it became the model for community-oriented primary care in many different parts of the world.

How do you look back on the decisions you made at various periods in your life?
Shula – I think they stemmed from the fact of being Jewish and the daughter of immigrant parents. I am not completely at home here and I am not completely at home there (South Africa) as an 'insider-outsider'. It amazes me that I have so many friends in South Africa, mostly new ones. It is a different kind of life there. You can pop into people there and phone up at the last moment to say you are coming. This is true for South Africa Jews particularly. I met friends from Cape Town in the Eastern Cape and there was an immediate bond between us, as CTJ's (Cape Town Jews). There is a set of shared assumptions between us, as citizens of the world.

Vivian Rakoff

Toronto
30/03/08

Vivian Rakoff was born in Cape Town in 1928. He was a member of Hashomer Hatzair and spent time on a kibbutz in 1948. He earned his BA and MA degrees at the University of Cape Town, after which he obtained his medical degree from the University of London and completed his psychiatric residency at McGill University.

Former director and psychiatrist-in-chief at Toronto's Clarke Institute of Psychiatry, Vivian received an honorary doctor of science degree for his contributions to the field of psychiatry and his work in establishing University of Toronto as a leader in the study of brain disease.

Rakoff's primary field of specialization is adolescence and the family. He was the first professor of psychiatric education at the University of Toronto's Faculty of Medicine and was known as an engaging teacher.

He has served as a visiting professor at a number of universities, including the National University of Ireland, Israel's Technion University, and the University of Manitoba.

He has written plays for radio and television and has also authored a number of peer-reviewed articles and textbook chapters. More recently he has reviewed books about psychiatry and general interest for major publications.

What were the intellectual influences on you as a young man?
Vivian - I've been lucky. I am an elaborately educated man, I have been to a lot of places and yet I think the most powerful intellectual influences of my life remain those adolescent years with that small cluster of friends in *Hashomer Hatzair* in South Africa. The intensity of both the emotional and intellectual involvement was amazing.

I left South Africa in December 1947 to read English at Cambridge. As it turned out I went with Ralph and Taibie Hirshowitz to Marseilles, from where they were due to be part of *Aliyah Bet* to Palestine. They were at a displaced persons' camp with concentration camp survivors. So it was, "Goodbye Cambridge, sorry dad." I spent a couple of months in Marseilles before sailing with a tourist visa on the S.S. Negba to Palestine. Within a short time my friend Ora who was with a group going to Kibbutz Shuval had me out of my blazer and shirts from dad and into the work clothes of a *chalutz*. I spent the rest of the year in Israel still thinking I would go to Cambridge. But I had no papers.

I returned to South Africa where I did another degree, in psychology this time very simply because I felt I was so useless on the kibbutz. I then went back to England but now to Oxford, putatively to do a PhD. However, I got into medical school in London. Aaron Klug was in England too and when he was in London we lived in a *bayit* with Shleim (Sam) Fanaroff. We reestablished the movement bond right in the middle of London.

Can you define the point at which you decided that kibbutz and Israel were not going to be part of your future?
Vivian - You know you have asked me one of the most difficult questions of my life. To this day, Geena, my wife and I talk about it. I was doing well academically, I suppose, made for an academic existence. And then there was the other side, the very powerful emotionally driven side of going to the kibbutz. But there was never a conscious decision. I was like a cork floating on the stream. I have never planned anything in my life in the ordinary sense. And there was always a fantasy that one day I would go back. Now I am eighty and the emotional bond has remained intense. But together with the bunch – Aaron, Shleim, Jack Halpern and Benny Kaminer we all went in an essentially academic direction.

Before you left South Africa in 1947 who was influential in pushing socialism and Marxism as the ideological direction of Hashomer Hatzair?

Vivian - I was a few years younger than people like Baruch Hirson. He was highly persuasive. To the end of his days he retained a kind of zealous, priestly quality. There was an intensity of belief that brooked no opposition. But I didn't want to join a monastery even if it were a Trotskyite monastery.

We studied you know, we studied, believe me. It wasn't Lenin and it wasn't Kropotkin, it was utopianism that got us. The kind of a life where people would share, and would be kind to one another, where there was a kind of bountiful sexuality. I can assure you, however, that most of it was more masturbatory than anything else. This was a youthful utopianism, more I think to do with Nietzsche's notion of young people forging their way up the mountain than with formal ideology.

I was ideology-prone. I was originally in *Betar* but only because I liked the fencing masks. Hashomer specifically denied the Diaspora and South Africa as such. We were utopian, and involvement in the struggle would have been real in the most ordinary way. We were in favor of a totally utopian vision of a kind of almost never-never land – the kibbutz. The romantic posters of the farmers, etc. were ready to eat us up saying, "There is a better land somewhere."

Do you think that your group of friends was unique in any way?

Vivian - I have met lots of Jewish boys of my time who were also part of an almost historical progression. We were stereotypical in many ways: the first generation, the small *gescheft*, the next generation maybe a little bigger *gescheft*. Then come the professionals, the intellectuals, the writers, artists, etc. I keep meeting myself in New York.

Can you identify any common denominator amongst those who followed through with their Zionist ideology as opposed to those who went a different route?

Vivian - I don't think they were as academically privileged as our little group which Shur has identified in the book on *Hashomer Hatzair*.

We were being rewarded at every step for a different kind of life possibility. We didn't train as fitters and turners. We were not the greatest
physically. Looking back I was a noisy, slightly eccentric kid with a
passion for poetry, literature and art. We were privileged and I suppose
in a sense different.

**The lofty utopian aspirations of your youth do not seem to have
given way to disillusionment or disappointment. Is that observation
accurate?**
Vivian - The only disappointment is with myself. I always felt that I
had failed. There were some years after I left Israel that I didn't go back
because I felt that I had lost my right to be there. There wasn't intense
disappointment with the idea of kibbutz. There were minor disappoint-
ments with the kibbutz itself – the gossip, the small town back-biting
and other stuff. I left the kibbutz with regret but somehow I had to do
something else with my life.

**As students in London did you and your friends join any movements
or organizations?**
Vivian - No. The Marxism we were exposed to in Hashomer was a
peculiar thing. Because our mentors were Trotskyites we never fell into
Stalinist orthodoxy. We remained on the left but critical and skeptical.
We were not joiners. We had been inoculated against orthodoxy. We
read the stuff and we knew the ideological currents but we weren't
believers. Our bunch remained a separate little group with its own dynamic and its own ideological intellectual fervor.

What was your feeling about the struggle against apartheid?
Vivian - I was disaffected, I hadn't been part of the struggle. In fact I
was pessimistic. If I had known then what I know now, might I have
stayed? I lacked nerve. I recognized the correctness of it but was I prepared to put my life on the line for it? I was definitely afraid.

**Would you elaborate a little on the role of William Reich in Hashom-
er Hatzair thinking?**
Vivian - There was confusion and hunger and yearning. In a sense, it

was quite splendid. How old were we? We were kids. The message was a world of unzippered sensual expression. Remember we were all South African Jews which meant we were Litvak, which meant repressed as all hell. We were South African Calvinist in a way that we didn't know either, just as repressive. But we came with the same equipment as everybody else in the world and here was a high flown ideology that allowed you to open your fly and not just have a good time, but to assert human freedom in the process.

Was the emphasis on Reich peculiar to South African Hashomer Hatzair?
Vivian – Yes it was. It was so exciting because we all knew a little bit of Freud, a little bit of Marx, and here they came together. As I said, my own thesis is that we were actually more Nietzschean although we didn't know it at the time.

What really appealed to us was the guitar playing, the nights in the mountain, youth, passion, sensuality, dreams, rejecting the authority of the father. This was a higher domain. My classmates in high school (SACS) had none of this.

There was also something going on in the wider context. In the period right at the end of World War II, it looked as though an entire new world was in the making. Old Europe had been destroyed and for a while left-wing movements did take over Europe. A utopian sense of possibility was abroad in the most extraordinary way. Out of the ashes of the war there was this dream, which never gets fulfilled anyway because people are lousy. But we were caught up in something far bigger. We didn't even know what tide it was that was carrying us.

Have you retained an interest in South Africa over the years?
Vivian - About 1950 or thereabouts I remember discussing it with Aaron and others. We decided we were not going to be exiles, people who remain forever in the homeland. I want to become a citizen of where I am. I don't want my life corrupted by perpetual nostalgia.

How do you feel about the way Israel has changed?
Vivian - Let me tell you the organizations I give money to: Peace Now, The New Israel Fund, a little to the UJA. All my friends in Israel remain on the left, remain critical. Even sitting as we did last year in a house in Savyon, the old *chavurah* sitting together, all of us were left-wing, critical, believing in the possibility of peace but no longer a bi-national state as we once believed. All of us are still committed to a notion of a social democratic society. I am critical but unavowedly supportive of the overall enterprise.

What does your personal and professional experience suggest as to whether there is such a thing as an ideological personality? Is there such an animal or is it more a question of adolescent ardor?
Vivian - That's a very good question. Eric Hoffer's book *The True Believer* gives an understanding of ideological fanaticism in a way nothing else does.

Idealism in a way is a manifestation of a generalized human desire to have a sense-making model or paradigm of the world. There are those who just accept what is given to them implicitly without it being explicit and there are those who try to make it explicit and if they haven't got a model, go looking for it. We seem to need a sense-making system that takes away the sense of frivolity in our existence because we have a real terror of meaninglessness.

You have described a number of key decisions in your life as being spontaneous, even impulsive. In retrospect, are there any roads you regret not having traveled?
Vivian - I should probably have read English at Cambridge and become a professor of English. It's more authentic than what I became because much of what I did become was based on fear. Despite all the apparent risk-taking and courage I was scared. In the end I settled for safety. I settled for this lovely room with all its books and tumbling papers, with its prints and its view of the ravine rather than going for something that might have been less comfortable but closer to who I might authentically have been. One will never know this.

I might have stayed on the kibbutz. I don't think that it would have worked out for me. The kibbutz was in the end a highly conformist society. I might have stayed in Israel like a number of my friends did and become an academic, but South Africa, never. I don't regret having left South Africa. It demanded a degree of political torment for a struggle that was fundamentally not mine. I must add that there was also a kind of snobbery on my part. South Africa is on the edge of the world. I wanted to be where the stuff happens - England or North America.

Michael Schneider

Jerusalem
20/12/07

Michael was interviewed while visiting Israel.

Michael Schneider has been the Secretary-General of the World Jewish Congress since September 2007.

Born in Paarl, South Africa, Schneider was an anti-apartheid activist engaged in activities prescribed by the African National Congress, including sabotage and providing an escape route for political fugitives from the South African Special Branch. He left South Africa in June 1964 in order to avoid arrest.

Prior to his present position Schneider was the Chief Executive Officer of the American Jewish Joint Distribution Committee from 1988 to 2002. Under his professional stewardship the "Joint" provided care and maintenance assistance for over 100,000 Jewish trans-migrants emigrating from the Soviet Union at transit stations in Vienna and Rome. During his tenure the "Joint" was engaged in a decade-long operation to rescue Jews from Syria, Yemen, and Bosnia by negotiating terms with those countries' regimes, and from Iran. It also played a major role in "Operation Solomon" which resulted in the now famous airlift of 12,000 Ethiopian Jews from Addis Ababa.

From 2002 to 2007 he served as the Chief Executive Officer of the World Jewish Restitution Organization, which is engaged in claiming restitution for communal and private property in eastern Europe, confiscated during the Nazi and Communist eras.

Schneider is a member of the Executive Committee of the Conference for Material Claims against Nazi Germany.

In July 2005 he was appointed Chevalier de la Legion De'Honneur by the Government of France.

Michael - I was born in Paarl. I grew up in Worcester. My parents were both deaf and dumb. My grandfather was a *rov* in Ceres. He moved from Dordrecht so my mother could go to the deaf school in Worcester.

At a young age, I had a single moment of horror which made me become dissatisfied with the apartheid system. My dad and his sister owned a hotel in De Doorns. On Saturdays I used to come in and pour the *Vaaljapie* for the colored population. A guy walked in and somebody said, "He's a *kaffir*." In those days you weren't allowed to sell liquor to Africans but you could sell to coloreds. Jim our barman took a *sjambok* and slashed the guy across the face. My father stood by, no reaction. What I thought at the time was, "Even a deaf mute has somebody to beat up in South Africa, if he's white."

The second incident was in my uncle's warehouse. I asked John, the black invoice clerk, to help move the barrels of very heavy electrical cable. He said, "No, I am an invoice clerk." I pointed a finger at him and said, "John if you don't do it, you are sacked." He got up and did it, but he never looked at me again. That was a moment of great shame for me. Those two things really turned me against apartheid.

In Johannesburg at a later stage I met people who were involved in anti-apartheid activities. A lot of these guys were Jewish of course. Monty Berman recruited me to join a group affiliated to the ANC in 1961. I started going to some discussion groups where I met some hard-line Communist Party members like Baruch Hirson, a Stalinist. They were uptight. It wasn't for me. They failed to indoctrinate me into hard-line communism.

In those days Mandela had issued an order to all the anti-apartheid groups to start committing sabotage. Monty taught me to make small bombs using Semtex and Westclox timers. I went down to Johannesburg where we did some knocking down of pylons. I was naïve, I must tell you. I mean we once brought Cape Town to a complete standstill by severing cables which put the whole suburban railway line to Simonstown out of action for the whole day.

When Tanzania became independent, the ANC decided to give them a gift of twelve African nurses in order to help the country develop. I was delegated to "borrow" the King David school bus in which I drove the nurses to the Bechuanaland border. I was dressed as a priest and had a forged letter from President Swart to say I was allowed to take them on an outing. Another activity was burning down half the South African government Pass Office in Johannesburg. I was the driver. Monty poured petrol through the letter box and set the place on fire. When Monty left for London, Adrian Leftwich, a guy called Eddy Daniels and I formed what we called the African Resistance Movement. We felt that in the ANC we were exposing ourselves to danger because we did not know who we were working with.

You were pulled deep enough into the anti-apartheid struggle to become an active saboteur and to put your own life at risk. What was it that led you to put your life on the line?
Michael - Anger, extreme anger. I met a lot of Africans at UCT as well. And then there was the Jewish anger. At that time, I was quite shocked that with its history of persecution the Jewish community didn't do anything, not only the Board of Deputies, but ordinary Jews. Why didn't they speak out? Years later I reached exactly the opposite conclusion, after working with the Joint and learning more about the pogroms etc. I realized that this was a community that came out of fear to a new country, were welcomed warmly by Afrikaners, and then later driven to greater fear when it was discovered that some of the people trying to lead the country were actually Nazi sympathizers. I don't think we have the right to single out South African Jewry as being culpable. The whole white population was culpable.

As I began to read more my thinking became more sophisticated and of course, other factors came in. But the real driving force was my own anger and my own guilt.

I don't know… maybe my grandfather's sense of Jewish morality played a part as well. When people asked me, "Why did you do all this?" I said, "Because I am Jewish and that is what Jews do."

When I finally escaped …

Escaped?
Michael - The Special Branch came to arrest me. There was a dragnet all around Cape Town, the papers were full of it, but I managed to walk right

through it. Then after a long meander through Africa I went to London.

What made you move into Jewish affairs in London?
Michael - There were two factors. I realized that my colleagues who had escaped beforehand were actually anti-Israel and that was a shock to me.

I took a job with the London Jewish Welfare Board who offered me a position at eighty-five pounds a year more than one I was considering with the Quakers. This ultimately led to my becoming the head of social services in the Jewish Welfare Board.

Later down the line the Joint Distribution Committee recruited me and eventually brought me to New York to run the organization. Now I am the General Secretary of the World Jewish Congress. Do I know how I got there? I have no idea. I never aspired to these positions but here I am brought out of retirement to try and resurrect the organization.

Did you become active in the anti-apartheid movement in London?
Michael - Part of my escape involved the head of the British secret service at the time. As a result of an agreement with him, I was proscribed from anti-apartheid activity. I still met people but I never attended ANC meetings. It sometimes occurred to me that had I done so I would probably have been the minister of something or other in South Africa or most ironically the South African ambassador to Israel. (laughter). It's amazing how one crossroad can completely change your whole life. I could have been a guerilla fighter in Tanzania, I could have been like Kasrils, God forbid but...

When you were most involved and active, did you imagine that your dream would be realized in your lifetime?
Michael - No never. What Mandela hoped when we started all the sabotage business was that it would stir the indigenous blacks to rise up, but they didn't. We were thirty years too early. No I never believed it then. It ran against the course of reasonable expectations, miraculous in many ways.

Are there any figures that stand out as being people who have changed the way you think about things?

Michael - Absolutely. Ralph Goldman. He was my predecessor as the head of the Joint. He was an inspirational figure, wise, smart. He taught me the value of modesty and understatement. I suppose also he was a bit of a father figure, my own father being a deaf mute, illiterate. Ralph is a legend in Jewish communal life in America.

You seem to have been involved in your work at so many different levels...

Michael - I think they brought me into the Joint because they thought I might become the rescue artist for the organization. It was not dissimilar to my work driving Africans to the border to escape the South African police. During my tenure, a big part of my activity dealt with escape. I smuggled Iranian Jews out of Iran after the Khomeini revolution. I paid bandits per head to *shlep* them across the border. I negotiated for four thousand Jews to leave Syria under Assad. We took out the last Yemeni Jews. We took out twelve convoys of Jews and Moslems during the Bosnian Serbian war.

What do you consider to be your special talent or strength that has enabled you to achieve what you have?

Michael - I don't know. I did assume responsibility at a very early age. I think that what really helped me was an ability to communicate. Having deaf and dumb parents, I had to communicate complicated ideas in very simple ways. I had to cut through to the quick. The other thing is I don't suffer bullshit lightly. I think I have the ability to cut through a lot of nonsense, sometimes to a fault. I tend to see only solutions rather than problems. This is not always good. I think a lot of this comes from my background and upbringing.

What drives you to work so hard for the Jews?

Michael - Part anger, still. Still angry. I mean I am going after Iran at the moment, pushing for sanctions. The truth is there will always be anti- Semitism. It is never going to go away. It is just like crime. It is a fact of life.

My lifelong commitment is to the security and the viability of the State of Israel. I am Jewish and I am a Zionist, always have been. Anti-Semitism is part of this but look, there are those who don't like us, *gesuntheid*. I mean there are nationalities I don't particularly like. It's those who wish to harm us that we have to go after.

Part of our brief is Jewish-Muslim relations. I previously worked in Indonesia for three years building a village there with Jewish money. They are not ready yet, but Indonesia is really a key to Jewish-Muslim relations. Two weeks ago we had the first national summit of Imams and Rabbis from all over America. My good friend Issy Liebler criticized me saying, "Some of those guys are against Israel." I feel differently. Like Rabin said, "You don't make peace with friends, you make peace with enemies."

If you were to revisit any of the critical choices that you have made in your life, are there any that you think you would do differently?
Michael – Maybe I should have gone into business. I can't eat more than I eat, I can't drive more than one car, but if I had gone into business and made a lot of money... I believe I could change the world with Bill Gates's money!

Conclusion

This book records a series of forty four interviews with South African and ex-South African Jews whose lives have been informed by ideology. The interviews reinforce the notion that Jews of conscience who grew up in South Africa during the period of white minority rule essentially faced three alternatives: 1) participation in the struggle for democracy; 2) the Zionist option; 3) emigration to other countries.

Influences

It appears that it is not easy to get rid of the pervasive (old) South African proclivity to think in terms of ethnic stereotypes and to identify people as members of groups: them and us; black and white; Jewish and non-Jewish. Living under apartheid necessarily shaped the world outlooks of those who grew up in that environment.

In addition, South African racist society produced people bearing a particularly high sensitivity to all forms of discrimination and oppression, who were determined to fight against injustice. They have engaged in activities intended to reduce prejudice, improve the lot of disadvantaged people, or campaign on behalf of oppressed minorities. Many of our interviewees fall into this category.

Paradoxically, this latter dynamic has not driven a significant number of ex-South Africans in Israel into politics, human rights activity or peace movements. Their activities have generally been restricted to community work.

Most interviewees began their explanation of what influences their commitment to different causes with an account of their parents and homes.

Our interviews with people of various ages, including first and second generation South Africans Jews, produced varying historical perspectives on the influence of values and beliefs in choosing a path of action. The first South African-born generation of interviewees generally spoke movingly about their parents' battle to acclimatize and survive in the new country. Mother and father might have been decent people with enlightened values but the exigencies of life did not generally allow them to take up humanitarian causes.

At the same time, parents expected their children to know what a *mensch* was, and to act like one. "If anybody was an example to me it was my mother saying, 'You must never hurt anybody that you don't have to hurt.' I trace the values that have guided my life to her." (Tzvi Pantanowitz). Siblings, too, were significant role models.

Jewish identity and Zionist belief were strong, both in the home and in the community. Mickey Korzennik describes the atmosphere in and around Jewish homes as "a tight tribal fortress," where the romantic picture of distant Palestine and the promise of the Zionist movement readily captured the imagination of young minds.

Unlike their parents, the new generation, often inspired by Marxist thinking or by graduates of youth movements in Europe and sometimes even driven by their own experience of poverty, was able to devote time and energy to matters other than survival. Many set out on a path that departed fundamentally from that of their parents, sometimes to the latter's chagrin.

The need to change the world seemed imperative in the period following WWII. It was essentially in the wake of the war that idealism flowered among the youth movements in South Africa, as it did in other parts of the world. Zvi Pantanowitz remembers the historical climate of the post-Holocaust era as one when you felt you were "being given a God-given chance to make a home for the Jewish people. It was now. You were history. It was a potent time historically."

Among those who were old enough to experience events surrounding the founding of the Israel and the Declaration of Independence, the excitement was palpable. "I arrived in Tel Aviv exactly two hours before Ben Gurion declared the establishment of the State... I ran to the museum in Rothschild Blvd. to hear him." (Moshe Ben Ami). Younger generations were strongly influenced both culturally and ideologically by the revolutionary aura of the sixties.

With regard to acquiring a social conscience, a number of interviewees told of a moment of epiphany – a seminal event. In one case it was overhearing blatant racist and anti-Semitic talk. In another it was witnessing crude '*baasskap*' in action. Michael Schneider sees his anger at what he witnessed as a boy and his subsequent guilt as the driving force behind his readiness to put his life on the line. A tour of Soweto with Selma Browde, who was instrumental in bringing electricity to the impoverished township, prompted Ronni Kahn to ask herself, "What difference have I made to anyone's life other than my own?"

Mention was made of *madrichim* and *shlichim*, who often had a powerful influence, as did certain teachers, writers, colleagues, and political figures. Dramatic events such as Sharpeville, the Soweto riots, and Biko's death also played a part in awakening sensibility to a need for change in South Africa. Chance factors, such as the proximity of a meeting place of a particular youth movement, or the actions of an older sibling often played a decisive role in determining which stream one became attached to.

A prime influence on the intellectual and ideological worlds of almost all the interviewees was the experience of growing up in a racist society coupled with being a member of a youth movement. The mix of contempt for apartheid and exposure to the values and attitudes of the Zionist youth movements created fertile ground for budding idealists. It was this political context that distinguished South African youth movements and student organizations from those of their counterparts in other western countries.

On the other hand, Alan Hoffmann suggests that the overall revulsion at apartheid made it almost too easy to assume a liberal, humanitarian stance and provided a legitimate reason for leaving the country. This relative ease of commitment did not properly test people's convictions, raising the possibility that their belief in 'freedom from oppression' and 'social justice' was not very deep.

Many of the people we spoke to remember their adolescent days in the youth movements as amongst the best times of their lives. Significantly, it is the powerful combination of intellectual and emotional intensity of the youth movement experience that is mentioned time and time again. The youth movements encouraged members to question the values of the society in which they lived, to posit alternatives, and to work towards change.

In addition, the movements in South Africa were in many ways an antidote to the repression of a school system that provided very little in the way of intellectual stimulation or challenging thought, and where questioning had no place outside of the exam room. It is little wonder that the well-organized youth movements and student organizations such as NUSAS were able to focus the beliefs and then channel the inchoate energy of young people into action.

Jewish values

For many of the interviewees, being Jewish centers on a sense of belonging to a historical and moral tradition, sometimes referred to as 'the tribe'. Being Jewish is a basic component of their identity and a basis for social relationships. At the other extreme, Geoff Budlender drifted away from the Jewish community in South Africa, "because I felt the community had nothing to say or declined to say anything about the society in which I was living. I lost interest."

Alan Hoffmann views the search for meaning as being at the heart of Judaism. However, he sees a degree of superficiality in the understanding of what being Jewish meant in the secular Zionist youth movements: "We mouthed this platitude about creating a national home for the Jewish people without thinking seriously about what we meant by the 'Jewish people'. And certainly we didn't know what we meant by the Jewish part of the Jewish people."

Interestingly, we heard from certain Israeli interviewees that living in Israel relieved them of the need to be self-consciously Jewish.

The vast majority of interviewees recognized the centrality of being Jewish to their value system. Lael Bethlehem: "I feel (being Jewish) is the bedrock of all my ideas." Others denied the existence of inherent Jewish values and suggested that one imposed one's own values, whether liberal or conservative, on a morally-neutral Judaism. David

Kretzmer pointed to the ambiguous nature of Jewish ethics, saying, "Our Jewish ethics are very different to the Jewish ethics of the hill people on the West Bank." There was very little evidence of a complete denial of any Jewish influence on people's way of thinking or acting. Although it was not always articulated, some notion of Jewish ethics often seemed to be hovering in the background of our discussions, either in the form of social democratic ideals or simple belief in justice.

Priorities

In deciding on priorities and how to put their values and beliefs into practice, divergence among the interviewees was clearly revealed.

The majority of interviewees we spoke to in South Africa were involved in what can broadly be called anti-government activities of one sort or another before and during the dark days of apartheid. Despite the risks involved, the more radical people engaged in illegal anti-government activities and were either imprisoned, detained, ostracized, or forced into exile. The liberals, on the other hand, managed to stay on the right side of the law and still actively take up the struggle by challenging the system, often through professions such as law or medicine, through some form of political protest, or by joining anti-government organizations. Mike Kuper adds a different perspective to living in a society, fundamental aspects of which you are opposed to: "Apartheid was an intractable issue but it did not dominate everything. I suppose the Palestinian issue is the same kind of thing. It seems to be intractable but everyone lives their own lives nonetheless."

Those who chose to leave South Africa explained their decision in different ways. The *Betar* leaders' belief in monism, "a single-minded objective, which is the Jewish community, the Jewish people, the creation of the Jewish State" (Harry Hurwitz) made their decision relatively straight-forward. *Hashomer Hatzair* leaders also put Zionism first, while respecting the decision of fellow-communists such as Baruch Hirson to leave the movement and fight for equality in South Africa. Vivian Rakoff adds a lesser-known rationale for taking a different line: "*Hashomer* specifically denied the Diaspora. We were utopian, and involvement in the struggle would have been real in the most ordinary way."

The 'push and pull' factor – being pushed by the iniquities of apartheid and pulled by the challenge of Israel - was particularly evident for people who chose the Zionist option. Those who left to go on *aliyah* considered their Zionist, Jewish and in some cases, socialist aspirations to be their top priority. However, some who left admitted that they were too afraid to actively take up the black cause and that, to a certain extent, *aliyah* may well have been a soft option.

Giddy Shimoni reminds us that although the decision to leave South Africa did not preclude heated discussion about issues such as involvement in the anti-apartheid student movement or campaigns such as the bus boycott, "the balance of opinion (in the Zionist movements) was definitely against serious involvement locally." David Kretzmer adds another point of view: "I thought the country was moving towards tremendous violence that would be fundamentally racial and I would be on the wrong side. I did not want to be part of it."

The nature of ideology

Certain questions put to the interviewees related to the extent to which their ideology was an expression of individual choice or of group mentality. While Jonathan Broomberg suggests that "ideology and beliefs are quite conditional on participation in a group," there are numerous examples in the book of people for whom belief was a very personal matter.

As was natural to expect, the adult view of ideology differed considerably from the way it was perceived when people were imbued with youthful belief in their ability to change the world. Ilona Tip is reluctant to describe what she did as ideological in any way. "I really do believe that whatever I did was circumstantial. I happened to be at a particular place at a particular time in history rather than sitting down and actually making well thought out decisions." Steve Aschheim is not convinced that ideology was the driving force behind his passionate commitment. "The most telling example that I can recall of my entirely non-ideological motivation was when I resigned from the movement on grounds of principle. I have no recollection at all what those principles were!"

Alan Apter has become very skeptical: "The ideology becomes more important than the people...Ideologies are dangerous." Sam Fanaroff compares then and now in this way, "In those days we wanted to destroy capitalism but we have all done pretty well out of it." Vivian Rakoff suggests that youth movement ideology "...was a utopianism, more I think to do with Nietzsche's notion of young people forging their way up the mountain than it had to do with formal ideology."

Yet, an abiding commitment to ideology of one sort or another has in some cases characterized people's lives. Richard Kuper: "...ideology has been a way of making sense of what I have seen around me."

While recognizing that idealistic fervor tends to wane with age, Giddy Shimoni raises real concern about the depth of people's belief in the first place: "... it is a great disappointment to find how many *olim* from South Africa, including graduates of the movement, have views that I would consider abominable on issues concerning conflict or peace with the Palestinians."

A salient feature of the sort of ideology we encountered was the precept that you should 'act on your belief.' Many of the people in this collection who believed in socialism chose to settle on kibbutz, though a lot did not remain. In South Africa people whose beliefs indicated they should help to ameliorate living conditions for the blacks or extend their civil rights, actively pursued those causes. People who felt strongly about human rights issues in Israel have become active in human-rights organizations.

An interesting question is: Why did people who, in their youth, were members of the same group and apparently held similar beliefs not act on those beliefs in the same way? In fact, the people we interviewed constitute a small minority of South Africa Jews who visibly translated their beliefs into practice in one of the three geographical arenas we investigated. Personal factors and circumstance obviously played a part, but is it the sometimes unarticulated idea that conviction and action go hand in hand that distinguishes them from the majority who merged into the privileged white society? A fuller explanation for this clearly complex question is regrettably beyond the scope of our book.

Narratives

Zionism has become a conundrum both for those who took the Zionist path and for those who rejected it, primarily because its nature has not been constant. Perceptions of Zionism and the Zionist narrative today are highly controversial.

It was interesting to compare to the interviewees' present perception of Zionism with that of their impressionable and youthful days. There was far less controversy about the nature of Zionism when Zionist leaders, *shlichim* and *madrichim* presented our interviewees with what seemed to be the totally logical answer to the Jewish problem – the right of the Jewish people to self-determination in their own national home. This was a national revival movement that embodied the highest humanitarian ideals. "Our conception was that through *aliyah* and one's life in Israel, one is participating ultimately in the most universal of causes." (Giddy Shimoni)

Many referred to the enthusiasm with which they went along with the romantic notions of the Promised Land, of "building and being built in it," as the song goes. For many Jewish youngsters pre-1967 Israel represented a version of arcadia where they would achieve personal fulfillment coupled with participation in an admirable, worthwhile, and exciting national endeavor.

In light of the realities of post-1967 Israel, various aspects of Zionism are being reviewed. People have begun to question how the Zionist narrative portrayed the Arabs and the Palestinians in particular, as an obstacle in the way of the development of the Jewish state, without national aspirations of their own.

People who accept the essentials of the Zionist narrative believe that the ideology they were brought up on reflected the urgency of the hour, the need for a single-minded sense of purpose and firm, unquestioning belief.

"The constraints of the Jewish people and the desperateness of the situation clearly contributed to the fact that they were oblivious to the effects of what they were doing on the indigenous population." (David Kretzmer)

Others recognize the exigencies of the situation but add that it was a myopic misrepresentation that raised false hopes and led them astray by ignoring the Palestinian question. Steve Aschheim suggests that this myopia might have been, "a necessary condition for pursuing the Zionist project."

Conclusive answers are few but the overall impression is that being a Zionist today feels distinctly different from what it did when it went together with wearing a scarf and woggle.

Given the importance that issues related to the Palestinians have assumed in our lives, a good deal of attention was paid to how the Palestinian question was presented to members of the Jewish youth movements and organizations in South Africa. The pervasive Zionist narrative tended to ignore much of what happened around the establishment of the State. With an incredibly unsophisticated 'good guys, bad guys' message, it managed to repress any suggestion that there might be a Palestinian entity at all.

The general view of whether the picture conveyed by the Zionist emissaries was conscious misrepresentation and propaganda or not, was that it was ubiquitous but not malicious. Interviewees were generally accepting of what they had been exposed to. "We were indoctrinated, but I don't think it was intentional. The people who were indoctrinating us were as blind as we were." (David Kretzmer)

As time has passed, our interviewees, along with most Israelis, have come to realize that there is a genuine conflict over this tract of land and the 'Palestinian problem', as it was called, is not going to disappear and cannot be ignored.

Leftist ideologies

Leftist ideologies played a significant role in the lives of a number of interviewees. Marxism was very much at the center of *Hashomer*

Hatzair ideology but differing interpretations were responsible for members leaving its ranks. A number of them became prominent anti-apartheid activists and parted ways with their peers for whom *chalutzik* Zionism took precedence. Some of those who subscribed to a Marxist ideology in their youth, still define themselves, more loosely perhaps, as Marxists.

Both *Hashomer Hatzair* and *Habonim* came to view *aliyah* to kibbutz as being the logical fulfillment of socialist values. Preparation was made for this move both through setting up *hachshara* farms and by pursuing trades rather than academic studies. In many cases, the decision to forgo an academic profession exacted a high price from those who did not remain permanently on kibbutz as well as from others who found they were not suited to physical labor.

Throughout the period in which South Africans came to kibbutzim, a high percentage did not remain permanently. Moshe Ben Ami remembers university graduates who came to kibbutz in the early days of the state who "wanted their life to revolve around interesting political and philosophical discussions." In general those who were more practically minded were able to accept the way in which a kibbutz way of life implemented socialist theory and had fewer difficulties in making kibbutz their permanent home.

It is interesting to note that not all those who were disillusioned and disheartened with their decision to settle on kibbutz actually left. Not wanting to repeat this pattern led to Ron Lapid's decision to leave kibbutz. He recalls observing "people who I held in very high regard, who had become disillusioned and bitter ... I was determined that this was not going to happen to me." This bitterness had to do largely with a sense of being stifled in the realization of talents and potential. Explanations for leaving kibbutz focused more on objective realities, personal irritants, and human frailty, than on ideological factors.

Pride in the role played by kibbutzim as well as personal satisfaction with different aspects of their kibbutz experience, were voiced by a number of ex-South African *kibbutzniks*.

It is important to note that our interviews were conducted after the privatization of most of the kibbutzim. It is likely that this has tempered enthusiasm for a social experiment that had been at the center of so many dreams. Those who no longer live on kibbutz sometimes offered a different perspective: "I still think that kibbutz was the most amazing social idea of the twentieth century." (Tzvi Pantanowitz)

Some of those with whom we raised the topic of the large numbers who left kibbutz had the impression that the people who were 'less radical' were the ones who stayed the course, while the real *verbrentes* often dropped out. Ray Melmed sees this as being true for *yerida* in general: "People who came without an ideology were more disposed to accept the reality, in the sense of riding the waves, whereas the ideologues were constantly being challenged by the imperfections they did not want to have to deal with."

Dissonance

Although natural optimism, naiveté, and the idealism of youth can often make everything seem possible, the transition to adulthood is filled with reminders of just how many issues remain unresolved, and how many new ones have arisen. It is not surprising, therefore, that there was much discussion about the ramifications of this transition for many of the people we interviewed.

Soul-searching questions of conscience are still high on the agenda. In the South African context: How does one relate to affirmative action in business, academia, and sport? Is there an element of betrayal in a decision to leave the country? To what extent has new South Africa altered the economic geography of the country? How different is the nature of privilege today from what existed in the apartheid era?

People living in Israel constantly face questions of moral imperative: To what extent is social, political, and economic discrimination against minorities to be a permanent feature of Israeli society? Is it true to say that you are complicit in bolstering the regime if you are not actively engaged in opposing it? Is a decision not to play an active role a sin of omission, rather than of commission?

The ability to cope with the dissonance when what is happening around you does not accord with your system of beliefs varies enormously. A number of the people interviewed noted the need to stretch their identities in some way. "We belong differently at different times of the day…Each of those moments in the day might reflect a different dominance of where in this fluid mixture of identities I happen to find myself." (Louise Bethlehem) Steve Aschheim points to learning to live with the "endless paradoxes, ironies, tensions, and contradictions in my position."

Hindsight

A number of interviewees related to the questions of how people feel today about the critical choices they made with regard to participation in the struggle in South Africa and whether they should have left the country or not. All of those who stayed in South Africa feel they made the correct choice and are gratified to have experienced the transition to a multi-racial society in South Africa. For those who left, whether to Israel or to other countries, the issue is more complex. Most of them do not regret their decision and are pleased they were able to leave the country where they saw no future for themselves. But a number feel strongly they should have done more while they were still in South Africa. "There have been many moments of regret. About inaction. Not about leaving South Africa, but about not fulfilling my moral responsibility." (Sidney Bloch)

The sad irony that emerges from this series of interviews is that the people who chose the South African option with little expectation of real change in their own lifetime, let alone peaceful change, have been amazed to see that change occurring far earlier than anticipated and in an almost miraculous way. "It is absolutely extraordinary. We never believed we would see this day in our lifetime and that made it worth fighting for." (Jules Browde).Whereas for those who uprooted for Israel with high expectations, the Promised Land has on the whole not yielded the milk and honey that was sung and danced about with such enthusiasm. Deep disappointment with how things have turned out and genuine concern about Israel's moral standing, as well as its physical future, characterized much of what we heard from ex-South Africans living in Israel.

Prism of memory

It is important to note that a lot of what we heard happened a long time ago. We all try to make sense of our personal stories and often impose a logic and coherence on them that were absent when the actual events occurred and decisions were taken. The prism of memory makes it unreliable but in some ways it produces even more intriguing insights into how we see ourselves.

Last Words

Steve Hellmann

As outlined in the introduction, this was not to be a tightly disciplined academic research. Our objective was to bring people's 'stories' in a way that would enable readers, many of whom might have had similar experiences, to compare, contrast, and draw conclusions if so desired.

This, however, was very theoretical. We had really little idea of what we were about to hear. After only one or two interviews we were hardly out of the door before I needed to check whether Lindsay was feeling as moved as I was. Time and again we agreed on how extraordinary the experience had been.

We had expected to learn a lot from the people we interviewed. We knew that their thoughts and opinions would offer interesting ways of looking at the subjects that we brought up. We anticipated gaining an understanding of what the passage of time had done with early beliefs and ambitions and we were not disappointed. The analytical thought and the conclusions were recorded and awaited our work on the transcripts at a later stage.

What was less expected was the power of the personal stories. The ability and willingness to share personal memories added a powerful emotional dimension. Perhaps close relatives and friends had heard some of these reminiscences, but at times, even the interviewees themselves seemed surprised, and grateful for the chance to go back in time to contemplate, what might have been defining moments. Whether it was Jerrold Kessel's nanny or Michael Hayden's mother; a fascinating panoply of characters and stories was laid before us.

In the best spirit of ancient oral tradition, each conversation enhanced an expanding collage of testimony being transmitted from one generation to another. What makes these stories all the more fascinating is wondering how differently the narrators might have perceived the situation at different times in their lives.

A natural outcome of this process has been to examine my own story and to realize how twisted and filled with contradiction, the road travelled from heady youth movement certainty to 'mature' skepticism and doubt has been. How easy it would have been at the age of eighteen, to dismiss Yehuda Amichai's suggestion that, "From the place where we are right, Flowers will never grow" and how difficult it is today, at sixty four, to deny that. "The place that we are right, Is hard and trampled."

Is it the gap between convictions once held and actions not taken, that spurs me to find reassurance in the authenticity of the story rather than the severity of analysis, or is it the subtle architecture of time that urges me to accept who I am?

Lindsay Talmud

Almost three years ago Steve and I decided to collaborate on this project, which sprung naturally from our common backgrounds and concerns. We have delved into the lives of real people as a way of exploring both personal and wider social issues, and in most respects the outcome has exceeded my expectations, even if certain conundrums remain.

Our study spans a period of history that has witnessed a shift from a world outlook based on belief, ideals, and commitment to one where such concepts, if at all existent, are confined to the fringes or are unrelated to politics. Yet the majority of our interviewees, in their individual journeys from youth to adulthood, have bucked this universal trend, challenging the adage that ideology wanes with age. Quite how far they are representative of South African and ex-South African Jews is, however, a matter of debate.

I certainly enjoyed the frisson of being catapulted back by interviewees' reminiscences to the heady days of movement involvement. I also identified strongly with those who recalled the thrill and romance of being free agents in the nascent Israeli state, as well as with their sense of belonging when they joined the ranks of the rejuvenated

Jewish people in their new homeland after the Holocaust. But I cannot help being astounded at the extent of our myopia, especially with regard to the fate of the Palestinians.

As to leaving South Africa, country of our birth, I concurred with those who saw no future for themselves in a racially-riven society that was bound to enter a period of prolonged violence. Moreover, like most of our interviewees, I abhorred the apartheid regime and was determined to live in a society based on social justice and democracy, which respected human rights and was free of oppression. In the early sixties Israel, and particularly kibbutz, appeared to provide the perfect alternative.

One of the beauties of the project was that it afforded me an insight into the thinking and feelings of people who chose to live in South Africa. My overall impression, albeit attained from the select few we interviewed, is of satisfaction and gratification. In fact, I felt envious of their experience and regretted that I had not witnessed the radical change in South Africa at first hand. More poignantly, my contact with politically active Jews in South Africa highlighted the issue of the small number of ex-South Africans in Israel who have chosen to be active politically or to be associated with causes many of us professed in the South African context. An explanation for this might be that it was easy to be 'liberal' and opposed to the regime in South Africa, whereas in Israel the need to feel part of the tribe is overwhelming.

When we were young, it was axiomatic that our ideals would be realized. 'Conviction **and** Action' was our rallying cry. I was curious to see to what extent people have carried through their ideals, and to understand how they view the changes that have taken place in their belief systems. While there were numerous references to the naiveté of our youthful perception of the world, the stories we heard bear testimony to the notion that the chronological divide between youth and adulthood need only temper what we held dear, not invalidate it.

At the same time, translating those ideals into practice has frequently proved problematic. One motif stands out from among the many conversations we had: the expectation to be a *mensch*. This worthy enjoinment may be open to interpretation, but I believe that it is a moral directive to minimize the disparity between one's ideals and one's daily life. That is the central message of our project, though I am left wondering how many of us think we are successfully complying with the spirit of the directive.

Acknowledgements

We wish to acknowledge the contributions of a number of people to this book.

We thank Bruce Oppenheimer, Tzvi Zaspan, the late Yehuda Peleg (Foggy), and Ian Dreyer in Israel, and Geoff Sifrin, Emmanuel Suttner, Anton Haber, and Milton Shain in South Africa, all of whom we consulted before and during the interviews. Their comments and suggestions were most helpful in shaping our approach to the project.

We would like to thank the Browdes for their generous hospitality in the use of their house in Fish Hoek, the Pillemers for hosting us so warmly in Durban, and the Leons for taking such good care of us in Johannesburg.

Our special thanks go to Daniel Goldfarb, who invested extensive thought in the cover design.

We thank Ora Baumgarten, who freely gave of her time and skill to suggest editorial changes in the text. We are extremely grateful for her invaluable contribution.

Glossary

Aliyah –immigration to Israel (lit. going up)

ANC – African National Congress

Assefah - plenum

Barmitzvah – 'coming of age' of a Jewish boy, aged 13

Batmitzvah - 'coming of age' of a Jewish girl, aged 12

Bayit – house, where certain members of movements lived

BEE – Black Economic Empowerment

Bet Midrash- Jewish place of study

Black Sash – women's protest movement in South Africa

Bnei Zion – Jewish youth movement

Bonim – builders, the middle age-group in *Habonim* (12-16 years)

Braai – barbecue

Chanichim – lit. pupils; rank and file of the movement

Chaverim – friends, members

Chavura – unit of the oldest age-group

Chevre – the "guys"

Chevrot noar - youth absorption schemes

Chug/chugim – evening classes

COSATU – Congress of South African Trade Unions

Drommie – South African

Dror – Jewish youth movement

Ekonom – catering manager

Eretz Yisrael – the Land of Israel

Ezrat ha'am - assisting the nation

Fatah – Palestine Liberation Organization

Fellahin – Arab/Palestinian peasants

Galut – exile, dispersion, diasporah

Garin – group of people going to settle together, usually on kibbutz

Gedud Trumpeldor – unit of Habonim in Johannesburg

Gescheft – business

Gizbar – treasurer

Golah – diasporah

Givat Hatachmoshet – 1967 battle site in Jerusalem, Ammunition Hill

Goldene medina – paradise (lit. the golden state)

Hachshara – training; training farm

Hadar – splendor, majesty

Hadracha – guidance, being a leader in the movement

Hagim - festivals

Halutz/halutzim - pioneer

Halutzik aliyah – immigration to kibbutz

Halutziut – pioneering; settling on kibbutz

Hamas – Islamic Resistance Movement

Hanhaga – steering committee

Hasbara – public relations

Hill people – West Bank settlers who live in hill outposts

Histadrut – Israeli Labor Federation

Hitcharut - competition

Inkatha – Zulu nationalist movement

Intifada – Palestinian uprising

Irgun – pre 1948 Jewish underground

Kaffir – derogatory term for blacks (lit. non-believer)

Ken – unit

Glossary

Koach kan – the power here

Kolboinik – waste bowl

Kol Yisrael - Israel Radio

Kotel – Western Wall

Kova tembel – lit. dunce cap; hat once commonly worn by workers in Israel (lit. dunce cap)

Kupah – kitty for communal money

Lehaim – a traditional blessing to life, cheers

Likud – right-wing Israeli political party

Lo naim – it's not comfortable; it's unpleasant

Machon – Institute for Youth Leaders from Abroad; one year study course

Machon Hahoref – winter course in Israel

Madrich/im – leader/guide, leaders

Machal – volunteers to the Israeli army from abroad

Machane/machanot - camp/camps

Manhig – the senior leader of *Habonim*, usually an adult

Makom –Jewish Agency youth course (lit. place)

Mapam – left-wing Israeli political party; now defunct

Masa –Jewish Agency youth course (lit. voyage)

Mashtela – unit of youngest age group (lit. Nursery)

Mazkir hinuch - education secretary

Mazkir klali – general secretary

Mensch – a decent person

Menschlichkeit – being a decent person; decency

Merakez – branch manager; head of section; activity coordinator

Meretz – left-wing Israeli political party

Miluim – reserve duty

Mitzvoth – precepts of Jewish religion; good deeds

Moatza - council

Nakba – Palestinian 'catastrophe'; a reference to events of 1948

NES - *Neged Sipuach* - against annexation (lit. *nes* = miracle)

Netzer Maginim – Jewish youth movement

N'kosi Sikalele – The national anthem of South Africa

NUSAS – National Union of South African Students

NAT – Nationalist Party

Olim – immigrants to Israel

PAC – Pan African Congress

Palmach - was the regular fighting force of the Hagana the unofficial army of the Yishuv (Jewish community) during the period of the Mandate

Reshimat Hashalom – Peace list

Rivonia – The *Rivonia* Trial was a trial that took place in South Africa between 1963 and 1964,

Rosh kevutzah miztayen -outstanding group leader

Rov - reverend

Sabras – people born in Israel

SACS – South African College School

Shaliach – emissary

Shalom Achshav – Peace Now

SHAWCO - Students' Health and Welfare Centres Organisation

Shetachim - territories

Shituf alef – original communal clothing store

Shmirat mitzvoth - religious observance

Shoah - Holocaust

Shomer kashrut – observer of laws of kashrut; keeping kosher

Shomer shabat – observer of the Sabbath

Shomrim – watchmen, the oldest age-group in *Habonim* (over the age of sixteen)

Shlichut – tenure of emissary

Shtilim – saplings, the youngest age-group in *Habonim* (aged ten to twelve)

Sichot - discussions

Siddur – Jewish prayer book

Sikui – chance

Sjambok - whip

SOAS – School of Oriental and African Studies

SRC – Students' Representative Council

Tarbut atzmit - self-culture

Tefila – prayer/service

Tefillin – phylacteries

Telfed - The South African Zionist Federation in Israel.

Tel Hai – place in northern Israel where Trumpeldor fell

Tikkun olam – repairing the world; making the world a better place

Tiyulim - hikes

Tochnit/tochniyot - program/programs

Turriyah – hoe

Tzedek - justice

Tzrif - shack

UCT – University of Cape Town

UJA – United Jewish Appeal

Ulpan – Hebrew language course

Umkhonto we Sizwe – military wing of the ANC

Vaaljapie – alcoholic drink

Verbrente – staunch person

Verligte – enlightened branch of Nationalist Party

Wits – University of the Witwatersrand (Johannesburg)

WIZO – Women's International Zionist Organization

Yediot – Hebrew newspaper

Yehuda and Shomron – the West Bank

Yerida - leaving Israel (lit. going down)

Yishuv – pre-state Jewish community in Palestine

Zochrot – Organization in Israel set up to perpetuate the memory of Palestinian society.

WHO WE ARE

Steve Hellmann and Lindsay Talmud are graduates of South African Habonim, Steve from Johannesburg, Lindsay from Cape Town. They came on *aliyah* in the sixties as members of Garin Etgar and settled on kibbutz Tzora.

Steve: Still lives on Tzora, where he has been actively involved in various aspects of kibbutz life. He worked as Central Shaliach in Johannesburg for South African Habonim in 1976-8. Steve has worked primarily in education, with English teaching and teacher training as his main focus. He is the co-author of Kidworld, an ESL textbook.

Lindsay: Was a member of Tzora for five years and then went to London to study Middle Eastern History and Arabic. He returned to Israel in 1998 and now lives on moshav Ramat Raziel, where he has his pottery studio. Lindsay's professional life has encompassed teaching history and special needs, designing furniture, translating, editing and writing.

* 9 7 8 0 9 8 3 1 8 2 0 1 6 *